Understanding English tenses

an analytic approach to the question of meaning of verb forms in English

A new program of advanced grammar

for teachers, translators and students of English

TOMASZ PILCH

Copyright © 2011 Tomasz Pilch

All rights reserved.

ISBN-10: 1463777167
ISBN-13: 978-1463777166

DEDICATION

To my family,
where everything begins and ends.

CONTENTS

ACKNOWLEDGMENTS 8
Author's preface 9
The verb as a communiqué 10
TENSE 11
  General introduction – what do tenses say and how 11
    Tense 11
    Aspect 11
      Aspect Continuous 13
        Aspect Continuous - Action aspect 14
          1. A single action or occurrence 14
          2. A rule governing the performance of an action or occurrence of events 15
            a. A rule made up of a continued activity 16
            b. A rule made up of a series of separate events 17
          3. A state 17
          24
        Aspect Continuous – Doer/speaker aspect 24
          1. Emotional attitude of the speaker to the situation described by the sentence 24
            a. Single action or event: 25
            b. Rule : 25
            c. State: 25
          2. Removal of the indication that the origination and continuation of the action is the effect of the intention/ decision of the speaker /doer 25
            a. A single action or occurrence 26
            b. A rule 26
            c. A state 26
          3. The Continuous vs. the non-Continuous in the narrative 27
          4. Attitudinal Continuous 28
      The Continuous vs. Lexical Aspect 29
      Lexical Aspect - classification of English verbs 29
        PUNCTUAL VERBS 31
          1. Punctual non-conclusive 31
          (the Continuous vs. the non-Continuous discriminating between a series of repeated occurrences and a single occurrence) 31
          2. Punctual conclusive 31
        DURATIVE VERBS 32
          1. Durative conclusive 32
          2. Durative non-conclusive 33
    Aspect Perfect 35
      Aspect Perfect in the main clause 35
        Variant 1 37
          Perfect non-Continuous vs. Perfect Continuous 38
            a. Single action/occurrence 38
            b. A rule 39
            c. A state 40
        Variant 2 40
          Perfect non-Continuous vs. Perfect Continuous 41
            a. A single action/occurrence 41
            b. A rule 41
            c. A state 42
        Variant 3 43
          Perfect non-Continuous vs. Perfect Continuous 44
            a. A single action / occurrence 44
            b. A rule 44
            c. A state 45
      Aspect Perfect in the subordinate clause 46
      The Perfect vs. non-Perfect in subordinate clauses 46
      Past Perfect as non-Perfect 47
      Past Perfect in hypothetical mood 48
Tenses 49
  Non-Perfect Tenses 49
    Present non-Perfect Tenses 49
      Present Simple vs. Present Continuous 49
        Action Aspect 49
          a. A single action/occurrence 49
            A present narrative 50

- A present report 50
- Performative verbs - Present Simple vs. Present Continuous 51
  - b. A rule 51
  - c. A state 52
- Doer/Speaker Aspect 53
  - 1. Neutral vs. emotional presentation 54
  - 2. Activity presented as intended vs. activity presented as merely happening 54
  - 3. Foreground vs. background activity 55
  - 4. Direct (blunt) address vs. less direct (more polite) address 55

Past non-Perfect Tenses 56
Past Simple vs. Past Continuous 56
- Action Aspect 56
  - a. A single action/occurrence 56
  - Performative verbs - Past Simple vs. Past Continuous 56
  - b. A rule 57
  - b. A state 57
- Doer/Speaker Aspect 59
  - 1. Neutral vs. emotional presentation 59
  - 2. Activity presented as intended vs. activity presented as merely happening 60
  - 3. Foreground vs. background activity 60
  - 4. Direct (blunt) address vs. less direct (more polite) address 60
- Attitudinal Past 61

Future non-Perfect Tenses 62
Future Simple vs. Future Continuous 62
- Action Aspect 62
  - a. A single action/occurrence 62
  - Performative verbs - Future Simple vs. Future Continuous 62
  - b. A rule 63
  - c. A state 63
- Doer/Speaker Aspect 65
  - 1. Neutral vs. emotional presentation 65
  - 2. Activity presented as intended vs. activity presented as merely happening 66
  - 3. Foreground vs. background activity 66
  - 4. Direct (blunt) address vs. less direct (more polite) address 66

Perfect Tenses 68
Present Perfect non-Continuous and Present Perfect Continuous 68
- The Continuous Action Aspect vs. the Continuous Doer/Speaker Aspect 68
- Variant 1 70
  - Present Perfect Continuous vs. Present Perfect non-Continuous 70
  - a. A single action/occurrence 70
  - Past Simple instead of Present Perfect 70
  - b. A rule 70
  - c. A state 71
- Variant 2 72
  - Present Perfect Continuous vs. Present Perfect non-Continuous 72
  - a. A single action/occurrence 72
  - b. A rule 73
  - c. A state 73
- Variant 3 74
  - Present Perfect non-Continuous vs. Present Perfect Continuous 74
  - a. A single action/occurrence 74
  - b. A rule 75
  - c. A state 76
  - Present Perfect non-Continuous vs. Present Perfect Continuous 76
- Present Perfect tenses in subordinate clauses 77
Past Perfect non-Continuous and Past Perfect Continuous 78
- Past Perfect non-Continuous and Past Perfect Continuous in the main clause 78
- The Continuous Action Aspect vs. the Continuous Doer/Speaker Aspect 79
- Variant 1 80
  - Past Perfect Continuous vs. Past Perfect non-Continuous 80
  - a. A single action/occurrence 80
  - b. A rule 81
  - c. A state 81
- Variant 2 82
  - Past Perfect Continuous vs. Past Perfect non-Continuous 82
  - a. A single action/occurrence 82
  - b. A rule 83
  - c. A state 83
- Variant 3 84
  - Past Perfect non-Continuous vs. Past Perfect Continuous 84
  - a. A single action/occurrence 84
  - b. A rule 85

- c. A state 86
- Past Perfect tenses in subordinate clauses...87
  - Past Perfect as 'Past Past' non-Perfect...88
  - Hypothetical and non-hypothetical use of Past Perfect.......................................90
- Future Perfect non-Continuous and Future Perfect Continuous..............................90
  - The Continuous Action Aspect vs. the Continuous Doer/Speaker Aspect...........91
  - Variant 1...92
    - Future Perfect Continuous vs. Future Perfect non-Continuous.......................92
      - a. A single action/occurrence...92
      - b. A rule..92
      - c. A state 93
  - Variant 2...94
  - Variant 3...94
    - Future Perfect non-Continuous vs. Future Perfect Continuous.......................94
      - a. A single action/occurrence...94
      - b. A rule..95
      - c. A state 96
    - Future Perfect non-Continuous vs. Future Perfect Continuous.......................96
- Tenses with mixed time reference 98
  - Present tenses to describe Past events..98
  - Present tenses to express futurity...98
    - The use of Present tenses in the main clause to express futurity.......................98
      - Present Non Perfect tenses – Continuous vs. non-Continuous........................98
        - 1) – A single decision of the speaker/doer...98
        - 2) - A single action resulting from a rule 99
        - 3) - A chain of actions..99
      - Present Perfect tenses – Perfect vs. non-Perfect...99
    - Present tenses used to express futurity in subordinate clauses........................100
      - Present Perfect vs. Present non-Perfect in adverbial clauses of time..............101
  - Futurity and the Past..102
    - Future tenses..102
    - Present tenses..102
    - Semi-auxiliaries and auxiliaries...103
    - Futurity from the perspective of the Past - relation to the moment of speaking...103
  - Future tenses to describe a present situation...104
- Passive Voice...105
  - Passive Voice and the Aspect Continuous..107
  - Conclusive and non-Conclusive in Passive Voice...108
  - Passive forms of verbal constructions...109
    - Tenses..109
    - Infinitives..110
    - Participles..110
    - Gerund...110
  - Passive Voice of di-transitive verbs...111
  - Placement of preposition following the prepositional verbs..................................111
  - Prepositional verbs followed by two objects...111
  - Indefinite agent omission..111
  - Passive Voice of compound verbs and verb groups...112
  - Passive Voice in the sentences containing a non-finite component.....................113
    - Infinitive constructions..113
      - Infinitive Object clause..113
      - The construction Nominative with the Infinitive 114
    - Participle constructions..115
      - Verbs followed by passive participle...115
    - Gerund constructions...115
- Reported Speech...117
  - Tenses in Reporting..117
  - Direct Reporting..117
  - Indirect Reporting...118
    - Personal and possessive pronouns in Indirect Reporting................................118
    - Adverbs of time and space and demonstrative pronouns................................119
    - Tenses..119
      - The main clause - Present tense..120
      - The main clause - Past tense...121
        - The Reported activity simultaneous with the act of Reporting...................121
        - The Reported activity earlier than the act of Reporting.............................122
        - The Reported activity future to the act of Reporting..................................123
      - The main clause - Future tense..123
    - Structures that are not modified by reporting...124
    - Syntactic structures – the interrogative, the affirmative, the imperative etc.)...126
      - The choice of the reporting verb..126
      - Affirmative sentences...126

- Interrogative sentences 126
- Imperative sentences 127
- Exclamatory sentences and exclamations plus incomplete clauses 127

Hypothetical mood 128
- The hypothetical in the main clause 128
- The hypothetical in the subordinate clause 129
- The hypothetical used to present hypothetical plans for the future 130
- Conditional sentences in English 130
  - The conditional construction - the basic recognitions 131
  - Hypothetical vs. non-hypothetical 131
  - Time reference in the non-hypothetical constructions 132
    - Special cases of tense choice 132
      - The main clause and the subordinate clause referring to the Future 133
      - The main clause expressed with a Past Perfect tense 133
      - Present tenses used to speak about the present plans concerning the future 133
      - The Future tenses used to suggest hesitancy of the speaker as to the present situation 134
  - Time reference in the hypothetical constructions 135
    - Time reference in the hypothetical main clause 135
    - Time reference in the hypothetical subordinate clause 135
      - Future-in-the-Past in the hypothetical subordinate clause 136
    - Mixed-time reference 136
  - The hypothetical combined with the non-hypothetical in a conditional sentence 137
  - Aspect Perfect in the conditional constructions 138
  - Aspect Continuous in the conditional constructions 138
- Hypothetical versus non-hypothetical conditional sentences - a table 142

ACKNOWLEDGMENTS

First and foremost, with all the humility, the author would like to acknowledge the intellectual indebtedness to the perspective on the grammar of the English verb forms opened by the monumental *A Comprehensive Grammar of the English Language* by R. Quirk, S. Greenbaum, G. Leech, and J. Svartvik, as well as *Tense, Aspect and Mood in English* by Henryk Kałuża, and *Klucz do Gramatyki Angielskiej* by Henryk Kałuża and Jan Kałuża – without the inspiration derived from these extremely insightful publications, this book might never have come into existence.

Additionally, the author wishes to express his heartfelt gratitude to all his colleagues and students who, more or less enthusiastically, agreed to talk with him on the subject of practical grammar, thus helping him clarify his concepts on different stages of development. The author is particularly indebted to Linda deVore, Anthony McCarthy, Anna Letovt-Vorbek, Jeff Hamblen and Steven Dewsbury, the addressees of his frequent requests for comment. The greatest thanks, however, are due to Tadeusz Lewandowski, phd for his unflinching readiness to read, comment upon and correct multiple samples, drafts, and finally the versions of the manuscript.

Last but not least, sincere thanks are due to Longman Group UK, the publisher of the invaluable *A Comprehensive Grammar of the English Language* by R. Quirk, S. Greenbaum, G. Leech and J. Svartvik for permission to quote the table presenting the types of verbs in English; to British National Corpus Consortium, the owner and manager of the British National Corpus, for the permission to quote selected sentences by way of illustration of the theses of this publication; and to Mark Davies of Brigham Young University for assembling and then making available to all their great Corpus of Contemporary American English – the author gratefully acknowledges that, without the chance of regular verification of his ideas with the databases and search engines of the two corpora, such publication as *Understanding English Tenses* might have taken additional two or three hundred years to write

Author's preface

This handbook has been written by a non-native speaker for non-native speakers. It addresses the problems which are encountered by students who do not have the talent to learn a foreign language 'not knowing how' but rather those whose learning must be based on rational and precise understanding of what they study and practice. *Understanding English Tenses*, as the title suggests, has been tailored to suit the needs of those who want to comprehend how English works (i.e. teachers, translators, and students of English Philology), rather than those whose ambitions do not reach beyond the acquisition of communicative Pidgin. At the same time, in view of the fact that the existing national versions of English, like American English, British English, Canadian English etc., make each a specific and incomplete use of the potential of the whole grammar, this book makes no effort to be either exclusively American or British or Indian or Australian etc. but rather tries to reconstruct the system that 'lies under' all of them, controlling the mechanisms of meaning formation and determining the shape of communication in each of the unique national realizations. Perhaps, with the post-colonial era so well under way, a time has come for the world to seek a decentralized communicative environment, on the one hand, independent of particular national 'usages' and, on the other, capable of offering each of the existing and future versions of English and users of English, both native and non-native, a precise descriptive and contrastive recognition of this language. If English is to strengthen its role as a communicative medium of the world, it should perhaps develop an ambition to become independent of what Nigel in Newcastle, Betty in Perth, Jill in Los Angeles or Nora in Christchurch might choose to use or disuse. Therefore, with all due respect of and grateful readiness to acknowledge the elder brotherhood of all the nations for whom English is the native tongue, this book tries to give justice to the richness and consistency of the system, with only a limited regard for the popularity of certain grammatical forms and structures.

Understanding English Tenses is a handbook of practical grammar but of a rare kind. With only a few exceptions, the existing presentations of English grammar try to make the learning easier and more practical by focusing their study on the final forms attained by verbs in typical situations. As a result, the backbone of the popular courses of grammar are tenses, the comprehension of which provides the foundation to build the understanding of the remaining finite forms. The advantage of this approach to teaching is speed and facility in acquisition of grammatical awareness on the least demanding and elementary level. The students obtain condensed recipes of how to deal with typical situations, presented with linguistic reflection and terminology reduced to the absolute minimum. The shortcoming of this methodology is the fact that it is done at the expense of precision and, often, accuracy of understanding of the studied phenomena. It is the consequence of the fact that, to borrow the terminology from physics, the tense forms in English belong to the grammatical 'macro' reality, whereas the question of their meaning is determined in 'micro' scale. The elementary 'particles' of which the English verb system is built are phenomena called Aspects: the grammatical aspect (i.e. the Continuous and the Perfect) and the lexical aspect – the final shape of the meaning of a given verb is always determined by a combination of these three. The probable reason why, despite their significance, the aspects are so rarely talked about in the teaching process is the fact that their study is apparently believed to require reserving a part of the classroom time to discussion of grammatical terms and phenomena treated directly and, therefore, lacking any visible link to immediate usage, which, in the competitive world of the language courses is a sin unforgivable.

An obvious question arises if it is at all needed to modify the method of teaching grammar particularly if it should require a detailed study abstracted from developing practical skills like 'greeting a friend,' 'buying food,' 'reading time tables' etc. The answer depends on the needs of the learners. If they have no use for reaching a near-native level of language competence, if they might be satisfied with merely an ability to communicate on an elementary level, in their case the answer is possibly that such an in-depth study of grammar is not needed. However, if their ambitions require a fully proficient use of the resources of the language, particularly when they have no talent to learn a foreign language 'subconsciously,' the analytical method of studying grammar is their only hope. Only by analysing the grammar on the level of operation of aspects can one learn how it really works.

The verb as a communiqué

When we come across a sentence, it is usually fairly easy to identify the part of it which describes the action performed. The overall meaning of this part is obviously dominated by the lexical meaning of the verb, however, the accurate and precise description (and/or understanding) of the actual shape of the meaning of the whole phenomenon requires taking into account grammatical considerations simultaneously broader and minuter than what is revealed in the popular understanding by the phenomenon of tense. The factors that are at work in producing the meaning are as follows:
- the tense
- the grammatical aspect
- the lexical aspect, i.e. the type of the verb
- the sentence context
- usage

TENSE

General introduction – what do tenses say and how

The English has a fairly developed system of tenses – there are 12 basic types plus past versions of future tenses, which makes 16 – which often discourages inexperienced learners. This number, however, does not represent 16 separate and distinctly different entities but an effect of combination of two systems, one made up of three units (tenses), and the other, of 2 (aspect). Therefore, to master tenses, one has to learn not 16 but three items.

Tense

The tenses in their basic form inform of the position of the action talked about with reference to the moment WHEN the action is being talked about – the so called, moment of speaking (about the event), which is the grammatical PRESENT TIME, always flowing with the conversation, passing from sentence to sentence. Each new sentence establishes a new moment of speaking (uniquely its own) for the action it presents. Now, with regard to this moment of speaking, the number of possible combinations is three:
 - at the moment when we speak about the action, it has not yet begun – so, we talk of it as future,
 - at the moment when we speak about the action, it already finished – so, we talk of it as past,
 - at the moment when we speak about the action, it has begun already but has not finished yet – so, we talk of it as present.

To use the tenses – Past, Present, and Future - we have to learn to recognize the above situations[1].

Aspect

The basic number of 12 tenses is a result of multiplication of the above three by four, which is the number of variations of using or not using 2 aspects: Continuous and Perfect. The effect of these combinations are four types of verb forms in each tense:
1. non-Perfect non-Continuous (e.g. Present Simple),
2. non-Perfect Continuous (e.g. Present Continuous),
3. Perfect non-Continuous (e.g. Present Perfect),

---

[1] For the sake of clarity, we leave aside here for presentation elsewhere the situation when we talk about present plans for the future and, most of all, subordinate clauses, in which the tenses are used to provide additional information about the activity described in the main clause, and, therefore, the main clause and not the moment of speaking is the reference point of such sentences and, consequently, such verb forms.

4. Perfect Continuous (e.g. Present Perfect Continuous).

As a result, in each of the three tense segments, we have four tenses, e.g. in the Present it is Present Simple, Present Continuous, Present Perfect, and Present Perfect Continuous. The English tense system is, therefore, made up of a simple repetition of the four types:

PAST	PRESENT	FUTURE
Past Simple	Present Simple	Future Simple
Past Continuous	Present Continuous	Future Continuous
Past Perfect	Present Perfect	Future Perfect
Past Perfect Continuous	Present Perfect Continuous	Future Perfect Continuous

If we look at any of the three tense segments of four, we shall note that, in each, there are two tenses which are Perfect and two that are not, and that within each of these pairs (non-Perfect and Perfect) there is one tense that is termed Continuous, and one that is not. So, the system does not contain four distinct and separate elements but, instead, is an effect of two decisions concerning the way the situation will be presented to the recipient of our communication: whether to describe it in the way called 'Perfect', and then, whether to mark the action/rule/state as Continuous or not.

One of the most important considerations that must be remembered when we try to master the tenses is the fact that the information added or removed by using or resigning from using any of the aspects (e.g. Continuous) remains the same in all finite verb forms, and, in consequence, the difference between Past Perfect Continuous and Past Perfect is the same as the difference between Future Simple and Future Continuous or any other such pairs.

At the same time, it is true that, when we compare two forms having the same aspect but different tense (for example Past Simple and Future Simple), we shall find them to a certain degree dissimilar. The phenomenon, however, is not a result of the fact that the component Simple (or should we say: non-Perfect non-Continuous) in the Present is different from Simple in the Future, but is a consequence of the nature of time flowing in one direction only. When we speak about the past, we encounter different situations to describe than if we speak about the future. When somebody says: *I will do it,* we may discuss the problem of it being or not being a promise, an expression of volition or a plan. However, in a normal situation, such questions would not even cross our minds if we were to talk about the past: *did it,* – in both cases, the potential of information offered by aspect remains the same but when combined with a reference to time and speaker, the result is not always the same. Future Perfect may have the same set of possible uses as Present Perfect, but we shall find it difficult to make use of them all because the situations that we might wish to describe as future will not be identical with those that we may find while speaking about the actions, rules or states that are present.

Summing up, to be able to make correct decisions about which of the English tenses should be used to describe a given situation, we must understand not the tense, which is a simple category, but the meaning of aspects of which the final verb forms are made. There are two of them, Continuous and Perfect, and now, they will be presented separately in the following chapters.

Aspect Continuous

To understand the direction in which this addition to the verb modifies its meaning, one should know the origin of the progressive form. It entered the English language fully not long ago, (about 18th cent., so it is not as old as the non-progressive) as a result of evolution of a complex phrase more or less equivalent to: *be in the middle of doing*[2] into a specific form of a single verb. The modification of meaning in consequence of shifting from non-progressive to progressive is very closely connected with the lexical meaning of the original phrase and has a potential of producing several modifications to the meaning of a verb (see below) but the question which of them will be perceived as prominent by the addressee of the message is determined by the category of the object of description. There are three basic categories:

1. a single action or occurrence, e.g. *She has done it / He appeared at the top of the stairs*,
2. a rule describing the regularity with which the actions or occurrences take place, e.g. *He always watches TV at eight / We are regularly meeting in this pub*,
3. a state, e.g. *He has a cat*.

However, the fact that in a given context certain meanings become more pronounced than others does not mean that the rest disappears – they become indistinct, though, a certain additional change to the context may make some more of them perceivable.

The above modifications of the meaning of a verb resulting from its interaction with aspect may be called **Action Aspect** because they inform about the nature of the action. However, in the case of the Continuous aspect, in the situation when either the rest of the sentence/context makes it sufficiently clear that the Action Aspect is non-Continuous, or the non-conclusive nature of the verb makes such distinctions negligible, the speaker has in its disposal, additionally, a parallel set of meanings which may be called **Doer/Speaker Aspect** because they provide information about either the doer or the speaker rather than the action. These meanings shall be discussed separately under the title Doer/Speaker aspect.

---

[2] cf. Kałuża, Henryk. *Tense, Aspect and Mood in English*. Wrocław: Wydawnictwo Uniwersytetu Wrocławskiego, 1983. Kałuża presents the following steps of this evolution:
He was on huntinge
He was a-hunting.
He was hunting.
As the above shows, what we today use as a Continuous form of a verb e.g. 'was hunting' evolved in the process of compression of a phrase originally built of the verb 'to be' and an adverbial of place built on gerund of the verb 'to hunt' (hunting = hunt), which is a derivative of a verb but, still, performing the function of a noun. The resulting form is, therefore, more similar to 'be (in the middle of) hunting' than to 'hunt'. The consequences of this origin still dominate the meanings of the progressive form.

Aspect Continuous - Action aspect

	Category of the object of description	the Non-continuous	the Continuous
1.	a single action or occurrence	tends[3] to be presented as a whole, in its entirety[4]	presented in the middle of being done
2.	a rule - continued activity	presented as unspecified rule, presumably primary, unrestricted by time, permanent	presented as restricted by time, understood as secondary, temporary, transitory
	a rule - series of acts or occurrences	presented as unspecified rule, presumably controlled, planned, regular	presented as chaotic and accidental or temporary, transitional
3.	a state	presented as not changing its intensity, steady, 'flat'	presented as a dynamic process, changing its intensity (increasing/decreasing its intensity) advancing towards completion

1. A single action or occurrence

When we talk about a single action or occurrence, the non-continuous form tends to represent, or 'name' it in its entirety, ignoring the temporal extent. It means that not only the momentary, punctual acts may be presented using this form, e.g. *I met him yesterday*, but practically any other as long as the speaker intends to view them as a whole. For example:

We came home at 5 yesterday, talked for an hour, then had supper and watched TV for 4 hours. At 10, we went to bed, slept for 8 hours and got up at 6.

The above sentence is a mixture of momentary and prolonged actions but because the sentence presents each of them in its entirety (e.g. *slept for 8 hours* – the whole act of sleeping is covered by this phrase), the continuous *being in the middle of doing* is recognized as inappropriate[5] and so they are expressed in the non-Continuous form. However, there is one consideration that must be borne in mind. The nature of the interaction between the non-Continuous and the meaning of the verb is not so much imperative as rather potential, towards realisation of which the non-Continuous inclines when permitted by the context. The question whether this potential is going to be realised or blocked depends upon the combination of the syntax and the nature of the verb (so called Lexical Aspect - for more details see the chapter on Lexical Aspect). If the latter is durative non-conclusive, depending upon the sentence structure in which the verb appears, it may be represented both in its entirety or in the middle - let us compare:

i. *At six, he watched her on TV.*

ii. *He watched her on TV for two hours, then returned to work.*

In the sentence *i.*, the action is presented in the middle of being performed (though differing in the overall meaning from the Continuous in the Doer/Speaker Aspect), whereas in the sentence *ii.*, the action is presented in its entirety. Thus, to be able to predict with satisfactory precision the meaning of the

---

[3] Although by nature, the non-Continuous tends to present the activity in its entirety, this potential may not always be realised due to contextual reasons - see discussion below concerning the consequences of expressing the single action or occurrence in the Continuous.

[4] Or in the middle but with a change in Doer/Speaker Aspect.

[5] A quite convenient method of determining whether in a given situation continuous form is appropriate is to extend the problematic verb forms into the *be in the middle of doing* form – so:

We came home at 5 yesterday, were in the middle of talking for an hour, then had supper and were in the middle of watching TV for 4 hours. At 10, we went to bed, were in the middle of sleeping for 8 hours and got up at 6. When my mother came, we were still in the middle of having breakfast.

It is clear that only in the last case of '*being in the middle of having breakfast*' the continuous seems justified by the context.

interaction between the verb and the non-Continuous, one must take into consideration also syntax and the type of verb (its Lexical Aspect) that is going to be used.

It must be remembered that the question whether the fact that a given activity is represented in its entirety is to be understood as meaning that the activity has been completed, that it reached its natural end beyond which there is nothing left to do, depends upon the Lexical Aspect. Only the combination of durative conclusive or punctual verbs with the non-Continuous can be interpreted as suggesting that the activity being the object of description is presented as having reached the state of completion, and not just the end of one of the segments into which the activity has been divided. Nevertheless, even in such situations, we can not be sure that what is described has reached the end unless the sentence uses any of the verbs denoting completion like *attain, accomplish, finish*, etc., or determines this fact by means of other lexical or syntactic devices - for example:

i. He wrote the letter yesterday.
ii. He wrote the letter for 2 hours.
iii. He finished the letter yesterday.

Only the last sentence, the sentence *iii.* states it directly that the activity has been finished, the other two offer such meaning as only one of two possible interpretations, the other being that the letter was written but not finished.

The Continuous, in keeping with its origin, when used to express a single action means that we want to present it in the middle of being done at some moment which is either specified or implied. The above mentioned *sleeping for 8 hours*, although long and continuing, is not presented in the middle of being performed at a specified moment, so it is non-Continuous, whereas, in the following sequel, the situation changes:

We came home... and got up at 6. When my mother came, we were having breakfast.

Here, the continuous is used because the action of *having breakfast* is caught in the middle of being done at the moment *when mother came*.

A series of successive steps advancing towards some goal naturally tends to present these steps in their entirety, since every next step requires completion of the preceding one. Therefore, the natural form of such presentation is the non-Continuous. There is, however, a situation when we might see it profitable to render these steps in the Continuous form - it is when our utterance is not just a description in words of the succession of events but illustrates the process actually being demonstrated to others step by step. In such a case, we might, on occasion, wish to draw the attention of the viewers to the fact that the steps constituting the series are also dynamic and changeable in nature - let us imagine a teacher's presentation of a chemical experiment. The teacher has a choice between two forms of presentation:

i. I **pour** liquid A into liquid B, and liquid B **changes** colour.
ii. (Look) I **am pouring** liquid A into liquid B, and (see) liquid B **is changing** colour.

The sentence *i.* presents the steps as complete acts with no regard to the temporal extension, treating each as stable, unchanging whole. The sentence *ii.* is more dynamic, since it tries to draw the viewers' attention to the transitional character of the successive acts, presenting them in *statu nascendi*, in the middle of happening and changing.

A separate category deserving our attention is the phenomenon that is called here 'a single occurrence'. It shares with the category of a single action its restriction in time (we may know when it begins and often predict how far it extends, besides, it usually has a self-terminating nature – it has some natural extension upon reaching which it will come to an end), and with the category of a state, its independence of human will (it is not presented as 'performed by' but, as 'happening to' someone). Let us analyse the following:

i. He came onto the landing of the stairs.
ii. He appeared on the landing of the stairs.

In the sentence *i.*, the action is presented as **performed by** the subject, who thus becomes an agent determining its shape, whereas in the sentence *ii.*, the action **happens to** the subject, who is thus put into a more 'passive' role, remaining rather 'involved in' than 'controlling' what happens.

The distinction between 'an activity' and 'an occurrence' may prove indispensable to reach satisfactory precision in describing involuntary verbs.

2. A rule governing the performance of an action or occurrence of events

When we talk of a rule, we often use the same verbs as when we describe an activity, but there is a significant difference. A rule describes not so much an activity being performed at a specified moment as rather the manner regulating the performance over a period of time (the latter specified or unspecified). Let us compare:

i. He is singing in the cathedral now. (actual performance)

ii. He sings in the cathedral. (rule - this is where he normally sings, which does not mean that he is singing there now)

iii. He often sings in the cathedral. (rule - like *ii.*, it does not describe any actual activity performed at an identifiable moment but a manner of his performing it, i.e. *often* and *in the cathedral*; it is different from *ii.* because it is not presented as an ongoing uninterrupted performance but a series of events).

A rule in its 'normal' i.e. intuited state is characterised by two properties - it is 'regular' and 'self-sustaining.' The first property, the regularity means that a typical rule has a recognisable and predictable manner of performance - we are aware how it operates and we can predict how it will operate. The second feature of its nature, the fact that it is self-sustaining means that it does not terminate of its own but continues until it is stopped by an external factor.

When we talk about a rule in English, we can use both progressive and non-progressive form. Naturally, making such a choice results in certain modification of the meaning of the utterance. The nature of the modification depends on what kind of activity constitutes the rule we describe. As it is presented above, there are two general types:

a. a continued activity - it is an activity that 'holds' continuously though it may be performed only sporadically, e.g. *live/work somewhere, sing in* (i.e. be a member of) *a choir, cooperate with somebody, produce something* etc)

b. a series of events (e.g. *regularly meet, frequently visit, rarely drink* etc.).

a. A rule made up of a continued activity

When we choose the non-Continuous, we simply present the rule without any additional information. As a result, its assumed character is what we normally believe to be the nature of a rule, namely, that it is unrestricted by time – timeless, permanent. Additionally, a common supposition concerning chiefly the rule made up of a single activity is that in comparison with other prolonged occupations, this one is a primary one, others merely subsidiary. Though it is usually the case, we must remember that it is only an assumption. The non-Continuous form of the verb does not define the rule as permanent, it simply states its existence – it is well illustrated by the following sentences:

I live in London permanently.

I live in London temporarily.

Since both sentences are correct and since there is no clash between *live* and *temporarily* the non-Continuous form must be regarded as, in itself, unmarked by either permanence or predominance. Having said this, we must repeat that, in the normal situation, without specification of the character of the rule, the typical assumption will always be that it is permanent, not temporary, and primary, not subsidiary.

At the same time, permanence if treated seriously, would limit the number of cases of application to close to zero, because from the perspective of the true permanence of the universe, there is no rule describing human life that is not temporary. So, a question arises what are the features of a rule that might qualify it as permanent. As can be inferred from the usage, it is the absence of a known 'terminus' of the rule at the moment about which we speak.

i. When my father was born, my grandfather usually went to work by bus.

ii. I work for IBM.

iii. If she gets this job, she will get up at 5 every day.

It means that, on the one hand, the rule has a self-sustaining character (it will not terminate of its own but will continue till it is stopped by an intervention from outside), and, on the other, at the moment about which we speak, the person or object to whom the rule applies does not know about the moment when it is to end. Having said which, we must admit that one might find situations which can relax particularly the second demand, like e.g. the situation of a person going to retire. The person knows when the rule will end but, nevertheless, will talk about it in a non-Continuous form: *I work for IBM*. What matters here is the fact that it HAS BEEN his permanent and primary occupation so far and will continue so, though for the length of time already known to him. What might be decisive is the fact that there is no alternative that would make his work for IBM, in the eyes of the person, a temporary or additional job, in comparison with this other permanent and/or primary occupation.

When we describe the rule using the Continuous form, we remove it from the unmarked form to the one that on the one hand is recognizably different and on the other, builds the added meaning by placing

the rule in the form of *being in the middle of being done* – like in the situation when we ask somebody where one lives:
> *Where do you live?*
> i. *I live in Glasgow.*
> ii. *I am living in Glasgow.*

The expected answer is the sentence *i.,* copying the tense of the question, but what if, instead, the answer received is *ii.,* presenting the activity not simply as *living* but as ONLY (?) *being in the middle of living*. The usual connotations reported by native speakers as associated with this shift of form are those of 'instability', 'impermanence', 'being liable to change', all of which can be subsumed under a general term of being 'impermanent'. The Continuous Action Aspect used to present a rule describing an ongoing single activity marks it definitely as being 'temporary', 'transitory' – unlike the non-Continuous form which means 'permanent' (though only by inference, being in fact neutral).

b. A rule made up of a series of separate events

Similarly to the mechanisms regulating the meaning formation in the case of a rule controlling an uninterrupted activity, the non-Continuous form used to describe a series of separate events tends to be recognised as unmarked by any additional meaning, though certain intuitions concerning the character of the activity seem to be more natural in connection with this form than with the Continuous - what is normally sensed is that the activity is regular, and the performer has a kind of mental control over the situation (i.e. it happens when the performer desires or expects it).
> i. *I often watch her on TV.*
> ii. *I am often watching her on TV.*

The sentence *i.* will naturally be perceived as not only stating the fact that this *she* is frequently watched by the subject but it will also permit an interpretation that the subject performs it rather regularly. Additionally, this form will be preferred if the *watching* does not happen by accident but is intended by the subject, e.g. that he seeks programs on TV with her (the latter modification belongs to the Doer/Speaker Aspect). The modification of meaning recognised as resulting from adding the Continuous form seems to go in two directions:
- removal of the intentional character of the performance - the utterance only records *who does what* and, therefore, would be preferred if the *watching* has an accidental character,
- although the frequency of the action is denoted by the same adverb, *often*, it will be recognised as differing from the impression made by the non-Continuous in the fact that it will not be perceived as regular, i.e. performed at similar and expected intervals.

The non-intentional, irregular character added to the description of the action is capable of modifying also the meaning of the adverbs of frequency, e.g. *always* or *regularly* will be perceived as rather *very often*, accidental and irregular.
> i. *I was always being ill with minor ailments such as earache or tonsillitis, and often spent as much as three consecutive weeks away from school as a result. (BNC - CEE 301)*[6]
> ii. *I was always ill with minor ailments such as earache or tonsillitis, and often spent as much as three consecutive weeks away from school as a result. (non-Continuous paraphrase of the above: BNC - CEE 301)*

3. A state

The combination of a state and the Continuous form is an area of controversy in the English grammar. Some users disqualify it completely, others report using it regularly, some grammar books ignore it, others discuss it, however, quite tentatively, with an ample use of adverbs of frequency, i.e. *usually, sometimes, rarely* etc. The following presentation, therefore, can not be regarded as representing the universal but rather potential usage, exploited by particular users to a degree consistent with their unique social background and individual preferences.

The heart of the problem seems to be the fact that the two phenomena to a certain degree both overlap and contradict each other – some of their features are similar, (which means that we seem to gain nothing by adding the Continuous to the state) some other, are practically opposite (which confronts us with a necessity to accept the fact that the Continuous, if used, will strip the state of some of its intuited

---

[6] Please, note that when a rule is made up of a series of states, the modification of meaning resulting from the use of the Continuous has the shape characteristic for a rule, not a state.

features). Let us begin by juxtaposing the constitutive features of the state with those of the Continuous modification to the meaning of a verb.

	state	the continuous
1	It is a non-dynamic, involuntary phenomenon whose meaning is always something akin to being, and which, therefore, can be paraphrased with the use of the verb *be* (e.g. *see* = *be aware through the sense of seeing*), it is not an activity but an experience.	Although it also originated from a phrase akin in meaning to *be*, namely from a phrase roughly equivalent to *be in the middle of doing*, so it was once a form of being, however, in the process of evolution it has acquired the status of a dynamic process, whose meaning derives more from the dynamic verb *doing* than from the static verb *be* (with durative non-conclusive verbs its meaning is almost identical with the *doing* component used alone, e.g. *It was raining* = *it rained*) – it is thus an experience turned process or activity. When we talk about permanent qualities, i.e. when the main verb is the verb *be* (e.g. *be patient*), the Continuous modification changes the meaning of the verb from the static permanent property into a kind of behaviour, e.g. *He is being patient* means that the person behaves in the manner that can be characterised as being a show of patience towards somebody at a given time: *He is patient* (it is his permanent quality). *He is being patient with me* (he is treating me with patience). Sometimes, this modification of the verb *be* is employed to load the utterance with irony, suggesting that the person described that way might not possess the quality spoken of but only pretends to have it.
2	It presents the subject in the middle of being something or somebody or experiencing something, in other words, in the middle of a static experience called a state.	It presents the subject in the middle of doing, performing, manufacturing something[7].
3	It is characterised by permanence - it is self-sustained and will not terminate of its own, therefore, it is expected to continue indefinitely till it is stopped by an agent acting from without.	It is perceived impermanent – it does not continue out of its own momentum, and must be upheld by a force from outside, so, therefore, it naturally leads towards its end, terminating of its own.
4	It is an uninterrupted, continuing phenomenon (experience or property).	It may change a continuing, uninterrupted state into a series of instances of it.
5	It is boundless – it makes an impression of having no identifiable beginning or end – if it exists at the moment of which we speak, there is no indication that it is ever going to end.	It is restricted temporally – we do not expect it to be endless, its borders might not be visible at the moment of which we speak, but they are perceived to be identifiable – it is being done then, and, possibly, only then.
6	It has a stable shape, characterised by some kind of 'natural' or 'normal' intensity,	It makes an impression of instability, suggesting transition, change, e.g. growth or

---

[7] With an exception of the usage described in the chapter on Doer/Speaker Aspect, which lists cases when the Continuous is employed to modify the meaning of acts presented in their entirety.

	which, in the course of its continuation, remains the same (it is understood as neither increasing of its own nor decreasing, it is 'flat').	decrease.
7	When it exists, it exists in a final, unchanging form.	It is often and naturally a process progressing from some beginning, through stages towards its completion.
8	It usually returns the meaning of the statement upon the subject, transforming it into a feature of the subject, e.g. *I still remember my father* lacks the delegation of effects upon the object[8], the latter is only quoted as a complement of the being of the subject as a person who still remembers his father.	It often 'delegates' the effects of the activity away from the subject, upon the object.

When a static meaning is expressed in the non-Continuous form, it is characterized by the features listed above. As it is clearly indicated by the point 2, if our intention is merely to indicate that the experience which we wish to present is not taken in its entirety but perceived in the middle, unlike in the case of the dynamic verbs, we do not need the Continuous modification because the nature of a state is exactly such.

Before we proceed, the reader must be reminded about a certain very significant consideration - whenever we use the term 'verb' or 'noun' or other parts of speech, what we mean is not THE WORD as a whole, but one of its MEANINGS. In English, one and the same word may often have multiple meanings, among them various types of verbs and nouns. Therefore, when we talk of *see* as a static verb, it should not be understood that we perceive the WORD *see* as being this particular type of verb only – what we mean is that we wish to concentrate on the one specifically named meaning, here 'static verb' equivalent to *being aware through the sense of sight*, excluding from our analysis, for example, the dynamic single occurrence also denoted by the word *see*, but, in this case, equivalent to *notice*, *spot* - both of them are involuntary, but the former is a state whereas the latter, an occurrence, located and restricted in time. The inclusion of the phenomenon of an 'occurrence' as distinct from both 'action' and 'state' makes it possible to recognize with greater precision the nature of such differences as for example in the following sentences:

i. *Mother did not see very well* (i.e. was not able to perceive).
ii. *Mother suddenly saw her at the other end of the room* (i.e. happened to spot/notice).
iii. *Mother looked at her* (i.e. decided to concentrate her eyesight on her).

The sentence *i.* denotes an ongoing, boundless and involuntary experience, whereas, the sentence *ii.*, though also involuntary, clearly refers to a phenomenon that has an identifiable beginning and, therefore, temporal dimensions. The sentence *iii* describes an activity remaining under the control of the subject, who thus turns from the passive recipient of the sentences *i* and *ii* into an active performer. Such situations are often encountered in the case of the so called 'stative' verbs, e.g.

i. *He told me he still remembered the times when they had lived in London.* (a state)
ii. *He suddenly remembered that he had a telephone call to make. (*an occurrence)
iii. *Please, remember me to your parents.* (an activity)

The difference may have significant consequences, since it may entail a difference in meaning of the modification into the Continuous form. In the case of a state, in the Continuous it becomes a description of a situation characterised by properties discussed above; in the case of an occurrence, (which may be recognized as a 'punctual' meaning), depending on whether its nature is 'conclusive' or 'non-conclusive', the Continuous would change it from 'a single event seen in its entirety' into, respectively, either 'a single non-conclusive event seen in the middle' or 'a series of separate, conclusive events'.

---

[8] Such delegation is typical for dynamic verbs, e.g.
He kicked the tyre
here the action has its doer – he – and its recipient – the tyre, the latter suffering the consequences of the kicking. In the sentence,
I believe in God
God is not the recipient of the belief but rather an element of the description of the character of the subject – I.

i. *I suddenly saw her standing by the opposite wall.*
ii. *All through the party, I was seeing her on and off at different parts of the hall.*
iii. *Mother is quite old and she does not see very well.*
iv. *Mother has finally begun this new therapy and she is seeing better every day.*

In the sentences *i.* and *ii.*, see denotes an occurrence of the punctual, non-conclusive nature, and, therefore, the Continuous form changes the meaning from a single, isolated event into a chaotic series of disconnected events. In the sentences *iii.* and *iv.*, see denotes a state. As a result, the change of form from the non-Continuous into the Continuous, modifies the meaning in a different way, transforming the state of neutral and static intensity into one whose intensity is changing.

If an event has a punctual and conclusive nature, the change from the non-Continuous into the Continuous entails the modification of meaning from an isolated, single event into a single event perceived in the middle of nearing its completion.

If we now focus on the static verb, the list of possible modifications of meaning resulting from putting it into the Continuous form must be in fact divided into two: General and Specific. The list of general characteristics enumerates all the potential changes to the meaning of the stative verb to which the Continuous may be employed. It comprises the following:

I.

It may change the feature no 1 (table above), namely, change the state into a kind of action performed by the subject. A good illustration of this category of transformations is the effect produced by the Continuous on the verb *be* used to describe permanent qualities - the Continuous changes them into something performed, a kind of behaviour or pretence at the moment described by the utterance. Let us compare:
i. *He is careful.* (a permanent quality)
ii. *He is being careful.* (acts in this manner)
iii. *He is brave.* (permanent quality)
iv. *He is just being brave.* (he merely behaves in a way that is called so, it, in reality, being not his nature but pretence)

Many native users declare that the use of this construction to describe how a person feels is unacceptable, i.e. **She is being angry.*

II.

It may reaffirm the feature no 2 (table above), particularly in the case of words having also dynamic punctual meaning like *see* or *hear* (as it was already mentioned above, many words having a stative meaning may also denote a punctual occurrence). In such cases, whenever what is meant is a state, to prevent ambiguity, the English may employ either the Continuous form or the combination of *can/could plus infinitive* - both constructions, though in a slightly different way, stress the fact that the described phenomenon is not a complete, concluded event but an ongoing experience perceived in the middle. Let us analyse the following:
i. *I suddenly understood what I was seeing.*
ii. *I now understand what I saw.*
iii. *He put on his glasses and finally could see what apparently everyone was seeing.*
iv. *To make sure that I was understanding the presentation correctly, the assistant kept explaining the details.*

The sentence *ii.* will be preferred to the sentence *i.* when what the speaker means is an involuntary experience perceived in the middle rather than a single punctual occurrence seen in its entirety - although the sentence *ii.* can be understood as meaning the same, it is more ambiguous because it can also mean a single event equivalent to ... *what I noticed*. For the sake of similar clarification, the speaker of the sentence *iii.* avoids using *saw* (which may mean both a state and an occurrence perceived in its entirety), replacing it first with *could see*, which arrests the meaning in the form of a state-like ability, and then with the Continuous, which prevents the object of description from assuming the shape of a single event seen as a whole. In the sentence *iv.* to prevent *understand* from becoming a single occurrence of the kind that we see in the sentences *i.* and *ii.*, the speaker uses the Continuous, which presents it in the form of an ongoing experience.

III.

It may change the feature no 4, i.e. breaking the intuited uninterrupted continuation of a state into a series of instances of such experience. Let us analyse:
- i. *...Neville Bain, said he <u>is seeing</u> many more inquiries from retailers currently buying from Far Eastern producers, while some continental suppliers which had been undercutting British producers are being forced to increase prices.* (BNC - K5H 2650).
- ii. *...Neville Bain, said he <u>sees</u> many more inquiries from retailers currently buying from Far Eastern producers, while some continental suppliers which had been undercutting British producers are being forced to increase prices* (non-conclusive paraphrase of BNC - K5H 2650).
- iii. *Already one <u>is seeing</u> cases with &Bgr;-lactamase-producing gonococci in London which have been acquired in Ghana, and there is little hope of preventing their eventual spread...* (BNC - ARH 276)
- iv. *Already one <u>sees</u> cases with &Bgr;-lactamase-producing gonococci in London which have been acquired in Ghana, and there is little hope of preventing their eventual spread...*(non-conclusive paraphrase of BNC - ARH 276).
- v. *... so that the County Council can demonstrate its commitment with consultations at a local level to demonstrate that, that members in particular <u>are hearing</u> what local people er say and to set up procedures...* (BNC - KN3 296)
- vi. *... so that the County Council can demonstrate its commitment with consultations at a local level to demonstrate that, that members in particular <u>hear</u> what local people er say and to set up procedures...*(non-conclusive paraphrase of BNC - KN3 296).

The non-Continuous of the sentences *ii., iv.,* and *vi.*, builds an impression that what is being described is a single, uninterrupted, flat phenomenon. The introduction of the Continuous modifies the overall impression, transforming the implied nature of the experience described from a single phenomenon into a series of instances of such.

IV.

It may change the feature no 5, implying a temporary, transient nature of the described state. Let us compare:
- i. *I don't see Mary very well - it is too far.*
- ii. *I couldn't believe what I was seeing.*

Unlike in sentence *i.*, the verb *see* in the sentence *ii.* no longer seems to denote a boundless state or ability. Although it avoids the possibility of being interpreted as a single point-like event (it suggests that it is an experience seen in the middle), nevertheless, it no longer reads as a limitless state but rather an isolated experience, located then and only then.

V.

It may change the feature no 6 (a stable shape), suggesting instability, and, therefore, being a clarifying structure employed to accompany the contexts representing the state as either focused upon at the moment when it changes its intensity (i.e. is growing or decreasing) or when its intensity has increased already above what is intuited as 'normal'. Thus, when we describe the permanent appearance of some object with the verb *look*, we normally use the non-Continuous form, e.g.

Her skin looks better.

However, when we describe the effects of some e.g. cellulite fighting cream, we may encounter a situation when Continuous becomes equally acceptable, perhaps, even preferred by some, for its obvious increased precision:

She has been using this new cream for 2 weeks so far, and her skin has been looking better (and better).

The above seems more accurate than the following non-Continuous alternative:

She has been using this new cream for 2 weeks so far, and her skin has looked better (and better).[9]

For the same reasons, a sports commentator may find the Continuous form preferable when describing some aspects of the famous Oxford-Cambridge rowing race, i.e. *The Oxford crew are looking tired.* The variant *The Oxford crew look tired* contains the same identification of the state, its object, and its quality

---

[9] What must be borne in mind is the fact that many users would avoid (perhaps, without even realizing it) such difficulty by using a different word of a dynamic meaning, here, for example *improve* or *get better*: *her skin has been getting better/has been steadily improving*. The above choice would be confronted if we decided to stick to the stative verb *look* in this situation.

but lacks the information about its changing character. Similarly, when we ask about the price of an article in a shop, we use the non-Continuous form because we do not expect to see it undergoing transformation in front of our eyes:
~ *How much does it cost?*
~ *It costs Ł 2.*
In a normal shopping situation, it will be difficult to find a case that would justify the use of the Continuous. However, if we take a few steps backwards, so far that we shall be able to see the economy as a whole, we might detect certain dynamism in the phenomenon of being a price, e.g. the case of talking about the rise of prices resulting from inflation caused by e.g. devaluation. If the prices have risen to a new level and stopped there, the proper form will be the non-Continuous:
After devaluation, food costs more.
However, if the devaluation has initiated a rising inflation and the prices keep growing, then an equally acceptable form shall be the Continuous:
After devaluation, food costs more and more.
After devaluation, food is costing more and more.
The same, practically, is the case with all the static verbs that we may find in situations in which they are liable of change. So, normally, *seeing* has a static quality:
We bought mother new spectacles and she sees better (the improvement has been effected and remains unchanged from then on)
but we can also find circumstances in which it is caught in the middle of a process of transformation, which would justify the use of the Continuous:
We bought mother new spectacles and she is seeing better every day.

The situation justifying modification towards suggestion of increased intensity is fairly easy to imagine (particularly in the case of verbs denoting involuntary states of mind or emotions/feelings) – we may illustrate it with a quotation from Virginia Woolf's *To the Lighthouse*: at the end of a long-awaited voyage, the sister observing her brother makes the following mental observation:
'There! Cam thought, addressing herself silently to James. You've got it at last. For she knew that this was what James **had been wanting**, and she knew that now he had got it he was so pleased that he would not look at her or at his father or at anyone.' (Woolf[10] *p. 150*)
In the above fragment, the removal of the Continuous form from *had been wanting* (if we changed it into *had wanted*) would deprive the communiqué of an indication of the speaker's conviction that her brother's wish was characterized by intensity above normal.

VI.

It may change the feature no 7 (i.e. an indication that the state exists in its final and stable form), accompanying and reflecting the contexts which emphasise the fact that at the moment being described, the presented state does not exist in its final stable form but progresses towards reaching it. Let us compare:
  i. *I understand it better now.*
  ii. *Thanks to your help I am understanding it better and better now.*
  iii. *He clearly resembles his father in every respect.*
  iv. *He is resembling his father more and more.*
The sentences *i.* and *iii.* present the state in its final and stable form. The Continuous used in the sentences *ii.* and *iv.* strengthens the impression that the phenomenon being described is a record of an ongoing transformation towards the final shape, i.e. a full understanding in *ii.*, and complete resemblance in *iv.*

The above list illustrates the potential for transformation of the meaning of static verbs, however, more often than not, the meaning of particular static verbs creates a context that, on the one hand, brings out some of the above, and, on the other, eliminates others. The following are some of the most readily recognizable classes of meaning together with the effect of their interaction with the Continuous:

a) The class of verbs which, when put into the Continuous, are generally recognised as characterised by intensification of the experience, comprises such verbs as *love, like, want, hate*. In the examples

---

10 Woolf, Virginia. *To the Lighthouse*. Ware: Wordsworth Editions Limited, 1994.

below, the Continuous version is usually recognised by native speakers as differing from the non-Continuous by suggesting an increased (above normal) intensity of the state:
  i. *Ever since being given a large stalk of them at the end of last summer, I <u>have been wanting</u> to make a design from them.* (BNC - CGV 578)
  ii. *Ever since being given a large stalk of them at the end of last summer, I <u>have wanted</u> to make a design from them.*
  iii. *I bought this motorbike twelve months ago and I <u>have been loving</u> it ever since.*
  iv. *I bought this motorbike twelve months ago and I <u>have loved</u> it ever since.*
  v. *It was five-thirty in the morning, and when I finally got to sleep I <u>was hating</u> those birds.* (BNC - FAP 3120)
  vi. *It was five-thirty in the morning, and when I finally got to sleep I <u>hated</u> those birds.*

b) The class of verbs which are put into the Continuous form to turn them into an ongoing process, possibly seen in the middle of progressing, are the verbs like *understand, cost, believe*.
  i. *I was now increasingly worried about my recurrent hamstring injuries, the treatment of which <u>was costing</u> a lot of money, paid for by parents and girlfriend.* (BNC - BMM 883)
  ii. *I was now increasingly worried about my recurrent hamstring injuries, the treatment of which <u>cost</u> a lot of money, paid for by parents and girlfriend.*
  iii. *To assess whether she <u>was understanding</u> what she read, I asked, 'Does that happen at your school?'* (BNC - B1Y 1365)
  iv. *To assess whether she <u>understood</u> what she read, I asked, 'Does that happen at your school?'*
In the above examples, the use of the Continuous creates an impression that the phenomenon being talked about is not static and final in its shape but dynamic, seen in the middle of progressing (possibly through a process of transformation) towards some end.

c) The class of stative verbs which share the same word with verbs denoting punctual occurrences. Let us compare:
  i. *Mother did not see him very well because it was too dark.*
  ii. *Mother saw me and waved to me.*
In the sentence *i. see* denotes a static ability, in the sentence *ii.*, a single, isolated occurrence akin to *notice* or *spot*. In such cases, the Continuous is sometimes used to clarify which of the meanings is meant, namely, that what is being described is not a single occurrence but a prolonged experience seen in the middle. A similar function is performed by a construction with the modal auxiliary *can*, however, the effect of using each of the two is different slightly. The construction with *can* represents a static ability whereas the Continuous is characterised by a certain dynamism, bringing to mind such intuitions as progression, transformation, incompleteness. The verbs that constitute this class are verbs like *see, hear, feel, taste, remember, understand, smell, accept, recognise*.
  i. *Cardiff moved to join them...and at last he <u>could see</u> what the others <u>were seeing</u>.* (BNC - G0E 1681)
  ii. *Cardiff moved to join them ... and at last he <u>saw</u> what the others <u>saw</u>.* (non-Continuous paraphrase of BNC - G0E 1681)
  iii. *Hundreds of these youngsters <u>were hearing</u> French or English for the first time at, for example, a lecture on the Lake Poets.* (BNC - AE8 1618)
  iv. *Hundreds of these youngsters <u>heard</u> French or English for the first time at, for example, a lecture on the Lake Poets.* (non-Continuous paraphrase of BNC - AE8 1618)
  v. *Suddenly, she <u>was remembering</u> what Jeff had told her.* (BNC - JXT 164)
  vi. *Suddenly, she <u>remembered</u> what Jeff had told her.* (non-Continuous paraphrase of BNC - JXT 164)
In the above examples, the non-Continuous sentences (*ii., iv., vi.*) seem to denote a conclusive occurrence rather than a state (this being, it must be remembered, merely the most natural surmise because the non-Continuous itself, in fact, neither eliminates nor strengthens any of the possibilities). Since, clearly, it was not the intention of the authors of the utterances, such interpretation is prevented by placing the stative verbs either in the Continuous (*i., iii., v.*) or in the *can+infinitive* construction (*i.*).

Aspect Continuous – Doer/speaker aspect

Whenever we deal with a situation that is characterized by one of the following:
- the Continuous Action Aspect is non-Continuous, and this fact is either indicated by or can be inferred from the rest of the sentence or the context,
- the non-conclusive nature of the verb makes the distinction between the Continuous and the non-Continuous immaterial,

the presence or absence of the Continuous form can no longer change the understanding of the status of the action in the way discussed in the chapter 'Continuous Action Aspect' and, therefore, the Continuous form may be employed to mean something else – the English grammar permits to use it to convey additional information about the speaker of the sentence, the doer of the action, or generally about the context of the utterance. One thing, however, must be borne in mind – the employment of this opportunity is not obligatory but optional – it may easily be replaced by more precise and conspicuous lexical means. Not all the native speakers interviewed by the author acknowledged using this instrument, some even recognized the use of certain elements of the system as awkward though not ungrammatical.

The Continuous Doer/Speaker aspect offers the following options of meaning modification:

	the non-Continuous	the Continuous
1.	Neutral presentation of the situation.	It indicates emotional attitude of the speaker to the situation described by the sentence.
2.	It may be intuited as identifying the doer or the speaker as the originator or controller of the action, i.e. somebody who keeps it up.	It removes the information as to who is the originator of the action, leaving it unmarked.
3.	In the narrative, the non-Continuous is the form reserved for the presentation of the foreground action.	In the narrative, the Continuous is the form indicating the background status of the action.
4.	In conversational English, this form is perceived as blunt and inconsiderate.	In conversational English, this form is perceived as more 'polite'.

The Doer/Speaker Aspect may may be attached to an utterance describing a single action, a rule and a state – the only restriction is the condition that it is clear that the Continuous form does not denote the action aspect.

1. Emotional attitude of the speaker to the situation described by the sentence

When the speaker is moved by the situation that he describes, he can underline it using the Continuous form, which will give the utterance a recognizably emotional character. The type of emotion connected with the described event is not determined by grammar but must be inferred from the context. Thus, the sentence:

You are always forgetting to lock the door.

to all probability expresses annoyance, whereas, a comment by a user of a certain book:

I bought this book a year ago and I have been loving it ever since.

seems to denote enthusiasm.

a. Single action or event:

  i. *I am meeting you again!*
  ii. *I meet you again.*

Sentence *ii.* is a simple observation upon the event, whereas *i.* is reported by some speakers as fitting the situation when the speaker is surprised, moved either positively or negatively.

b. Rule :

  i. *He is always forgetting his money at home.*
  ii. *He always forgets his money at home.*

Again, the sentence *ii.* is a simple statement of fact, a recognition of a rule, whereas *i.* seems to express an emotion, which here, as the context suggests, seems to be annoyance. With a changed context, the identification of the emotion may change, e.g.

  i. *Her son is always reading serious books.*
  ii. *Her son always reads serious books.*

In the above pair, the emotion attached to sentence *i.* seems to be something positive, e.g. admiration.

c. State:

  i. *I bought this book a year ago and I have been loving it ever since.*
  ii. *I bought this book a year ago and I have loved it ever since.*

Here, like in the previous pairs, the sentence *ii.* is a statement of fact, whereas in sentence *i.,* the speaker apparently chooses the Continuous form to stress that he/she is enthusiastic about it. At the same time, it must be remembered that, in the case of utterances produced by somebody else, it may sometimes be difficult to work out an exact interpretation of such uses of the Continuous aspect because it overlaps with the already mentioned case of using the Continuous to signal an increased intensity of the state (Action Aspect). Isolating the problem area for the sake of illustration: it is obvious to a speaker of sentences – *I have been loving it* or *I have been wanting it* – if he/she is agitated or wishes to express additional intensity of the state. If, however, the sentences were produced by another speaker and, additionally, referred to still somebody else, it would be difficult to determine on the basis of the verb form alone if the Continuous used in the sentences – *she has been loving it* or *she has been wanting it* – denoted emotional attitude of the speaker or notification of the increased intensity of the state.

2. Removal of the indication that the origination and continuation of the action is the effect of the intention/ decision of the speaker /doer

The non-Continuous form is generally reported by native speakers of English as apparently pointing towards the doer or speaker as the one who has initiated and keeps up the action performed. The addition of the Continuous form removes this information, leaving only the identification of the elements of the situation, i.e. the doer, the action, the recipient etc.

In view of the fact that a large part of the English verb system is made up of verbs whose Continuous and non-Continuous forms roughly or perfectly overlap[11] as far as the description of the activity is concerned, this fragment of the English system of Aspect seems to be particularly important because it is often the primary consideration determining the choice between the Continuous and non-Continuous forms. Let us compare:

  i. *He watches her on TV.*
  ii. *He is watching her on TV.*

If we were to paraphrase the above sentences into equivalent constructions capable of illustrating the nature of their meaning the sentences would look as follows:

  i. *He watches = He continuous watching her on TV.*
  ii. *He is watching = He is in the middle of watching her on TV.*

The performance of the activity in *i.* is thus presented as possibly an effect of the subject's initiating it and/or keeping it up, whereas the sentence *ii.* seems to be free of any suggestion as to who is the originator of the action.

---

11 See below the discussion on the Lexical Aspect and the Continuous, i.e. the relation between the type of a verb and the modification of meaning resulting from addition of the Continuous form.

Thus, we may encounter a number of variants dictated by the Continuous Aspect.

a. A single action or occurrence
i. I will be going to London on Friday.
ii. I will go to London on Friday.
The above sentences may be variants of an answer to a request to deliver something to somebody in London, e.g.
Mary: *Can you deliver that parcel to my aunt in London?*
John: *All right, I will go to London on Friday, and deliver it.*
or
John: *All right, I will be going to London on Friday, so I will deliver it then.*

The answer *i.* sounds as if the person has made a declaration that he/she will go to London specifically to deliver that parcel (presenting the action as a result of a decision taken in connection with the situation). If, however, this is not the case because, e.g. he/she already expects to be going to London on Friday, he/she may avoid the above interpretation by choosing the answer *ii.*, which removes this suggestion, leaving only the information who will do what and when.

Unlike it is suggested by some grammar books, the above meaning of the non-Continuous does not seem to be the effect of the use of the auxiliary *will* (historically originating from an indication of volition, i.e. *I will=I want*), but simply the non-Continuous form itself, because a similar choice will be found in the Past and Present tenses, e.g.
i. John: Mary asked me to deliver a parcel to her aunt in Warsaw, so I went to Warsaw on Friday and delivered it.
ii. John: Mary asked me to deliver a parcel to her aunt in Warsaw. Well, I was going to Warsaw on Friday (anyway), so I took it with me and delivered without any problem.

The sentence *i.* sounds like an expression of volition – *I was asked so I decided to go there*. In the sentence *ii.*, the speaker expresses two different types of attitude to the action – *was going* and *took*. The Continuous form, by removing the suggestion that the action is performed as a result of the decision of the doer/speaker indicates only that John did it but does not say that it was done in connection with Mary's request. It rather sounds as if he was going to Warsaw anyway, and only used this coincidence to satisfy Mary's entreaty. In the case of *took*, the non-Continuous seems to point in the direction of the doer, John, as the one who takes the decision to do so and at the moment described by the sentence.

A similar situation is illustrated by the following pair of sentences:
i. He talked to her about this affair yesterday.
ii. He was talking to her yesterday and she informed him about this fact.

The sentence *i.* permits twofold interpretation, i.e. on the one hand, merely that the *talking* happened and, on the other, that the doer willed it to happen, that it was done as a result of his initiative. The sentence *ii.* is free of the latter suggestion, and, therefore, is more suitable in situations in which we wish to present the event as an accident, i.e. he came across her in the street by accident, without seeking her or having decided to talk to her.

b. A rule
The above mechanism is not restricted in its operation to single events only but offers the same choice when we speak about rules. Let us compare two sentences:
i. We regularly meet in this pub.
ii. We are regularly meeting in this pub.
Thus, when we make regular appointments with somebody in *this pub*, the more accurate expression of this fact will be sentence *i.* above, whereas, when we only regularly bump against somebody there, the form that would be indicative of this (additional) information will be sentence *ii.*

c. A state
Due to the fact that one of the features that characterize a state is the fact that generally it is not voluntary, it is difficult to make full use of the meaning of the opposition the Continuous vs. the non-Continuous as suggesting (or removing the suggestion) that something is in existence as a result of the initiative of the speaker or subject of the state. Such sentences seem to be bound to remain quite rare and such interpretations quite indistinct although they seem to exist. Unlike, however, in the case of a single

action or a rule, in which the Continuous and the non-Continuous make up pairs of opposite meaning, here only the Continuous marks the verb in an identifiable way, leaving the non-Continuous clearly unmarked, at least not marked as an opposite to what is suggested by the Continuous. Thus, the Continuous apparently stresses the non-intended, unintentional, perhaps accidental character of the state, whereas the non-Continuous leaves it neutral, unmarked. The phenomenon may be illustrated by the following sentences:
  i. Summing up all the licence costs and initial outlays, which are unavoidable, **the enterprise is already costing** you a lot of money though it hasn't generated a single dollar of profit yet.
  ii. Summing up all the licence costs and initial outlays, which are unavoidable, **the enterprise already costs** you a lot of money though it hasn't generated a single dollar of profit yet.

It is true that the sentence *ii.* neutrally states the fact that the enterprise, at that stage, already costs some money, without any indication that the costs are actually specifically 'intended'. On the other hand, it is the 'unintended' character of the costing that seems to be stressed and added to the meaning of the sentence *i.* by the Continuous.

3. The Continuous vs. the non-Continuous in the narrative

To all probability, a splinter phenomenon of the above mechanism regulates the use of the Continuous and the non-Continuous in narratives. Due to the fact that, in the case of many verbs (particularly durative, non-conclusive, though not only), the characterisation of an action by the non-Continuous and the Continuous forms are not significantly different as far as the suggested Action Aspect is concerned e.g.
  i. He wrote. (meaning: he continued writing at the time),
  ii. He was writing. (meaning: he was in the middle of writing at the time)
  iii. It rained. (it continued raining)
  iv. It was raining. (it was in the middle of raining)

In the case of such verbs, the choice between the non-Continuous/Continuous forms is regulated by the question whether the events constitute the main plot or the background of the action. Thus, we may come across the use of the non-Continuous even when what is spoken of are several actions performed at the same time and seen in the middle – a good illustration may be a fragment of an introductory paragraph in the novel by Thornton Wilder, *The Woman of Andros*:

„ *The sea was large enough to hold a varied weather: a storm **played** about Sicily and its smoking mountains, but at the mouth of the Nile the water **lay** like a wet pavement. A fair tripping breeze **ruffled** the Aegean and all the islands of Greece felt a new freshness at the close of day."* (Wilder 1)[12]

The three highlighted verbs above denote continued actions which remain parallel to each other. Since it is the main stream of the narrative, they are expressed in the non-Continuous form to avoid the impression that would be created if they had the Continuous form, namely, that it is a preparation of the background for the beginning of the actual narrative, which would be entered with the non-Continuous form. Let us compare two fragments:
  i. He **watched** over her while I **made** the necessary preparations for transportation. Then we lifted her and ...
  ii. He **was watching** over her while I **was making** the necessary preparations for transportation when suddenly the door opened and Harry rushed in.

In the sentence *i.* the highlighted actions constitute the central thread of the narrative while in the sentence *ii.* they make only the background for Harry's rushing in, which begins the actual action of the plot.

Similar considerations regulate the use of the Continuous and the non-Continuous in the following sentences:
  i. He wrote in semi darkness...
  ii. He was writing a letter and she was reading when suddenly the door opened and Mary came in.
  iii. The pears ripened in the mellow sun.
  iv. The pears were ripening in the mellow sun when ....

The above phenomenon is a by-product of the opposition between the non-Continuous perceived as containing an intentional component (presenting the performance of the action as a result of intention or persistence), and the Continuous perceived as free of such identification. Thus, the latter becomes the

---

12 Wilder, Thornton. *The Woman of Andros*. Harmondsworth: Penguin Books Ltd., 1969.

natural choice for the expression of an action continuing, in a way, of itself, and belonging to the setting of the events of the plot, the former, at the same time, in turn, as acts of volition, will be expressed using the non-Continuous.

The employment of the above opposition in descriptions of a state seems to constitute a rare case, since there is little that we can gain from using it. The state by its nature makes an impression that it constitutes background to the dynamic action, so there is no significant benefit of denoting it additionally as such. However, perhaps for the sake of emphasis, this possibility seems to be occasionally employed - there are sentences produced by native speakers which permit interpretation in the above direction. Let us consider the following:

i. I did not know till I started talking to her if she <u>was understanding</u> the situation, but I found that she was.

ii. I did not know till I started talking to her if she <u>understood</u> the situation, but I found that she was.

iii. To assess whether she <u>was understanding</u> what she read, I asked, 'Does that happen at your school?' (BNC - B1Y 1365)

iv. To assess whether she <u>understood</u> what she read, I asked, 'Does that happen at your school?' (non-Continuous paraphrase of BNC - B1Y 1365)

Among possible interpretations of the use of the Continuous in the sentences *i.* and *iii.*, the above explanation appears quite legitimate, i.e. that in each case the preference for *was understanding* was motivated by the desire to strengthen the background status of this element of the situation being described.

4. Attitudinal Continuous

One more consequence of the fact that the non-Continuous is perceived as a form expressing intention/declaration of the speaker/doer is avoidance of non-Continuous in the situations when we do not want to sound arrogant because we are talking to people who deserve or demand respectful treatment (e.g. superiors, customers etc.). In these cases we shall encounter an increased preference for the Continuous, often coupled with back-shift of the verb tense. Thus, an employee wishing to go on holidays in June may choose from the following options arranged from the more precise but arrogant towards grammatically less precise though more polite:

i. I want to go on holidays in June.
ii. I think of going on holidays in June.
iii. I'm thinking of going on holidays in June.
iv. I thought of going on holidays in June.
v. I was thinking of going on holidays in June.

The same considerations would clearly regulate the choice between the following options by a stewardess making an announcement:

i. The passengers are requested to remain on their seats – we <u>shall take off</u> soon.
ii. The passengers are requested to remain on their seats – we <u>shall be taking off</u> soon.

This manipulation of the grammatical structure is recognised as particularly natural in questions asked to our superiors. The non-Continuous form of a question, by determining the form of the answer, would force the superior to make a statement that would be declarative in form. Thus, the question in the non-Continuous might be regarded as our overstepping our position by „demanding" some kind of a promise – the solution here would be to use the Continuous, which, as we remember, removes the indication of intentionality of the performance of the action. Let us compare:

i. What will you do tomorrow?
ii. What will you be doing tomorrow?
iii. What did you do yesterday?
iv. What were you doing yesterday?

Question *i.* and *iii.* would be natural for a superior because they might be regarded as demanding a declaration, whereas questions *ii.* and *iv.* would be the natural choice of an employee requesting just information about the occupation of the superior tomorrow and yesterday.

The Continuous vs. Lexical Aspect

Modifications resulting from combining the Continuous with different types of verbs

Lexical Aspect - classification of English verbs

The formation of the final meaning of a verb depends not only on the grammatical form we use to express it but also on the character of action with which this grammatical form combines. It has to be remembered that, first of all, words usually have more than one meaning and, therefore, may denote more than one type of action. Additionally, a given type of action may be considerably modified by the content of the sentence by which it is to be expressed. Thus, whenever we wish to predict the result of combination of a verb and a grammatical form, we must be sure that we identify correctly the category of action which will finally appear in the sentence. For example, the verb *write* in the sentence *he is writing* is a non-conclusive activity; when, however, we add an object, *he is writing a letter*, the character of the overall meaning changes into possibly a conclusive phenomenon, although it might not be recognised in all contexts, as in the above, where there is practically no difference between *he is writing a letter* and *he writes a letter*. However, if we change the sentences into Past Simple, the difference will be recognised between *he wrote*, which seems to denote an ongoing activity that may not have produced a result, and *he wrote a letter*, which suggests that the letter was finally completed, finished[13]. The following classification[14] should, therefore, be understood as listing merely the types of activities alone, whose character, however, can be modified by the structure of the phrase in which they are made to function, incorporating a verb, an object, and other syntactic units.

---

[13] The interpretation of the second sentence as denoting accomplishment is not, in fact, required by the grammatical form, it is rather a common inference, however, one that most users would subscribe to. From the grammatical point of view, the sentence *he pumped a tyre* may be used also to denote an equally unaccomplished activity as *he pumped*.

[14] The table together with its contents were derived from: Quirk, R., S. Greenbaum, G. Leech, and J. Svartvik. *A Comprehensive Grammar of the English Language*. London and New York: Longman Group UK Ltd, 1985.

stative	quality		be tall, have two legs, be a mammal
	state		be angry, be ill, love (t), resemble (t), think (that), own (t)

	stance		lie, stand, sit

dynamic	durative	conclusive and durative	agentive– accomplishments	write (t), eat (t), drink (t), fill up (t), discover (t)
			nonagentive- processes	ripen, grow up, improve, separate, turn red
		non-conclusive and durative	agentive- activities	drink, sew, write, hunt, play (t), talk
			nonagentive– goings-on	rain, snow, boil, shine, glow
	punctual	Conclusive and punctual	agentive– transitional acts	sit down, catch (a ball), shoot (t), begin (t), stop (t)
			Nonagentive– transitional acts	drop, receive (t), catch (t), take off, arrive, die
		non-conclusive and punctual	agentive– momentary acts	tap (t), nod (t), fire (a gun), kick (t)
			nonagentive– momentary events	sneeze, explode, blink, flash, bounce

The first category, i.e. the stative verb, comprises verbs that bear the features of a state – we do not perform them but rather remain inside of them. Apart from that they are involuntary (neither begin nor terminate as a result of a decision of the subject referent of this situation), they do not change intensity (neither intensify in time nor diminish), their meaning does not contain the implication of a natural beginning or end (they can be stopped only by an external agent, not upon reaching any finishing point). Within this category, we have two subdivisions: permanent and inalienable features of the referent, called qualities, and passing, transitory situations characterising it, called states.

A separate category is constituted by stance, which is different from state because it is performed but at the same time, similar to state as it denotes a position occupied by the referent.

A category opposite to stative is dynamic. It comprises activities that either:
- are performed by the subject (they are voluntary) - they do not seem to characterise any permanent properties of the subject but only his/her occupation at the moment,

or
- happen to the subject (they are involuntary) within certain definable or intuited time bounds - they are not perceived as spreading into an indefinite past and future of the point in time of which we speak.

The dynamic can be divided into two basic subcategories: durative and punctual. The durative activities extend over a period of time, whereas the punctual are momentary events and acts that happen as if in an instant of time.

A further subcategory is the division into conclusive and non-conclusive phenomena. The conclusive activities are those whose meaning involves a notion of the beginning or ending of the activity, e.g. go and come. When we say He went there it means that the person already left for the place, and when we say, He came there, it means that the person arrived at the place. The non-conclusive activities like e.g. walk lack such element and therefore make no distinction in description of the activity between she walked and she was walking (the two do contain a difference in meaning but of a different type).

Still another category is the division into agentive and non-agentive phenomena. The agentive are activities performed by a doer capable of making decisions about beginning and terminating the activity like *write*, *nod* etc. The non-agentive is the term applicable in the situation when the performance of the activity is a result of some sort of a natural process, beyond, at least the capacity of the subject of it, to begin, control or terminate, e.g. *snow, ripen, sneeze, catch [cold], arrive* and the like.

PUNCTUAL VERBS

1. Punctual non-conclusive
(the Continuous vs. the non-Continuous discriminating between a series of repeated occurrences and a single occurrence)

Since it is recognised that such phenomena as *nod* or *blink* have the nature of points without any temporal extent, they can not be perceived as a single event caught in the middle of happening. As a result, the Continuous form turns the meaning of such utterance into a description of a series of such phenomena seen in the middle. When there is a need to describe a single event of that kind in the middle of happening, it can be done with the use of special expressions added to it to convey such idea, e.g.:
  i. *He was kicking the door* (a series of kicks seen in the middle),
  ii. *He was caught in the act of kicking his sister* (can be understood as him being seen in the middle of giving just one kick).
In the non-Continuous form, this kind of meaning describes a single event, e.g.
He kicked the door (the usual interpretation will be that it was one kick only although the form kicked could as likely mean several kicks).
If, in the above case, we wanted to be precise as to whether there was one or more kicks, we would have to resort to lexical means, i.e.:
  i. *He kicked the door only once.*
  ii. *He kicked the door several times.*
As it is illustrated by the sentence *ii.*, the non-Continuous can also be employed to describe what is denoted by the Continuous (i.e. a series of events instead of a single one) adding, at the same time, an intended character of the action, but we would have to use a combination of the form with lexical means like adverbial expressions, e.g.
  i. *He kicked the door several times.*
  ii. *He kicked the door for 5 minutes.*

2. Punctual conclusive
(the Continuous vs. the non-Continuous discriminating between a single occurrence presented in the middle and an occurrence seen in its entirety)

Although the occurrences described by such meanings are also perceived (similarly to punctual non-conclusive category) as points without any temporal extent, they are a part of a larger entity, whose end or beginning they are, therefore, in the Continuous form they may denote a single event caught in the middle of being performed or occurring, e.g.
  i. *He was beginning to understand* (denotes the progression towards full understanding seen in the middle of happening).
  ii. *We were finally arriving at an agreement.*
  iii. *The bus was stopping* (the bus, upon nearing a bus stop, began the process of slowing down for the purpose of coming to a halt at the stop).
In the non-Continuous form, this kind of meaning describes a single event, e.g.
  i. *The plane took off.*
  ii. *She will arrive at 10.*
  iii. *We arrived at an agreement.*
  iv. *The bus stopped.*

DURATIVE VERBS

When we view these meanings from the perspective of action aspect only, the difference between the Continuous and the non-Continuous is fairly easy to establish – but when we take into consideration also the Doer/Speaker Aspect, the context becomes the primary determining factor

1. Durative conclusive

The nature of the modification of meaning resulting from making a choice between the Continuous and the non-Continuous depends on whether we view the situation in terms of Action Aspect only or broaden the scope to incorporate also the Doer/Speaker Aspect. Consequently, if we take into consideration also the latter, the difference between the Continuous and the non-Continuous falls into three binary choices.

a. The action perceived 'in the middle' (the Continuous) vs. action perceived in its entirety (the non-Continuous).

Let us consider the following:
  i. *In March, he was still writing this short story.*
  ii. *He wrote (=completed) this short story in March, 1972.*
  iii. *When I came, she was making tea.*
  iv. *When I came, she made tea.*

If we take into consideration the Action Aspect only, the above sentences must be interpreted as representing the opposition between presenting the action in its completeness (sentences *ii.* and *iv.*), or showing it in the middle of being performed at a given moment (sentences *i.* and *iii.*).

b. The form pointing at the doer or speaker as the initiator of the action (the non-Continuous) vs. the form merely identifying the doer and action, removing the information about the authorship of the event (the Continuous).

Another choice that we have when the meaning of the verb is durative conclusive is between the simple presentation of an action (the Continuous) and the presentation of the action as having come into being as a result of the intention of the doer or speaker (the non-Continuous). The latter form points at the doer/speaker as the originator and presents the action as willed and kept up, therefore, continued not so much on its own as rather due to the speaker's/doer's decision. All such additional information is removed when the action is presented in the Continuous form. Let us recall an example already analysed above:

Mary: Would you be so kind as to deliver that letter to my aunt in Warsaw?
Peter:
(a) All right, I will go to Warsaw on Friday and deliver it.
(b) All right, I will be going to Warsaw on Friday, so I will take it with me and deliver.

The sentence (a) employs the form that 'looks' like an expression of the speaker's decision, which, in this context, suggests that the journey to Warsaw will be undertaken as a result of and in order to satisfy Mary's request. The sentence (b), removing the indication of the speaker's will with regard to the trip to Warsaw, breaks the connection between the trip and Mary's request. It, therefore, suggests that the journey has been expected or predicted for some time when Mary voiced her wish, and so, Peter takes a decision not so much to take the trip (if it happens, it will be determined by an independent factor) but to agree to take the letter, hence the difference in aspect between '*will take*' and '*will be going*'.

Here are some more examples of similar oppositions:
  i. *I talked to Mary about this incident an hour ago.*
  ii. *I was talking to Mary about this incident an hour ago.*
  iii. *At five, I will write the letter to Susan* (will finish, but also possibly will merely keep up the effort to continue writing it).
  iv. *At five, I will be writing the letter to Susan* (I will be in the middle of doing it - no indication of who wills it, just notification of the fact that the action is expected to be being performed at the specified time).

c. The 'foreground' action perceived 'in the middle' (the non-Continuous) vs. the 'background' action perceived 'in the middle' (the Continuous).

In the case of durative meanings, both the Continuous and the non-Continuous may denote actions which, at the moment of which we speak, are in the middle of being performed. The difference results from the distinction within the Doer/Speaker Aspect.

As was said above, in point b., the non-Continuous is perceived as pointing at the doer/speaker as the initiator of the action, and the act as being started, controlled and upheld by him, whereas the use of the Continuous erases these suggestions, leaving only the identification of who does what. Consequently, the non-Continuous is preferred as the form appropriate to present the main stream of a narrative of events, its foreground, since it is the form naturally suited to relate the acts which are an effect of the doer's decision to start the performance and effort to continue it. Let us compare:

i. *I wrote and watched them play.*
ii. *They played in silence while I was writing. After a while, they asked me to leave them.*
iii. *The pears ripened quickly in the mellow sun, and when the winds came everything was ready for the harvest.*
iv. *When we finally reached the valley, the pears were already ripening and there was no time to lose.*
v. *At five, I still struggled to make it work.*
vi. *At five, I was still struggling to make it work, when John phoned and told me that it no longer mattered.*

In the sentence *i.*, *writing* constitutes the foreground of the action, hence it is represented in the form suggesting the resolution of the doer to continue it at that time. In the sentences *ii., iv.* and *vi.* was *writing/were ripening/was struggling* constitute the background to the main stream, and so, the form chosen as indicative of this status is the Continuous. Similar considerations are responsible for the use of the non-Continuous in the sentences *iii.* and *v.*

2. Durative non-conclusive

Unlike in the case of the punctual or even durative but conclusive type of meaning, the durative non-conclusive does not permit for a sharp distinction between the Continuous and the non-Continuous within the Action Aspect. The perceivable difference, when recognised, derives its meaning from the considerations of the Doer/Speaker Aspect. Consequently, the addition or removal of the Continuous will modify the meaning between the following poles:

a. Emotional attitude towards the activity spoken of (discriminating between the mere description of an activity and representing it in a form suggesting the speaker's agitation in connection with it)
Let us compare:
i. *He plays the drums again.*
ii. *Damnation, he is playing these drums again.*

The sentence *i.* merely states the facts, i.e. who does what and when. The Continuous form of the verb suggests agitation of the speaker and, therefore, is more appropriate in the sentence *ii.* where it is employed to additionally reflect the speaker's annoyance with the playing.

b. Intentionality (pointing at the doer or speaker as the originator or controller of the action) vs. absence of intentionality (free of any suggestion as to who originates and controls the action).
Let us consider the following:
i. *I talked to him in the office yesterday and he told me everything about this affair.*
ii. *I was talking to him in the office yesterday and he told me everything about this affair.*

The non-Continuous form in the sentence i. permits the interpretation of the event of *talking* as resulting from the will and initiative of the *I* (i.e. that the speaker sought the interview, perhaps went there specifically for the purpose of finding the person in order to talk to him), whereas the Continuous form in the sentence *ii.* states merely the fact that the conversation took place in the office yesterday, removing, however, the information as to whose will brought the event about.

c. Foreground vs. background plane of the narrative (representing the foreground with the non-Continuous and the background with the Continuous form).
Let us consider the following sentences:
i. *We walked with undiminished speed and I pondered our situation. Finally, I decided that she had a right to know the truth so I stopped and turned to her.*

ii. We _were walking_ and I _was considering_ our situation when suddenly we saw a car approaching from the right across the field.

The non-Continuous was preferred for the sentence i. because here the events of *walking* and *pondering* constitute the foreground of the narrative. In the sentence ii., the *walking* remains in the background to the event of noticing the car, and this fact is indicated by the use of the Continuous for the form of the verb.

d. Polite vs. neutral/blunt (using the Continuous to sound more polite)
Let us consider:
i. _Will you walk_ home today or _will you need_ a taxi, sir?
ii. _Will you be walking_ home today or _will you be needing_ a taxi, sir?

Of the above two utterances, the sentence ii. will be considered more polite and, therefore, preferred to address a person whose position entitles him/her to the speaker's respect. The sentence i., although its factual content is identical, will be considered blunt, and, in certain situations even inconsiderate due to the fact that it requires the answer in an equally declarative form as the question, i.e. in the non-Continuous. The non-Continuous, as it is noted in the point b. above, sounds like an expression of volition, which, therefore, permits many interpretation (e.g. that by responding in the same form, the person asked will be making a declaration of will or a promise), which might not always be regarded as very convenient by the person thus accosted.

Aspect Perfect

In finite verb clauses, the Aspect Perfect creates two similar, but not identical systems of meaning formation - **the Perfect in the main clauses**, and **the Perfect in subordinate clauses**. Therefore, for the sake of clarity and precision, the following discussion is split to address each of these systems separately, beginning with the presentation of the nature of meaning modification introduced by the Perfect in the finite main clauses, and then proceeding to discuss the consequences of the use of the Perfect in the subordinate clauses.

Aspect Perfect in the main clause

In the normal course of the study of English, students encounter the form called Perfect when they confront Present Perfect after having learned Past Simple, and it is usually the latter that serves as a comprehensible background in the process of explanation. The fact, however, that Perfect is studied through comparison between Past Simple and Present Perfect is neither felicitous nor profitable. A student is introduced to a construction which is presented through its relation with the past, however, with a warning that the past event is mentioned because we are interested in bringing to mind its results, or because we wish to stress the effect etc, which leaves the learner with a question if this form actually refers to past or present – if the former, then, what is the use of calling the recipient's attention to the result (present or also past?), if the latter, then, why is the form founded upon the past event rather than addressing the present directly. The result is a serious difficulty (some teachers admit that often insurmountable) encountered by students of English and frequently discouraging many in their efforts to master the language.

To understand properly the nature and purpose of modification of meaning resulting from addition of this form to a verb, one should begin with its origin. According to Henryk Kałuża's *Tense, Aspect and Mood in English*, it evolved from the phrase equivalent to *have something as done*. Thus, the phrase *I have written a letter* derives from and is, therefore, similar in meaning to the structure of *I have a letter (as) written* and, consequently, is closer in grammatical nature to *I have a written letter* than *I wrote a letter*. At the same time, it should be remembered that the sentence *I have written a letter* is also significantly different from *I have a letter* due to the fact that the former 'spans' two points in time - covers two verbs/actions/events (*have* and *written*) - while the latter is built of only one (*have*).

If we look at the basic types of uses to which Perfect form is put, we shall see that they consist of three simple variants of what can be done with two points in time, one primary 'P' (where the speaker's attention is focused, represented by the verb *have*), and the other secondary 'S' (always preceding the primary and represented by the 'main verb'). These variants are as follows:
1. the situation represented by 'P' is described with the use of the meaning of 'S',
2. the situation in 'P' is used as a basis to make guesses about or offer an explanation on what produced it, namely 'S',
3. the situation existing in 'P' is presented as having continued since or as long as 'S' (depending on whether 'S' represents an earlier moment in time or some continuum beginning before 'P' and extending to the point parallel with 'P').

For the person who has neither a native competence nor a precise knowledge of grammar, the situation is further complicated by the fact that the Aspect Perfect overlaps with the Aspect Continuous, both the Action Aspect and the Doer/Speaker Aspect. To make it clearer how these three (the Perfect Aspect, the Continuous Action Aspect and the Continuous Doer/Speaker Aspect) influence the meaning formation, the above three variants will be discussed in detail in their interrelation, i.e., each of the three variants of the Perfect Aspect in combination with the Continuous Aspect, both the Action and the Speaker/Doer Aspects.

Theoretically, the combinations of the Perfect/non-Perfect and the Continuous/non-Continuous should not create new phenomena of a nature that would be different from its constituent parts (Perfect and Continuous) - when we combine the two Aspects, potentially, we do not create a grammatical 'alloy' but a mixture, in which each of its ingredients is capable of retaining its separate identity. It is the consequence of the fact that although the Perfect and the Continuous may be employed to modify the meaning of the same verb, they do not refer to the same elements of the act of communication - the Continuous reveals an opinion about the nature of the activity or its relation to the subject (i.e. what kind of an action/rule/state is being presented) whereas the choice between the Perfect and the non-Perfect is the choice between two different methods of presenting the same (i.e. the choice shows in which of the alternative manners (i.e. the Perfect or the non-Perfect), one and the same situation is presented - most often it is a matter of choice of individual or stylistic preference).

However, like in the non-Perfect tenses, when we wish to employ the Continuous Aspect in the cases which are inconsistent with the elementary intuitions connected with the Continuous/non-Continuous opposition in the Action Aspect, we will have to take special care so that the intended meaning might become clear and unambiguous. In the case of the Perfect Aspect, the above is the consequence of the fact that the basic intuitions associated with the three variants of use of the Perfect form are not neutral in relation to the Continuous – some of the variants seem intuitively to suggest that we are dealing with a situation of the nature characteristic for what is described with the use of the non-Continuous, others, with a situation resembling the Continuous. To remind, Variant 1 is used to describe a situation by means of what caused it, and Variant 2 presents a guess as to what has caused the situation existing at the moment of reference. For example:
  i.   Susan tells me that your report has arrived.
  ii. I guess your smile means that you have won.

As a result, in the case of these two variants, at the moment which is the temporal point of reference of the sentence (in the examples above, it is the Present, i.e. the moment of speaking), the activities spoken of no longer continue, they finished before and, at the moment described, we see only their results. This naturally suggests that the activity about which we talk is taken as a whole, and this, in turn, makes the non-Continuous the more natural option. On the other hand, Variant 3 describes the situation in which, at the moment described by the sentence, the activity spoken of has been in progress for some time beginning earlier. For example:
  i.   She has been watching this program for 15 minutes already.
  ii. We have been writing this report for two months (now).

In other words, at the moment which is being described by the sentence (in the examples above, the Present), the activity of the verb is still in the middle of continuation, and this, obviously, suggests the Continuous as the correct choice in the Action aspect.

In consequence, somebody who wishes to exploit, in the Perfect Aspect, the possibilities offered by the Continuous Doer/Speaker Aspect must be aware of this tendency to associate the use of the Continuous or non-Continuous with specific variants of the Perfect. The shape of these common assumptions is as follows:
  –   the use of the Perfect non-Continuous tends to be interpreted as suggesting that the Perfect has been used in the meaning of Variant 1 or 2,
  –   the use of the Perfect Continuous is likely to be understood as an indication that the Perfect has been used in the meaning of Variant 3.

If, therefore, we wished to use the Continuous in Variants 1 and 2, or the non-Continuous in the Variant 3 (in other words, if we need to defy the above prejudices and/or expectations of the addressee of our communiqué), we will have to make sure that the combination of syntactic and lexical means indicate the real meaning of our use of these constructions with sufficient precision.

At the same time, additional consideration that has to be taken into account if we wish to attain precision in understanding and being understood is the nationality of the recipient of our communication. The above-described regularity seems to be clearly felt in the American usage, whereas in the British English the Perfect tends to be treated as a more autonomous structure, dominating the Continuous, and, thus, offering a greater freedom in creating meaningful combinations of the Perfect with the Continuous. Let us analyse some examples:
  i.   I am telling you that he is talking to the doctor.
  ii.   I am telling you that he has talked to the doctor.
  iii. I am telling you that he has been talking to the doctor for some time.
  iv.   I am telling you that he has been talking to the doctor.
  v.   I am telling you that he has talked to the doctor for some time.

The sentence *i.* presents *talking* as being in progress at the moment described by *am telling you*. The sentence *iii.* will be interpreted both in American and British English as describing the same moment and situation (i.e. the *talking* in progress at the moment of *telling*) as sentence *i.* but enriched with information for how long the activity has been in continuation. At the same time, a Briton could accept this sentence also as meaning the activity of *talking* as earlier than now, continuing (but in the Past) *for some time* (belonging to Variant 1). The first and natural guess of both an American and a Briton as to the meaning of the sentence *ii.* will be that it is a case belonging to Variant 1 or 2, i.e. that it describes the *talking* as earlier than the moment of *telling*. The sentence *iv.* is likely to be interpreted by an American as similar to the sentences *i.* and *iii.*, i.e., describing the activity of *talking* as being in progress at the moment of *telling*. The same sentence, when interpreted by a Briton, tends to be understood as describing a situation similar to that of the sentence *ii.*, the modification of meaning resulting from the use of the Continuous communicating one of the notions described by the Doer/Speaker Aspect rather than changing Variant 1/2 into Variant 3. The sentence *v.*, in American usage, tends to be understood as belonging to Variant 1/2, whereas in the British use, may be regarded as Variant 3, describing the activity of *talking* as being in progress at the moment of *telling*, the use of the Continuous intended to suggest something within the modifications of Doer/Speaker Aspect (e.g., such choice might be interpreted as intended to present the activity of *talking* as being initiated and kept up by the doer rather than resulting from a chance meeting).

Summing up, it seems that the combination of the Continuous with the Perfect, in the British English is dominated by the Perfect, permitting the use of the Continuous in each of the three Variants of the Perfect, whereas in the American English, the usage and interpretation seem to be dictated by the Continuous Action Aspect, thus making it more difficult to exploit the complete potential of the combination of the two.

Variant 1

One of the most specific uses of the Perfect is the case when we employ it to describe a situation by means of what brought it about, whose effect this situation is. Unlike in the case of the non-Perfect forms, which address the situation directly, here, in the Perfect form the meaning (namely, what is intended to be communicated) is indirectly given to understand, instead of being named directly. This method of communication is not very precise and requires the context to reach satisfactory accuracy. Let us look at the following sentences:

  i.   I have written the letter.
  ii. I wrote the letter.
  iii. I write the letter.

Due to the nature of the verb *write* and the sentence context, all three sentences leave unspecified the question of accomplishment of the action – it may or may not have reached the stage of completion. What is the primary difference, apart from the time reference, is the method of communication. In *ii.* and *iii.*, the activity and the point in time are named directly – the sentences are about *writing* 'then' (*ii.*) and 'now' (*iii.*) - whereas the sentence *i.* does not so much talk about *writing* as uses it to communicate what is hiding under *have* – the possible range of meanings goes beyond the simple *The letter is written by me and, therefore, ready* and may cover also such readings as:

i. (due to the fact that the letter is finished) I am ready to do something else.

ii. (due to the fact that the letter is finished) I am free, unoccupied.

and everything that in a specific context may be suggested as being a result of *writing the letter*. Similarly, the sentence *I have finished the report* may be used to mean not only that *the report is ready* but also *I am no longer occupied and, therefore, free to ...* or *stop worrying – you have the report ready*. Thus, the features characterising the formation of meaning of the above sentences about writing the letter are as follows:

1. at the moment at which our attention is focused, the activity mentioned in the sentence is no longer continued – therefore, the sentence i. is not equivalent to sentence iii.,
2. like in the sentence ii., the sentence i. mentions the activity that, at the moment at which our attention is focused is already past, however, our communicative intention standing behind the choice of the structure i. is not to talk about 'writing' but to talk about what may be given to understand as a result of this past activity and which resides in the present – the sentence i. does

not talk about the past but wishes to communicate something about the present, and, therefore, is not equivalent to the sentence ii.[15]

An interesting indication of the fact that the focus of the sentence in the Perfect form lies at the verb *have* rather than the main verb may be the question of correctness of the following sentences:
  i. I have written the letter today.
  ii. *I have written the letter yesterday.

Almost every student of English knows that the sentence *ii.* is incorrect while the sentence *i.* is not. The fact would be unexplainable if we looked upon the sentence as information about *writing* – why should then the mention of the time of action be allowed when it is present but not if it is past. The puzzle is solved when we look upon the sentence as focused on *have* – the sentence *ii.*, then is the case of incongruity, the verb *have* is in the present form whereas the adverbial is past. It may be regarded as a further indication that the actual 'main verb' of the Perfect construction is *have*, rather than the other element.

Perfect non-Continuous vs. Perfect Continuous

As we know, the Aspect Perfect combines with the Aspect Continuous, both Action Aspect and Doer/Speaker Aspect, creating a number of binary oppositions which, following the internal structure of the Continuous, are of a triple kind, split into utterances relating single occurrence/actions, rules, and states.

a. Single action/occurrence

As it is dictated by the Aspect Continuous, the opposition between the Perfect Continuous and Perfect non-Continuous will be perceived as stemming, in Variant 1, from the consequences of producing a result by an action/event taken in its entirety (the non-Continuous) or in its incompleteness (the Continuous) – in other words, as producing an effect by finishing something or by merely performing it. Thus, the Perfect non-Continuous form will be used when the situation described is produced by the completion of an action/occurrence, and the Perfect Continuous form, when the situation is an effect of simply performing the action, not necessarily reaching its end. A good illustration might be a situation that one might encounter at a party. Let us suppose that the hostess has promised some of her guests that her husband will drive them home at the end. Now, the time has come when they desire to leave. They see the husband sitting in front of a TV clearly not occupied with anything important, so they find his wife and ask to be driven home. However, what they do not know, it is impossible because the husband is drunk. In reply to their request, the hostess may inform them about that fact responding in the following way:
  i. He can't drive you home because he is drunk.
  ii. He can't drive you home because he has drunk two bottles of wine.
  iii. He can't drive you home because he has been drinking.

The content of the above three sentences is practically the same: the husband is not able to do it because he is intoxicated as a result of having been drinking alcohol. This communiqué has three different forms. In the sentence *i.*, the meaning is presented directly, in the remaining two, indirectly, given to understand. In the sentence *ii.*, the meaning is suggested by referring the recipient to the predictable effects of accomplishing something, here, drinking two bottles of wine – as it is suggested by the non-Continuous tending to present a single action in its entirety, the effect is produced not by drinking two bottles but by having drunk them. In the sentence *iii.*, it is suggested that the result, namely the fact that the person is not able to drive, is produced not so much by reaching the end of some activity but by merely performing it, i.e. drinking alone in almost any quantity produces this result - the sentence avoids setting the limit and discussing its having or not having been exceeded. It is based upon an assumption that any drinking results in this incapacitation.

---

15 Paradoxically, though the sentence *i.* can not be equivalent to the sentence *ii.*, in some specific contexts, the sentence *ii.* may be equivalent to the sentence *i.* Let us take, for example, the sentence *The train has arrived*. If, for some reason, it were significant for the speaker in the present that the train arrived 10 minutes ago, such information could not be given with the use of the Present Perfect construction (for reasons discussed below). At the same time, the sentence *The train arrived 10 minutes ago* does not naturally refer to the present. However, if the sentence *The train arrived 10 min. ago* is uttered by a person rushing into the waiting room and yelling to his friend sitting there, it is rather unlikely that the friend should fail to understand the message as having reference to the present moment. What is material here is the fact that this present time reference is a result of extra-grammatical circumstances, without which the sentence would loose its present significance and would return to its normal time reference specified by grammar, i.e. the past form of the verb.

At the same time, we remember that the choice of the Perfect Continuous or the Perfect non-Continuous may be dictated by the considerations described by the Doer/Speaker Aspect. Let us take two sentences:
  i. *He has talked to her.*
  ii. *He has been talking to her.*

The preference for the non-Continuous will be shown in the cases when the *talking* is an effect of the subject's intention, initiative, whereas, if it is merely a coincidence, the Continuous is likely to be preferred because it removes the suggestion that the doer or speaker is responsible for the performance of the action. The precision of communication by means of this form largely depends on the type of meaning that is handled by it. For example, if we take a durative, conclusive *write the letter*, the meaning is never absolutely clear in all its aspects – let us analyse the following:
  i. *He has written the letter.*
  ii. *He has been writing the letter.*

In the Action Aspect, the sentence *i.* would be appropriate if we wished to say that the performer completed the writing of the letter. The same sentence, if chosen for the sake of what it offers in the Speaker/Doer Aspect, could be preferred above the sentence *ii.* if the doer wanted to say that the action was willed and kept up by him – the question of completion is not specified precisely by this form, it could mean both completed and merely performed. In the case of the sentence *ii.*, in the Action Aspect, this form would be chosen if the doer wanted to say that the result is produced by a mere performance, without reaching the state of completion (e.g. this sentence might be quoted as an explanation why the speaker is exhausted or gloomy). In the Speaker/Doer Aspect, the sentence would be preferred if the speaker wanted to remove from it the indication that it was performed because of his initiative or will, leaving only the information who performed what. It must be remembered that the Continuous here does not say that the writing was not the initiative of the doer, the sentence simply does not contain any information as to whose initiative it was.

Sometimes, an addition of merely one more element may significantly change the distinction between the Continuous and the non-Continuous, e.g. an addition of specification of the number of items upon which the action operates. Let us compare:
  i. *We have cleaned the windows.*
  ii. *We have been cleaning the windows.*

In the above two sentences, the question of completeness of the action is as indistinct as in the previously discussed example with *writing a letter* - the non-Continuous may be employed to suggest that either the job has been completed, all the windows having been cleaned, or that it has not been completed, the non-Continuous having been chosen to present the action as 'willed' and 'kept up' by the performer. The Continuous would be interpreted as suggesting the incompleteness of the job, the content of *have* being an effect of mere performance, without reaching the end. However, if we add the number of items operated upon, the situation changes. Let us analyse the following:
  iii. *We have cleaned 10 windows.*
  iv. *We have been cleaning 10 windows.*

The number of windows makes the Doer/Speaker Aspect indistinct in the sentence *iii.*, thus leaving the opposition between the Continuous and the non-Continuous determined by the Action Aspect alone, identifying the non-Continuous with the completeness and the Continuous, with the non-completeness of the action.

b. A rule

Here, as dictated by the Action Aspect, the choice between the Perfect and the Perfect Continuous is:
- either the choice between the result produced by a permanent/primary rule contrasted with those produced by a transitory/ secondary one,
- or the results of a 'regular'/predictable rule contrasted with those produced by a hectic series of repeated accidents, without perceivable predictability.

For example, let us imagine a conversation about the chances that a certain person may help us in locating a certain file in the office – one of the participants voices his belief that it is possible in one of the following ways:
  i. *He may know the answer because he knows this place.*
  ii. *He may know the answer because he has worked here for 20 years.*

iii. He may know the answer because he has been working as her substitute for 2 weeks.

It is not the case that the person is still employed in this place. What is suggested is that he enjoys the effect of working here, namely, the thorough knowledge. The sentence *i.* presents the meaning directly, whereas the sentences *ii.* and *iii.*, indirectly – the meaning is given to understand by them. In the sentence *ii.*, the choice of the non-Continuous is a result of the fact that the effect, i.e. the knowledge of the place is produced by a permanent rule. The Continuous form of the sentence *iii.* is a result of the rule being temporary and secondary.

Here, too, (although it seems to be a rare case) the choice between the Continuous and the non-Continuous may be governed by the Doer/Speaker Aspect. For example, let us imagine the situation of somebody contemplating the idea of persuading his friend to join her on a flight by British Airlines. The other person participating in the conversation may voice her doubts saying:

A: *I don't think she'll join you.*
B: *Oh, won't she? And why?*
A: (using one of the following)
i. *She prefers to fly Lufthansa.*
ii. *She has always flown Lufthansa.*
iii. *She has always been flying Lufthansa.*

The sentence *i.* explains the situation directly stating the reason, in the sentences *ii.* and *iii.*, it is given to understand. The sentence *ii.* will be preferred if the person wishes to express her conviction that this flying Lufthansa is not an accident but a result of choice and pursuance of such resolution (that it has been intended and that effort has been made to continue it), whereas the sentence *iii.*, merely states that such practice has existed - in this situation it would be tantamount to adding some kind of reservation like *it <u>seems</u> that she prefers to fly Lufthansa* as opposed to the suggestion of the sentence *ii.* being *it is clear that she has been resolved to fly Lufthansa*.

c. A state

In accordance with the Action Aspect, when we wish to talk in Variant 1 about the effect produced by a state, the Perfect non-Continuous will be appropriate for talking about the results of a state characterised by neutral and stable intensity, whereas the Perfect Continuous will be chosen when one intends to employ the additional modification of the meaning listed and discussed in the chapter on the Continuous Aspect. For example, the Continuous may suggest an increased intensity of the state - let us consider a situation when two people are talking in a situation when one has requested an opinion if there is any sense in asking a colleague from their office to resign from taking holiday at a date planned by him. The person voicing her opinion may choose:

i. *No, he is too keen to go.*
ii. *No, he has wished it too much.*
iii. *No, he has been wishing it too much.*

In the sentence *iii.*, the Continuous seems to be placing additional emphasis on the strength of the desire to go, suggesting an increased intensity.

Variant 2

Sentences of the Variant 2 are deceptively similar to those of Variant 1. In both cases, the activity denoted by the verb and by *have* are disconnected (the main verb activity is no longer continued at the point of time at which *have* is located). In Variant 1, we use a phenomenon that we hope is known to the recipient of the information to suggest something that the recipient does not see or realize, e.g. *Her husband can't drive you home because he has been drinking*. The invisible fact that the person is drunk is described with the help of something whose meaning and consequences, we hope, are known to the listener. We do not see what is to be communicated – we are given to understand what it is. In the sentences of the Variant 2, the meaning formation is realized in the opposite direction. Let us imagine a situation when a person famous for irascible temper returns home bruised and with his clothes torn and bedraggled. The natural commentary might be:

You have been fighting again.

In the above statement, unlike in the sentences of the Variant 1, at the moment of time reference (here, the present moment) we see effects of something that happened at an earlier time. On the basis of what we see, we either make a guess as to the likely cause or present information that explains the existing situation by naming its reasons. Therefore, here, the speaker uses what is seen to guess at or inform of what brought it about – in the Variant 1 the direction is the opposite. For example:

i. I can't answer the phone because I have been making a cake.
ii. He won't help you at the moment because he has been oiling the car.
iii. You have been drinking again.
iv. You have not put an end to that affair – I can see lipstick on your collar.

In the sentences *i.* and *ii.*, we see the construction employed to explain the reasons for the existing state, whereas the sentences *iii.* and *iv.* are a form of guesses about the causes of what the speaker sees.

Perfect non-Continuous vs. Perfect Continuous

As dictated by the Continuous Action Aspect, this opposition is divided into three situations recognized by it – speaking about a single occurrence/action, a rule, and a state.

a. A single action/occurrence

In this category, the non-Continuous is chosen when we want to present an opinion that what we see is a result of completion of an action. On the other hand, the Continuous form will be preferred when we wish to express the belief that the described situation is an effect of merely performing the action/occurrence mentioned; in other words, the result to have been produced did not require the completion of the action denoted by the verb. A good illustration of the use of the Continuous will be found above in the sentence discussed already:

i. You have been fighting again.

To illustrate the situation deserving the use of the non-Continuous let us imagine a writer with a habit of locking himself in his cottage till he has finished writing his novel. Upon seeing him in the street after some time, we are justified to voice a supposition that it is an indication that he has finished it, namely:

ii. I see you have finally written that novel.

In the case when the result is an effect of performed rather than completed activity, we may encounter a situation (particularly with non-conclusive verbs) offering a choice within the Doer/Speaker Aspect, namely, between representation of the activity as intended and kept up by the doer, or as just performed, e.g. a modification of the above examples:

i. (I see) You have worked on that play of yours.
ii. (I see) You have been working on that play of yours.

In the above examples, the sentence *ii.* merely states the *working* as a probable cause of the situation witnessed by the speaker, whereas the sentence *i.* adds to this information additional dimension, namely, a suggestion that we believe the performance of the activity is an effect of will and resolve to do and continue it. Thus, the latter example will be fitting when, for example we know that to work on that play the doer must brave, overcome difficulties, or force himself/herself to continue the activity.

b. A rule

In this category, the non-Continuous will be preferred when we wish to express an opinion that what we see is a result of a permanent rule - for example:

i. (I see) You have often travelled on this line.
ii. (I gather) She has never taken sugar in her coffee.

The Continuous form will be a more accurate indication of the nature of the situation if we want to present conjecture or inform that what is seen is an effect of not so much a regular, predictable rule as rather an irregular series of events - for example:

iii. (I see) You have been taking your medication regularly for a change.
iv. (I gather) You have been attending the lectures a bit more systematically this semester.

In this category, the combination of the Perfect with the Continuous tends to produce most often the variant building its meaning upon the considerations listed under the Speaker/Doer Aspect. Thus, the sentence *iv.* above may be also put into a pair with its opposite, i.e.

v. (I gather) You have been attending the lectures a bit more systematically this semester.
vi. (I gather) You have attended the lectures a bit more systematically this semester.

However, the choice, we might have above, is not so much the distinction between a rule represented as permanent and regular (*vi.*) contrasted with an irregular, accidental series (*iv.*), or permanent vs. impermanent, but rather between the mere presentation of the existing regularity (*v.*) contrasted with the regularity represented as intended and consciously kept up (*vi.*). In this context and with this pair of sentences, the sentence *v.* is satisfied with just stating the fact, whereas the sentence *vi.* adds the suggestion that the speaker perceives it as an effect of resolution and deliberation of the doer. Similar considerations will be found in the choice between the following statements:

vii. (I see) You have regularly been visiting the beach.
viii. (I see) You have regularly visited the beach.

The sentences above may be perceived as fitting a situation of making conjectures on the olive colour of somebody's body. The sentence *vii.* makes merely a guess that such past regularity might be responsible for the looks of the person. The other sentence (*viii.*) may be regarded as more fitting in the case when the speaker guesses that the regularity was not a coincidence but that it was consciously upheld and maintained by the person.

Sometimes, the operation of the Speaker/Doer Aspect may have significant consequences for the meaning of the verb, like for example in the following pair:

ix. (I gather) You have regularly met in this pub.
x. (I gather) You have regularly been meeting in this pub.

Due to the intuitions embedded in the use of the Continuous (discussed in the chapter on the Continuous Aspect), the sentence *ix.* seems to be a suggestion that the people in question regularly made appointments in this pub, whereas, by removing intentionality, the sentence *x.* apparently presents these meetings as a work of chance, not deliberation, i.e. accidental coming across each other at that place.

c. A state

As dictated by the Continuous Action Aspect, the choice of the Perfect non-Continuous will indicate the fact that the speaker considers the state which is guessed at as being the cause of the described situation to be characterised by the properties natural for a state (see chapter on Aspect Continuous). The situation when we may encounter such uses of the Perfect may be e.g. a conversation about some aspects of somebody else's behaviour which seems to suggest that the person has recognized a woman present on the scene (sentence *i.*, below). A similar case may be an observation upon the behaviour which clearly indicates that the person talked of is familiar with e.g. responsibilities involved in possessing a cat (sentence *ii.*, below)

i. Clearly, he has known her.
ii. Apparently, she has had cats already.

The use of the Perfect Continuous would require a situation that would justify it - the list of such will be found in the chapter on the Continuous Aspect discussing, among other things, the possible modifications of meaning of stative verbs by the Continuous. Below will be found a presentation of selected cases which seem most obvious but, what must be borne in mind, all other cases of combining the Continuous with the stative are possible on condition that we encounter a situation that permits making use of it - the decision whether to use the Perfect or not does not affect the considerations responsible for the use of the Continuous[16]. Let us consider the following sentences:

iii. It seems she has seen a lot more than she wishes to admit.
iv. It seems she has been seeing a lot more than she wishes to admit.

The above sentences express a guess that the behaviour of the person talked of suggests that she might have more knowledge about something than she is ready to admit. The sentence *iii.*, as a result of the combination of the non-Continuous form and the verb *see*, is ambiguous about the nature of the phenomenon that is the basis of the conjecture of the speaker - the verb *see* may denote both a state of seeing and a single occurrence (similar to the meaning of the verbs *notice, spot*) seen in its entirety. As a result, the decision whether the basis for the conjecture is a single occurrence or a state is left to the reader. The use of the non-Continuous in this case may indicate that it is not material for what we wish to be understood whether it is an effect of a state or an occurrence. If, however, we considered it important that the basis of the conjecture should not be perceived as a single occurrence but a prolonged state or at

---

16 Actually, in the American English, the opposite is the case.

least series of occurrences, such meaning may be made more prominent by putting it into the Continuous form, like in the sentence *iv*.

Another possible situation that would justify the use of the Continuous could be a wish to suggest that the state described is characterised by changing or increased intensity. Such cases in which we would make guesses that a situation in existence at the moment of reference is a result of a state which, at that moment, is no longer continued but is, at the same time, characterised by changing or increased intensity seem to be quite rare, therefore, the potential of this instrument might not be exploited very frequently, however, such cases exist, like for example the following pair of sentences. The sentences might be used to express observations upon some regrettable aspects of somebody's physique, betraying the fact that the person overused alcohol in some previous period of life.

   v. Clearly, he has loved alcohol quite a lot.
   vi. Clearly, he has been loving alcohol quite a lot.

The sentence *v.* simply identifies the insuperable disposition towards alcohol as responsible for the person's looks. The sentence *vi.* enriches the information of the sentence *v.* by laying additional stress upon the *loving* of alcohol, inviting to perceive it as intense enough to justify the ironic loading of the statement.

The above examples do not constitute the complete list of the possibilities but just an illustration that the use of the Continuous also in this variant is determined by the mechanisms of meaning formation controlled by the Aspect Continuous. To avoid overloading the presentation of the Perfect with the repetition of the notions already discussed in the chapter on the Continuous Aspect, the reader is requested to refer there for the complete information concerning the modifications resulting from using or not using the Continuous in different situations and with different types of verbs.

Variant 3

This variant addresses the cases when we wish to say that an activity, a rule or a state present at a given moment in time (past, present, or future) continues or is repeated for some time. Let us take a present situation of somebody writing a letter:

   i. He is writing a letter.

The activity occupies the present moment, but naturally it began earlier. Now, as long as we want to continue talking about previously chosen moment in time (the moment of speaking in the above sentence) and, apart from that, if we wished to add information about the length of the activity or its starting point, we must not use the non-Perfect tenses. Therefore, a simple extension of the sentence *i.* is forbidden:

   *ii. * He is writing a letter for 2 hours, now.*

The above sentence is ungrammatical in English - the only permitted way leads through the use of the Perfect, i.e.

   iii. He has been writing a letter for 2 hours, now.

or

   iv. He has written a letter for 2 hours, now.

Using sentences of this kind we must remember that although they denote a segment whose borders are determined by the position of *have* (past, present, or future) and the main verb (located in the anteriority of the verb *have*), our attention and, hence, the attention of the recipient of the communiqué is focused only on the point were *have* resides, not on the activity leading to this moment from its anteriority or on all the segment. It is different, therefore, from what is presented by non-Perfect tenses in a similar situation - let us compare the following sentences[17]:

   i. He was writing the letter at 7 yesterday.
   ii. He was writing the letter for 2 hours yesterday.
   iii. He was writing the letter from 5 to 7 yesterday.
   iv. At 7 yesterday, he had been writing the letter for 2 hours.

The sentences from *i.* to *iii.* denote either a single point (*i.*) or its enlargement, a segment (*ii.* and *iii.*) - in each case, we focus upon the entirety of the time reference (i.e., the whole point, the whole segment). In the sentence *iv.*, however, the situation is different - this statement focuses only on the end of the segment, on 7 o'clock, the rest of it (the activity going from 5 to 7) serving only as additional information, providing a supplementary dimension to what the speaker concentrates upon and describes, namely, the activity in progress at 7 o'clock. Thus, if we were to locate on a time line the point described by the

---

17   We must remember that all four sentences in the examples may be rewritten in the non-Continuous form, with, however, difference in the Speaker/Doer Aspect.

sentence *iv.*, we would find that it is the same as in the sentence *i.* (i.e. *7 o'clock yesterday*), though the former contains some more information about the history of the activity. The full list of possible situations that are produced by the three basic points of reference, past, present, and future will be discussed in detail in the chapters devoted to Perfect Tenses.

Another, no less significant consideration that has to be borne in mind while using this variant is that, due to its nature, it imposes upon the described situation the character of a segment (some grammarians call the Perfect tenses, segmental tenses) - no matter what is the nature of the verb, whether it is durative or punctual, in the syntactic context created by this variant of the Perfect it will denote a continuum rather than a point.

Perfect non-Continuous vs. Perfect Continuous

a. A single action / occurrence

The combination of Variant 3 of the Perfect and a single action/occurrence may be baffling to incautious students because it defies the fundamental intuitions acquired at the early stages of English language acquisition (dominated by the Action Aspect of the Continuous) suggesting that the non-Continuous represents a single action/occurrence in its entirety, as a more or less conclusive, independent point. Due to its nature, the Variant 3 imposes its segmental nature on even punctual verbs, presenting everything in the middle of continuation or repetition, i.e. in the middle of an ongoing segment. The meanings attributed by the non-Continuous and the Continuous forms in Variant 3 are determined by the Doer/Speaker Aspect and derive from the opposition between the action presented as willed and kept up by the doer/speaker (the non-Continuous), or just continuing (the Continuous). As a result we can choose between the following pairs of sentences:

i. *When she came, he had written the report for 2 hours already.*
ii. *When she came, he had been writing the report for 2 hours already.*
iii. *He has hammered the lock for a couple of minutes and does not seem to be going to stop soon.*
iv. *He has been hammering the lock for a couple of minutes and does not seem to be going to stop soon.*

All four sentences present an ongoing segment arrested at a specified moment. The first pair of sentences (*i.* and *ii.*) present a single durative action seen at the moment *when she came* being then in the midst of continuation for 2 hours. In the second pair (*iii.* and *iv.*), a single punctual action is multiplied into the form of a series perceived at the moment of speaking in the midst of being repeated. In each of the pairs, we have a choice whether to represent the performance as willed and kept up by the doer (sentences *i.* and *iii.* - the non-Continuous), or (after removing the information about who originates or controls the action) just to present the situation identifying who does what and when but withholding the information who is responsible for the origination or continuation of it (sentences *ii.* and *iv.* - the Continuous).

b. A rule

The fact that a rule naturally describes a certain period over which the activity described continues makes its properties similar to those characterising the modification of meaning imposed upon the verb and the structure of the sentence by this variant of the Perfect. In consequence, the description of a rule in the Perfect and the non-Perfect form look, to some extent, similar with, however, one significant difference. The non-Perfect form (both the Continuous and the non-Continuous) describes a rule in force at a point specified by the sentence, presenting it as being in the middle of operation then (neither at the beginning nor at the end). When we use the Perfect, a rule is also presented at a certain moment but not in the middle of continuation but as having been in force so far, till the moment of reference. Let us compare the following sentences:

i. *She always goes on holiday in June.*
ii. *She is always going on holiday in June.*
iii. *So far, she has always gone on holiday in June.*
iv. *So far, she has always been going on holiday in June.*

The first two sentences, *i.* and *ii.*, present the rule at the moment of speaking in the middle of operation, i.e. the rule started earlier and is expected to continue beyond now, our attention focused upon now. The sentences *iii.* and *iv.* also focus the reader's attention upon 'now' and present the same rule but they handle the presentation in a different way - they present the rule not so much in the middle of an ongoing continuum of unspecified boundaries but now as having operated so far, till the moment of reference (which is 'now'). The latter form excludes the inevitability of future continuation, which is naturally implied in the case of the non-Perfect form. The suggestion indicated by the decision to use or not to use the Continuous may be described by the elements of both the Action and Doer/Speaker Aspect - they are quite close. The use of the non-Continuous will indicate that the speaker perceives the rule as originating from and remaining under control of the will of the doer and, in consequence, being 'regular' and 'predictable', whereas the use of the Continuous will remove this suggestion, representing the rule as a series of occurrences or tendency rather than a realization of some policy of the doer. Similar considerations seem to be standing behind the choice of the Continuous and the non-Continuous in the following sentences.

i. *He sometimes drinks tea instead of coffee.*
ii. *He is sometimes drinking tea instead of coffee.*
iii. *Since 1999, he has sometimes drunk tea instead of coffee.*
iv. *Since 1999, he has sometimes been drinking tea instead of coffee.*
v. *He never played with us.*
vi. *He was never playing with us.*
vii. *Since he had lived there, he had never played with us.*
viii. *Since he had lived there, he had never been playing with us.*

Another of the more obvious modifications of meaning introduced by the selection of the Continuous or the non-Continuous operates between two opposing notions: on the one hand, a primary and permanent rule (the non-Continuous) and, on the other, a secondary/subsidiary and impermanent one (the Continuous). Let us compare:

i. *I have worked for IBM for 15 years.*
ii. *I work in the Accounts Department but since Friday, I have been working in the Human Resources as Mrs White is away and I am substituting for her.*

In the sentence *i.*, the non-Continuous was chosen as better reflecting the fact that the work is probably the primary and permanent occupation of the doer (although, as it was stated in the chapter, it is only a conjecture, not a fact determined by grammar). In the sentence *ii.*, the Continuous was chosen to warn that the work in the Human Resources has a temporary status, the primary job of the doer being that in the Accounts Dept.

Generally speaking, if the context permits, the whole range of meaning modifications described by the Continuous Aspect may be combined with the Perfect.

c. A state

Like in the case of a rule, the natural temporal properties of a state naturally coincide with the characteristics of the Variant 3 - both denote an ongoing 'situation' continuing for some time with, however, the same reservation as in the case of a rule. If the state is presented by the non-Perfect tense, it is presented at some point of reference as being in the middle of continuation, stretching, at the same time, naturally into the past and the future of that point. When a state is described by the Perfect form, it is denoted as present at a moment of reference and continuing for some time since a moment (specified or not) in the anteriority of the point of reference - there is no suggestion (common for the non-Perfect form) that the state is expected to continue beyond the point on which we focus. Let us compare:

i. *At 5, he will be at home.*
ii. *At 5, he will have been at home for 2 hours.*

Both sentences focus upon *5 o'clock,* when the state is to be located. In the case of the sentence *i.*, there is a natural expectation that the state will begin before and will continue beyond *5 o'clock*. The sentence *ii.* 'sees' the state only till *5,* giving no grounds to suppose that it will be bound to continue. The use of the Continuous, as in all other cases of the combinations of the Perfect with the Continuous, is regulated by the Continuous Aspect (the reader is requested to search the information on these matters in the chapter on the Continuous Aspect).

Aspect Perfect in the subordinate clause

The catalogue of functions performed by the Perfect when it is used in the subordinate clauses comprises several additional points, i.e. whenever the situation is characterised by the properties discussed in the chapter on the uses of the Perfect in the main clause, the Perfect obviously is the only choice, however, there are also a few other cases in which the choice of a tense in the subordinate clause is specific for the subordinate clause only. Below, the reader will find a catalogue of these cases.

The Perfect vs. non-Perfect in subordinate clauses

The problem that deserves a special attention of the student of English is the choice between the Perfect and the non-Perfect in subordinate clauses, like time or conditional clauses - the use of the Perfect, although in fact consistent with the natural uses of the Perfect form, is often reported to be a source of serious difficulties. A good illustration of the circumstances determining the choices of that kind is the case of the adverbial clauses of time. The function of the time clause is to locate the moment of the action of the main clause in time. The temporal mutual arrangement of the actions of the main and subordinate clause (i.e. whether they are simultaneous or succeed each other and in what order) is determined by temporal conjunctions like *before, after* (with an exception of conjunctions representing simultaneity like *when*[18]) and can not be changed by the choice of the Perfect or the non-Perfect. The information conveyed by this choice determines the part of the action of the subordinate clause which is the actual reference point for the main clause. Making a choice between the non-Perfect and the Perfect, we choose between referring the main clause to the location of the entire action of the subordinate clause (the non-Perfect) or (in the case of the Perfect) to the location of the moment when the action of the subordinate clause exists either in the form of an effect (like the use of the type of Variant 1), or (like in Variant 3) in the form of an activity perceived at a moment of reference preceded by what of the activity has been being accomplished by that point (i.e. at a given point, the activity of the subordinate clause is in continuation for some time). In other words, whenever we wish to define the temporal location of the action of the main clause by reference to the moment in time when the entire action of the time clause is placed, we use the non-Perfect tenses in the time clause. Thus, the main action will be located as remaining e.g. *'before'* or *'after'* the entire action of the subordinate clause. Whenever we wish to describe the placement in time of the main action by reference to the moment when the action of the subordinate clause exists in the form of effect or at a moment when it has existed so far, we shall use the Perfect form. Let us compare:

i. He left before we had lunch.
ii. He left before we had had lunch.
iii. He left before we had been having lunch for an hour.

As it is suggested by the choice of the non-Perfect in the time clause of the sentence *i.*, the action of the main clause took place before the entire *having* of the lunch. The use of the Perfect in the time clause of the sentence *ii.* and *iii.*, indicates that the moment of reference is either the point when the *having lunch* came to an end (*ii.*) or before the expiration of one hour (*iii.*). Thus, the most obvious difference between the three sentences is that, in the first, the action of the main clause preceded the entire action of the time clause, whereas in the second and third, it may have happened during the action of the time clause but before its end or the expiration of the time specified. In the case of the sentences of the kind of the sentence *ii.* the choice between the Perfect and the non-Perfect makes little difference when we use the conclusive verbs, particularly those which denote the beginning or end of activity like *finish, end, start* or *begin*, e.g.

i. He left before we finished lunch.
ii. He left before we had finished lunch.

As the difference between *finished* and *had it (as) finished* is negligible, in the case of such verbs, the choice between them has no other function as stylistic - the Perfect places emphasis on the fact of completion of the action at the moment described.

---

[18] In the case of conjunctions representing simultaneity, like *when, while, as* etc, the Perfect will mean that the action of the subordinate clause is earlier that the action of the main, and the non-Perfect, that it is simultaneous. Let us analyse:
i. He came when we had watched the show.
ii. He came when we were watching the show.

As it was stated above, the nature of the modification of meaning resulting from employing the Perfect form derives from its origin, i.e. from the structure similar to 'having something (as) done'. Due to this fact, the Perfect is all the more likely when the character of the object of description is close to a static situation, a result of this 'having something (as) done.' When the nature of the object of description is more akin to a dynamic succession of events, the non-Perfect forms are perceived to reflect this fact better. With regard to this fact the English employs two different forms in what seemingly are identical contexts - let us compare:

i. *When I opened the case, the mouse jumped out and escaped.*
ii. *When I had opened the case, I started laying my clothes on the bed to make a selection.*

In the sentence *i.* the *jumping* and *escaping* succeeds directly the *opening* of the case, the latter being treated as a complete event, followed by the others. In the sentence *ii.*, the situation is presented differently - instead of presenting the *opening* as an entire, conclusive event, which, therefore, is 'ready' to be succeeded by other similarly complete events, the structure describes the moment when the subject 'had the case as opened', thus moving the focus onto the static situation suggested by the verb *have* and, therefore, transforming it into a background situation rather than the beginning of a series.

Past Perfect as non-Perfect

Past Perfect, apart from the function consistent with the nature of the Perfect, performs also the role of the non-Perfect tense in the Past, similar to the role played by Past Simple with reference to the Present, i.e. when we choose Past Simple, we indicate that the action is located in the past to the present point of reference and is separated from it (unlike Present Perfect, which uses the past to describe the present). When a point of reference established by the location of the main clause is a past moment, the past version of the Perfect, i.e. Past Perfect is used to describe not only situations characteristic for the Perfect but also such which are incompatible with it, namely, it may be employed to say that some action is in the past of the past moment (since in the past it performs the role played by Past Simple with reference to the present, Past Perfect in this use might be called Past Past Simple). Let us analyse the use of the Perfect in the following sentence:

At 5, he had already learnt that he had failed the exam two days before.

In the main clause, we find Variant 1 of the Perfect (with the help of the *learning* located in the past of 5 o'clock, the speaker describes the situation denoted by *had* at 5, namely, that this *he knew* the result of the exam then). The situation in the object clause is different. Here we have an adverbial of time which clearly refers the clause to the past of 5 o'clock. The adverbial describes the location of the *failing the exam*, focusing the predicate on the main verb rather than on *had,* which is incompatible with the Perfect and suggests that we deal with a form of non-Perfect hiding under the Perfect. Such phenomena are quite common in Reported Speech when the point of reference is in the past, and in the situations that might be called the cases of reverse order. When the English sentence enumerates verb forms in Past Simple, the assumption is that the events described, happened in the order reflected by the order of presentation in the sentence. If, however, any of the events in fact happened earlier than it is manifested by the order of utterance, it is indicated by the use of Past Perfect - for example:

i. *She said that the thief had stolen the ring from her flat.*
ii. *She came home and found that a thief had broken into it during her absence.*

The sentence *i.* illustrates the fact that in Reported Speech, when the main (reporting) clause is in the past, Past Simple is reserved for the situation when the reported event is simultaneous with the act of reporting. When the reported event is earlier than the reporting clause in the past, this fact will be indicated by the use of Past Perfect. Such usage of the Perfect is clearly incompatible with the nature of the Perfect Aspect described above. The usage of the Perfect in the sentence *ii.*, is dictated by the fact that Past Simple would be misleading because it would permit interpretation that this *breaking* was not earlier but that it followed the *coming home.*

Making a choice between the Perfect and the non-Perfect while talking about the past non-Perfect situations, we must bear in mind the fact that in complex sentences with multiple subordinate clauses, Past Perfect is reserved for the situation when the act it denotes remains in the past to the action of the clause that is directly main to it, when it is simultaneous (even to a clause expressed with Past Perfect tense) we use non-Perfect forms instead - for example:

i. *She said that the thief had stolen the ring which was lying on the table.*
ii. *She said that the thief had stolen the ring which had been given her by her late husband.*

In the sentence *i.*, the *lying* is simultaneous to its main clause expressed with Past Perfect; in the sentence *ii.*, the *giving* of the ring by the late husband of that lady was earlier than its main clause, i.e. *stealing* of the ring. In consequence, in the sentence *ii.*, Past Perfect is used, indicating that the event is earlier than *stealing*. However, if the type of the communiqué of the subordinate clause is any of the three variants reserved for the Perfect form in English, the past subordinate clause will be expressed with Past Perfect regardless of the fact that the subordinate clause is simultaneous with the main clause expressed with Past Perfect - for example:

i. *She said that they had discovered a tomb that had been buried in the sand for four thousand years.*
ii. *He said that he had talked to Peter who had lived in this place for over 5 years.*

The sentence ii. is ambiguous because it can mean both that Peter *had once before lived in this place for over 5 years* and that Peter *had been in residence there at that moment for more that 5 years* - in the first case, Past Perfect is used as Past Past Simple, to signal the fact that the living there is earlier than the moment of talking about it, whereas in the other case, the situation is one of the variants reserved for the Aspect Perfect, and the *living*, therefore, is contemporary to the moment of talking.

Past Perfect in hypothetical mood

In hypothetical mood (which is discussed in a separate chapter), Past Perfect is one of two possible forms of the subordinate clause and has two functions to perform. One the one hand, its use indicates that the clause refers to the past of the utterance (not the moment of speaking, but the moment of expressing the sentence to which the Past Perfect construction is a subordinate clause, e.g. in Reported Speech, its reference point of the reported clauses is not the moment of speaking but the location of the reporting clause). At the same time, Past Perfect remains the only available construction to express the grammatical information reserved for the Perfect form, and, thus, when the context requires, will be used not only to refer to the past of the reference point but (in the case of the three variants of the Perfect discussed above) also to describe the situations contemporary and future to the point of reference. Let us analyse the following:

i. *Which house would you buy if you had got that job?*
ii. *Which house would you buy if you got that job?*
iii. *She asked him which house he would buy if he had got that job.*
iv. *If, tomorrow, we had been married for five years, tomorrow, I would have been happy for five years.*

In the sentences *i.* and *iii.*, Past Perfect marks the action (*getting the job*) as earlier than the moment of expressing the utterance, and, therefore, refers to the Past. In the sentence *iv.*, the speaker wishes to express the meaning reserved for the Perfect form (Variant 3, above), and has no choice but to use Past Perfect to talk about the future.

Tenses

Non-Perfect Tenses

Present non-Perfect Tenses

Present Simple vs. Present Continuous

When at the moment of speaking about an action/occurrence, a rule or a state, it has already begun but has not yet come to an end, the situation is recognised by the grammar as Present.

There are two Present tenses which handle the communication in a non-Perfect manner - these are Present Simple and Present Continuous tenses. The choice between the two is dictated by the Aspect Continuous and, therefore, falls into two systems of meaning attribution, Action Aspect and Doer/Speaker Aspect.

Action Aspect

Action Aspect is the primary of the two and conveys information about the status of the action. When the grammatical form of the verb is the only or primary information about the nature of the action with regard to the Continuous, the meaning attributed to the verb by the choice to use or not to use the Continuous will be determined by the Action Aspect. In consequence, it will fall into three basic categories distinguished by the Action Aspect: a single action/occurrence, a rule describing the regularity with which the actions or occurrences take place, a state.

a. A single action/occurrence

the non-Continuous (Present Simple)	the Continuous (Present Continuous)
presents the action or occurrence either in its entirety (or continuing - see Doer/Speaker Aspect)	presents the action or occurrence in the middle of being performed

In the Action Aspect, Present Continuous presents a single action or occurrence in the middle of being performed or happening at the moment of speaking. Present Simple (or: Present non-Continuous) presents it as a whole, in its entirety. One thing, however, has to be remembered - with an exception of punctual verbs, the use of the non-Continuous, here Present Simple, does not, in itself, mean that we present a homogeneous, solid point, like an event. Most English verbs are durative and non-conclusive, and in such cases, the use of Present Simple must be understood as representing the occurrence seen in its entirety, even though this entirety is not so much a point but a defined period.

The act of reporting a present event usually is a variant of two general situations:
- conducting a present tense narrative,
- reporting events that really happen simultaneously to the act of speaking (like, e.g. sports commentaries).

This fact has a significant bearing upon the question of choice between the Continuous and the non-Continuous particularly when we describe a single action and a state. In a narrative it is up to the speaker (who, like the narrator of a fictitious event, has a bird's eye view upon the described situation) how the activities are presented, i.e. as a whole or in the middle. When the speaker conducts a running commentary upon events that actually happen at the moment when he speaks about them, a problem arises as to what should be the criterion that will determine the question whether the activity should be presented as a whole or as being in the middle of happening - the status of durative verbs can not be arbitrarily determined by the speaker (by 'naming' the whole duration and thus presenting them as a whole, e.g. *he reads the paper for 2 minutes*) and has to be recognized with regard to the context in which they appear.

A present narrative

A good illustration of the narrative situation we shall find in e.g. jokes and stage instructions appended to the text of a drama. Let us analyse the following:

He enters the stage from the left, comes to the table and picks up one of the newspapers. He reads it for a few seconds, then drops it back on the table, turns and walks to the window, where he stops. When he is looking through the window, Mary enters through the door on the right.

As we can see, the choice of Present Simple ignores the question whether the event described has the form of a point or a period (compare *enters*, *picks up* or *stops* with *reads for a few seconds* and *walks*). Present Continuous is used only when we present an action in the middle of being performed at some moment (specified or implied). In the example above, the reason why the Continuous is used is the fact that the activity of *looking* is not seen in its entirety but in the middle at the moment *when Mary enters the stage*.

A present report

A similar though not identical situation to the above case of a narrative is the use of non-Perfect Present tenses to report the events happening at the moment of speaking. Here, in consequence of the properties of the situation, i.e. talking of events at the moment when they happen, we need some method that would make it possible to determine what kind of occurrences are to be represented with the use of the non-Continuous (presenting them, in the Action Aspect, in their entirety) and which, with the use of the Continuous. The circumstance which apparently determines such choices is the temporal relation between the act of speaking and the event spoken of:
- when the act of speaking tends to be longer than the action spoken of, the event may be perceived in its entirety, therefore, the preferable form in the Action Aspect will be the non-Continuous,
- when the act of speaking tends to be shorter than the action spoken of, the event may be perceived from within, which means, in the middle of happening, therefore, the preferable form in the Action Aspect will be the Continuous.

Let us compare the following situations:
i. *Green passes the ball to Jones, Jones intercepts and shoots to Brown, but Brown is looking somewhere else. He misses it.*
ii. *The horses are galloping with tremendous power, Morning Cloud is steadily moving towards the front of the group.*

The sentence *i.* may be a fragment of a football match commentary. During such an event, the actions reported by the speaker are so short that the act of naming them is longer than what it names. As a result, the act of speaking naturally can address them as entire items, hence the use of the non-Continuous. A different situation is encountered in the case of *looking somewhere else* which is longer than the act of speaking, and, therefore, is addressed as something unfinished, seen in the middle of happening, hence the Continuous form. The sentence *ii.* is a commentary on a horse race. In such a situation, the act of speaking is shorter than the activities named by it, therefore, the natural form will be the Continuous, which presents the action as being 'in the middle of happening.'

Performative verbs - Present Simple vs. Present Continuous

There is a class of verbs and expressions in whose case the utterance of the phrase is, at the same time, the performance of the action that they denote. Since the utterance and the action are one, in the situation of simple communication of a single action or occurrence, the verb always names the action in its entirety, therefore, the natural form for such verbs is the non-Continuous, hence Present Simple.

 i. I <u>swear</u> that she has been with me for the last half hour.
 ii. I <u>promise</u> you to remain here till you come back.
 iii. I <u>give you my word</u> she will pass the final exams.

Although the verb *give* is not as such a performative verb, in the sentence *iii.* it is a part of a phrase equivalent to the performative *promise*, and, therefore, in this case, its form is the effect of the same mechanism.

b. A rule

	the non-Continuous (Present Simple)	the Continuous (Present Continuous)
prolonged, uninterrupted activity	presents it as primary, permanent, endless (at the moment of reference)	presents it as temporary, subsidiary
a series of events	presents them as governed by a rule - orderly, predictable, primary	presents them as disorderly series of accidents, transient, subsidiary

When we talk about a rule in the Continuous Action Aspect in English, we make a choice within two binary oppositions:
- permanent, primary vs. transitory, secondary,
- orderly vs. accidental.

The use of Present Continuous presents the rule either as temporary/transitory (in the case of prolonged uninterrupted activities as *work, live*), or as a disorderly series of occurrences (in the case of a series of disconnected actions). When we use Present Simple, the natural assumption will be that we wish to mark the rule as opposite in nature to the above, namely, as primary, permanent and orderly. However, we must remember that the non-Continuous does not mark the rule as specific in any way, stating merely the existence of the activity or a series. Thus, the interpretation that the rule expressed by Present Simple is permanent and primary must be understood not so much as communicated by the grammar as rather a permitted inference from the fact that instead of the Continuous, the non-Continuous has been used. In other words, Present Simple may be used both to represent a permanent and a transitory rule, though the common natural assumption is that the choice of Present Simple is an indication of a wish to mark the rule as primary, permanent and orderly.

A separate question is the criterion that is to be employed in determining whether a present, and, therefore, unfinished rule should be regarded as permanent or temporary. This determinant is the speaker's knowledge (or its absence) of when the rule is to end. If the rule is still qualified as permanent at the moment of which we speak its end is unknown to the person to whom it applies. When the end, at the moment of which we speak, is already known, the rule may be considered temporary. This choice is independent of the comparative lengths of the two types of rules. Let us consider a situation of a student passing entrance exams to a university in a different town and, simultaneously, moving his home to a still different town. He will move his furniture to his new residence and after a few weeks will leave to live in the university town where he will remain for a few years of his education. Majority of this time will be spent at the university, away from his new 'home town'. Nevertheless, while speaking about the infrequently visited 'home town' he will be saying *I live there* and talking about the university town, *I am living there*. The latter choice of the Continuous, indicative of the fact that the rule is of a temporary nature, is not obligatory and will only be made if one wished to inform with the use of grammar about this fact. It would not be ungrammatical to use the unmarked non-Continuous - the only difference between the two forms in this case is the fact that the Continuous would be more precise in rendering the nature of the situation. However, if we judged that our interlocutor does not deserve to be informed so precisely (being e.g. an inquisitive barber or pumping station attendant) or that we do not need to state the fact because it is known to the listener, the non-Continuous (Present Simple) would be an equally acceptable choice.

An additional consideration that must be taken into account in making a choice between the Continuous and the non-Continuous is sometimes the question whether the rule is of a primary, basic type or additional and subsidiary - a good illustration is a permanent job and some temporary, additional one. If the rule is primary, the preferred form will remain the non-Continuous (Present Simple) even if the end of the rule is known like, e.g. in the situation when a person already knows the date of his retirement - throughout the remaining years or months while talking about where he works he is likely to prefer Present Simple to Present Continuous.

c. A state

The Continuous is to a large extent antagonistic to what is intuited as constituting the nature of a state, therefore, the combination of the Continuous with the stative verb frequently not so much enriches its meaning as rather alters it, modifying certain elements making up the character of the described phenomenon. Thus, whenever, in the present, we wish to present a state in its 'natural', commonly intuited form, we use Present Simple. The addition of the Continuous will change significantly certain properties of the state described (a detailed discussion will be found in the chapter on Aspect Continuous). An additional consideration that must be borne in mind is that the actual shape of the modification of meaning produced by the Continuous when combined with a stative verb depends often upon the meaning of the verb, different combinations producing different effects (the list of these verb categories will be found in the chapter on the Continuous Aspect), therefore, the presentation below must be regarded as a certain approximation, not a complete list.

- The Continuous may change a state into a kind of action performed by the subject.
    i. *He is patient.* (permanent neutral state)
    ii. *He is being patient with me.* (he acts in this manner)

- The Continuous, in the case of words having also dynamic punctual meaning, like *see*, may be used (as an alternative to the construction with auxiliary *can*) to reaffirm the fact that what is presented is, at the moment described, an ongoing experience/situation seen in the middle.
    i. *I can't believe what I am seeing.* (BNC - H8M 2191)
    ii. *'... Parmedes, you do realise what you are hearing is highly confidential material, don't you?'* (BNC - AD9 3893)

This modification produces significant changes in the Past and Future utterances, in which the possibility of the alternative punctual meaning is clearly perceived to be a conspicuous option, which, therefore, requires clarification. In the Present, it seems to be the effect of a habit formed in the other two time references (Past and Future) than a distinct modification of the original meaning of the verb, i.e. the meaning of the above two sentences would not be changed if the non-Continuous were used instead of the Continuous:
    i. *I can't believe what I see.* (non-Continuous paraphrase of BNC - H8M 2191)
    ii. *'... Parmedes, you do realise what you hear is highly confidential material, don't you?'* (non-Continuous paraphrase of BNC - AD9 3893)

- When expressed with the non-Continuous form, a stative verb is intuited as describing a state as an uninterrupted phenomenon. The use of the Continuous may change this intuition, transforming the object of description into a series of similar static instances.
    i. *Nonetheless, as a long-established reader of the medical journals, it does strike me that we are hearing much more about increasingly curious self-administrations.* (BNC - B7N 1525)

ii. *'My head's cleared now, the cigarettes are tasting good again...'*[19]

The use of the Continuous implies that what is denoted is neither a single uninterrupted phenomenon, nor a rule but a series of incidents of a similar nature.

- The Continuous may be used to emphasise the temporary nature of the experience, stressing the impression that what is being described is not a boundless ability but a passing experience.
    i. *Again, the viewfinder image will alert you to the problem by showing you how the camcorder is seeing the scene.* (BNC - CBP 505)
    ii. *Again, the viewfinder image will alert you to the problem by showing you how the camcorder sees the scene.*

In the above examples, the Continuous changes the nature of what is represented by the verb *see* from the characteristic feature of the object (i.e. Present Simple - how, by nature, the camcorder as such always sees the scene) into reference to a particular experience each time it happens (i.e. how a/your camcorder, at a given time, is seeing it, in other words, how the situation looks, at a given time, when seen by a/your camcorder).

- The Continuous may be used to reflect the fact that the state described is not natural and 'flat' but characterised by an increased or increasing intensity.
    i. *Son, we must finish this call - it is costing you a fortune.*
    ii. *I think she is understanding slowly what her situation really is.*
    iii. *I am loving every minute of this film.*

All the above three sentences can be rewritten in the non-Continuous but we would lose a warning/indication that the intensity of the state is changing (the sentences *i.* and *ii.*) or has increased (the sentence *iii.*).

- The Continuous may be used to emphasise the fact that the state, at the moment described, exists not in its final shape but progresses towards it.
    i. *He clearly resembles his father in every respect.*
    ii. *He resembles his father more and more.*
    iii. *He is resembling his father more and more.*

The sentence *i.* presents the resemblance between the two as a finally established fact, hence the non-Continuous, which merely names the state in its fully-developed shape is sufficiently precise. The sentences *ii.* and *iii.*, describe a process progressing towards reaching its fullness determined by the meaning of the verb. This fact may be expressed with the use of lexical items alone (*more and more*), but the fact may be rendered with increased clarity if we use an accompanying structure of the Continuous, stressing the instability of the described phenomenon.

As it was stated above, the above list must be perceived as only an introduction to the consequences of the combination between the Continuous and the stative, the complete presentation to be found in the chapter on the Continuous Action Aspect.

Doer/Speaker Aspect

This chapter presents the cases when the choice of the Continuous signals an intention to inform about the speaker or doer rather than about the activity. Using this fragment of the Continuous Aspect we must remember that it is secondary to the Action Aspect, i.e. that it is recognisable only when either the situation or the context has independently established the shape of the Action Aspect as non-Continuous or the non-conclusive nature of the verb makes the distinctions of the Action Aspect negligible. There are four types of modifications resulting from such use of the Continuous. Since these are all auxiliary structures, employing the same grammatical form, their use requires exercise of sufficient caution lest the meaning should become ambiguous - as the situations that legitimise the use of the Continuous are not mutually exclusive, the significance of the Continuous in one and the same sentence may be interpreted in different ways, which makes it additionally important to clarify with the syntax or extralinguistic components of the situation, which of the following cases the use of the Continuous addresses.

---

19 Rabinowitch, Willa. *Heavier Than Air.* Sewanee Review, Summer97, Vol. 105 Issue 3, p299, 17p. 1997. Corpus of Contemporary American English. http://www.americancorpus.org. Accessed: 02.08.2009, 07:00.

	the non-Continuous	the Continuous
1.	Neutral presentation of the situation.	It indicates emotional attitude of the speaker to the situation described by the sentence.
2.	It may be intuited as identifying the doer or the speaker as the originator or controller of the action, i.e. somebody who keeps it up.	It removes the information as to who is the originator of the action, leaving it unmarked.
3.	In the narrative, the non-Continuous is the form reserved for the presentation of the foreground action.	In the narrative, the Continuous is the form indicating the background status of the action.
4.	In conversational English, this form is regarded as blunt and inconsiderate.	In conversational English, this form is perceived as more 'polite'.

1. Neutral vs. emotional presentation

When either the Action Aspect is determined as non-Continuous by the context (the rest of the sentence, the situation) or the non-conclusive nature of the verb makes the distinctions of the Action Aspect negligible, the Continuous may be employed to indicate that you are moved by the described event. Thus, in such cases, Present Simple will represent the situation in a neutral shape, without disclosing any feelings of the speaker or doer whereas Present Continuous will give the utterance a perceivably emotional character. This grammatical modification is most often employed when the non-Continuous nature of the described event is most obvious, namely in the case of talking about a rule and a state, though in the case of a single action/occurrence it is also possible.
    i. He is always forgetting his money at home.
    ii. He always forgets his money at home.
    iii. I love it.
    iv. I'm loving it.
    v. Well I never, I'm meeting you again.
    vi. Well, I meet you again.
The Continuous alternatives in the above sentences may indicate that the speaker is moved by what is described. We must remember that the actual nature of this agitation (i.e. whether it is positive or negative: a sign of admiration or criticism) is not determined by grammar but must be inferred from the context.

2. Activity presented as intended vs. activity presented as merely happening

The non-Continuous creates utterances which seem to point towards the doer/speaker as the one who has initiated the action and keeps it up, i.e. is responsible for the fact that the activity continues. This impression is removed by the use of the Continuous. Thus, Present Simple is used when the activity is intended or kept up by the speaker/doer, and Present Continuous is chosen when we wish to avoid such identification and are satisfied with merely naming the elements of the action, i.e. who does what.
    i. He watches her on TV at the moment.
    ii. He is watching her on TV at the moment.
    iii. I seldom meet her at Peter's.
    iv. I am seldom meeting her at Peter's.
Present Simple used in the sentence *i.* sends a strong signal suggesting that the activity is kept up and willed by the doer, whereas Present Continuous removes this suggestion, leaving just a bare statement of fact. In the case of a rule (the sentences *iii.* and *iv.*), Present Simple may be read as a neutral statement of fact or an indication that the continuance of the rule is intended, and that possibly, the events that make it up are also such. Thus, the sentence *iii.* may be additionally interpreted as stating that the subject seldom

makes appointments at Peter's. Present Continuous, by removing the element of intentionality, will make an impression that what is being described is a series of accidents.

In the case of a state, since by nature it is involuntary, it can not be represented as willed or kept up. Thus, Present Simple will make a neutral statement of fact. The use of Present Continuous, on the other hand, will strengthen the impression that what is presented is accidental and unintended.
   i. Summing up all the costs at this quite initial level, the enterprise is already costing us a fortune.
   ii. Summing up all the costs at this quite initial level, the enterprise already costs us a fortune.

3. Foreground vs. background activity
In a narrative (when permitted by the Action Aspect), the intentional character of the activity suggested by the non-Continuous (Present Simple) makes it a more appropriate form to express the foreground actions, whereas the fact that the Continuous (Present Continuous) is perceived to represent neutrally what is in the middle of happening at a given moment, makes it a more likely choice to present the activities which remain in the background of the main plot:
   I enter the room and I see them occupied. Mary is listening to music and Henry is writing in a notebook. I yell at them, and they jump from their seats and run to me.

4. Direct (blunt) address vs. less direct (more polite) address
Since the non-Continuous is recognised as expressing the intentional character of what is said, it is regarded inappropriate in situations when we wish to show our deference and avoid the impression that we impose on our interlocutor (particularly when asking questions or requesting something - see Continuous Doer/Speaker Aspect). In the situations when we want to show our respect, we will use Present Continuous. If we do not care if we sound blunt or even arrogant, we may use Present Simple.
   i. I think of going on holidays in June.
   ii. I am thinking of going on holidays in June.
   iii. I wonder if I could ask you a favour.
   iv. I am wondering if I could ask you a favour.
   v. Do you leave, Mr Smith?
   vi. Are you leaving Mr Smith?
The fact that Present Simple seems particularly blunt in interrogative constructions may be owing to the intentional character of the non-Continuous – its use in the question makes the interlocutor respond in the same construction, which forces him/her to make a statement of a character of a declaration/ a promise. In consequence, the interrogated persons may feel that instead of just describing the situation, they are called to oblige themselves to do something. Consequently, when people feel they are not in a position to demand such declarations (e.g. talking to their superiors), they tend to avoid the non-Continuous forms, here, Present Simple. In the opposite situation, namely when people have authority over others, they are free to choose either the direct but blunt and impolite address of the non-Continuous, or wrap their statements in a more polite, and, therefore, more palatable Continuous form[20].

---

20 A step further in the direction of making the statement sound more polite is to express it in the past form - this construction is discussed in the chapter Past non-Perfect.

Past non-Perfect Tenses

Past Simple vs. Past Continuous

When, at the moment of speaking about an action/occurrence, a rule or a state, it no longer continues because it came to an end before the moment when we speak of it, the situation is recognised by the grammar as Past. There are two Past tenses which handle the communication in a non-Perfect manner - these are Past Simple and Past Continuous tenses. The choice between the two is dictated by the Aspect Continuous and, therefore, falls into two systems of meaning attribution, Action Aspect and Doer/Speaker Aspect.

Action Aspect

Action Aspect is the primary of the two and conveys the information about the status of the action. When the grammatical form of the verb is the only or primary information about the nature of the action with regard to the Continuous, the meaning attributed to the verb by the choice to use or not to use the Continuous will be determined by the Action Aspect. In consequence, it will fall into three basic categories distinguished by the Action Aspect: a single action/occurrence, a rule describing the regularity with which the actions or occurrences take place, and a state.

a. A single action/occurrence

the non-Continuous (Past Simple)	the Continuous (Past Continuous)
presents the action or occurrence either in its entirety (or continuing - see Doer/Speaker Aspect)	presents the action or occurrence in the middle of being performed

In the Action Aspect, Past Continuous presents a single action or occurrence in the middle of being performed or happening at a specified or implied moment in the past. Past Simple (or: Past non-Continuous) presents it as a whole, in its entirety. One thing, however, has to be remembered - with an exception of punctual verbs, the use of the non-Continuous, here Past Simple, does not, in itself, mean that we present a homogeneous, solid point, like an event. Most English verbs are durative and non-conclusive, and in such cases, the use of Past Simple must be understood as representing the occurrence seen in its entirety, even though this entirety is not so much a point as a defined period.

In the situations regulated by the Action Aspect, Past Continuous is used to present a single action/occurrence only when there is a specified moment at which the action is perceived as 'caught' in the middle of happening. In all other cases of both punctual verbs and durative, the nature of Past Simple (which, after all, is nothing more than a name of the activity marked as past) is broad enough to render these situations with precision sufficient for the English grammar.

Performative verbs - Past Simple vs. Past Continuous

There is a class of verbs and expressions in whose case the utterance of the phrase is, at the same time, the performance of the action that it denotes. Since the utterance and the action is one, in the situation of simple communication of a single action or occurrence, the verb always names the action in its entirety, therefore, the natural form for such verbs is the non-Continuous, hence Past Simple.

    i. *He swore that she had been with him for the past half hour.*
    ii. *She promised me to remain there till I came back.*
    iii. *I remember you gave her your word that her son would pass the final exams.*

Although the verb *give* is not as such a performative verb, in the sentence *iii.* it is a part of a phrase equivalent to the performative *promise*, and, therefore, in this case, its form is the effect of the same mechanism.

b. A rule

	the non-Continuous (Past Simple)	the Continuous (Present Continuous)
prolonged, uninterrupted activity	presents it as primary, permanent, endless (at the moment of reference)	presents it as temporary/transitory, secondary
a series of events	presents them as governed by a rule - orderly, predictable, primary	presents them as disorderly series of accidents, transient, subsidiary

When we talk about a rule in the Continuous Action Aspect in English, we make a choice within two binary oppositions:
- permanent, primary vs. transitory, secondary,
- orderly vs. accidental.

The use of Past Continuous presents the rule either as temporary/transitory (in the case of prolonged uninterrupted activities as *work, live*), or as a disorderly series of occurrences (in the case of a series of disconnected actions). When we use Past Simple, the natural assumption will be that we wish to mark the rule as opposite in nature to the above, namely, as primary, permanent and orderly. However, we must remember that the non-Continuous does not mark the rule as specific in any way, stating merely the existence of the activity or a series. Thus, the interpretation that the rule expressed by Past Simple is permanent and primary must be understood not so much as communicated by the grammar as rather a permitted inference from the fact that instead of the Continuous, the non-Continuous has been used. In other words, Past Simple may be used both to represent a permanent and a temporary rule, though the common natural assumption is that the choice of Past Simple is an indication of a wish to mark the rule as primary, permanent and orderly.

A separate question is the criterion that is to be employed in determining whether a past, and, therefore, finished, rule should be regarded as permanent or temporary (after all, from the moment of speaking, all past rules are finished and, therefore, temporary). The circumstance that decides this question is the knowledge or attitude of the subject of the rule – if, for this person, at the moment of which we speak, the rule was primary, permanent, orderly, the form proper for this situation will be Past Simple; if, however, for this person, the rule was temporary, disorderly series of accidents, the form preferred will be Past Continuous.

The student of English needs to remember that the choice of the Continuous, indicative of the fact that the rule is of a temporary nature, is not obligatory and will only be made if one wishes to inform about this transitory nature with the use of grammar, i.e. by giving the verb a Continuous form. It would not be ungrammatical to use the unmarked non-Continuous - the only difference between the two forms in this case is the fact that the Continuous would be more precise in rendering the nature of the situation. However, if we judged that our interlocutor does not deserve to be informed so precisely (being e.g. merely an inquisitive barber or pumping station attendant, etc.) or that we do not need to state the fact because it is already known to the listener, the non-Continuous (Past Simple) would be an equally acceptable choice.

An additional consideration that must be taken into account in making a choice between the Continuous and the non-Continuous is sometimes the question whether the rule is of a primary, basic type or additional and subsidiary - a good illustration is a permanent job and some temporary, additional one. If the rule was primary, the preferred form will remain the non-Continuous (Past Simple) even if the end of the rule was known at the moment of which we speak, like, e.g. in the situation when a person already knew the date of his retirement - talking about the remaining years or months of his working there we would be likely to prefer Past Simple to Past Continuous.

b. A state

The Continuous is to a large extent antagonistic to what is intuited as constituting the nature of a state, therefore, the combination of the Continuous with the stative verb frequently not so much enriches its meaning as rather alters it, modifying certain elements making up the character of the described phenomenon. Thus, whenever, in the past, we wish to present a state in its 'natural', commonly intuited form, we use Past Simple. The addition of the Continuous will change significantly certain properties of the state described (a detailed discussion will be found in the chapter on Aspect Continuous). An additional consideration that must be borne in mind is that the actual shape of the modification of meaning produced by the Continuous when combined with a stative verb depends often upon the meaning of the verb, different combinations producing different effects (the list of these verb categories will be found in the chapter on the Continuous Aspect), therefore, the presentation below must be regarded as a certain approximation, not a complete list.

- The Continuous may change a state into a kind of action performed by the subject.
    i. He was patient. (permanent neutral state)
    ii. He was being patient with me. (he acts in this manner)

- The Continuous, in the case of words having also dynamic punctual meaning, like *see*, may be used (as an alternative to the construction with auxiliary *can*) to reaffirm the fact that what is presented is, at the moment described, an ongoing experience/situation seen in the middle.
    i. I couldn't believe what I was seeing. (past version of BNC - H8M 2191)
    ii. I was informed that what we were hearing was no longer classified.

- When expressed with the non-Continuous form, a stative verb is intuited as describing a state as an uninterrupted phenomenon. The use of the Continuous may change this intuition, transforming the object of description into a series of similar static instances.
    In those days, we were hearing many similar stories.
The use of the Continuous implies that what is denoted is neither a single uninterrupted phenomenon, nor a rule but a series of incidents of a similar nature.

- The Continuous may be used to emphasise the transitory nature of the experience, stressing the impression that what is being described is not a boundless ability but a passing experience.
    i. To assess whether she was understanding what she read, I asked, 'Does that happen at your school?' (BNC - B1Y 1365)
    ii. To assess whether she understood what she read...
In the above examples, the Continuous changes the nature of what is represented by the verb *understand* from the apparently permanent property of the person (i.e. Past Simple indicating her *understanding* as a stable and final phenomenon) into something that is rather a particular experience in the shape existing only when it takes place (i.e. the *understanding* is presented as changing and progressing, following the altering sense of the text).

- The Continuous may be used to reflect the fact that the state described is not natural and 'flat' but characterised by an increased or increasing intensity.
    i. After devaluation, the food naturally was costing more and more.
    ii. I saw she was understanding slowly what was the meaning of what she was seeing.
    iii. She was loving every minute of her stay there.
All the above three sentences can be rewritten in the non-Continuous but we would lose a warning/indication that the intensity of the state was changing (the sentences *i.* and *ii.* -with the exception of *seeing*, which rather belongs to the point immediately preceding this one) or had increased (the sentence *iii.*).

- The Continuous may be used to emphasise the fact that the state, at the moment described, exists not in its final shape but progresses towards it.
    i. He clearly resembled his father in every respect.
    ii. He resembled his father more and more.
    iii. He was resembling his father more and more.
The sentence *i.* presents the resemblance between the two as a finally established fact, hence the non-Continuous, which merely names the state in its fully-developed shape, is sufficiently precise. The sentences *ii.* and *iii.*, describe a process progressing towards reaching its fullness determined by the meaning of the verb. This fact may be expressed with the use of lexical items alone (*more and more*), but

the fact may be rendered with increased clarity if we use an accompanying structure of the Continuous, stressing the instability of the described phenomenon.

As it was stated at the beginning of the presentation of the state, the above list must be perceived as only an introduction to the consequences of the combination between the Continuous and the stative, the complete presentation to be found in the chapter on the Continuous Action Aspect.

Doer/Speaker Aspect

This chapter presents the cases when the choice of the Continuous signals an intention to inform about the speaker or doer rather than about the activity. Using this fragment of the Continuous Aspect we must remember that it is secondary to the Action Aspect, i.e. that it is recognisable only when either the situation or the context has independently established the shape of the Action Aspect as non-Continuous or the non-conclusive nature of the verb makes the distinctions of the Action Aspect negligible. There are four types of modifications resulting from such use of the Continuous. Since these are all auxiliary structures, employing the same grammatical form, their use requires exercise of sufficient caution lest the meaning should become ambiguous - as the situations that legitimise the use of the Continuous are not mutually exclusive, the significance of the Continuous in one and the same sentence may be interpreted in different ways, which makes it additionally important to clarify with the syntax or extralinguistic components of the situation, which of the following cases the use of the Continuous addresses.

	the non-Continuous	the Continuous
1.	Neutral presentation of the situation.	It indicates emotional attitude of the speaker to the situation described by the sentence.
2.	It may be intuited as identifying the doer or the speaker as the originator or controller of the action, i.e. somebody who keeps it up.	It removes the information as to who is the originator of the action, leaving it unmarked.
3.	In the narrative, the non-Continuous is the form reserved for the presentation of the foreground action.	In the narrative, the Continuous is the form indicating the background status of the action.
4.	In conversational English, this form is perceived as blunt and inconsiderate.	In conversational English, this form is perceived as more 'polite'.

1. Neutral vs. emotional presentation

When either the Action Aspect is determined as non-Continuous by the context (the rest of the sentence, the situation) or the non-conclusive nature of the verb makes the distinctions of the Action Aspect negligible, the Continuous may be employed to indicate that the subject is moved by the described event. Thus, in such cases, Past Simple will represent the situation in a neutral shape, without disclosing any feelings of the speaker or doer whereas Past Continuous will give the utterance a perceivably emotional character. This grammatical modification is most often employed when the non-Continuous nature of the described event is most obvious, namely in the case of talking about a rule and a state, though in the case of a single action/occurrence it is also possible.

   i. He was always forgetting his money at home.
   ii. He always forgot his money at home.
   iii. It was clear that he wanted it very, very much.
   iv. It was clear that he was wanting it very, very much.
   v. I saw you! You were meeting him again!.
   vi. I saw you. You met him again.

The Continuous alternatives in the above sentences may indicate that the doer was moved by what is described. We must remember that the actual nature of this agitation (i.e. whether it is positive or negative: a sign of admiration or criticism) is not determined by grammar but must be inferred from the context.

2. Activity presented as intended vs. activity presented as merely happening

The non-Continuous creates utterances which seem to point towards the doer/speaker as the one who has initiated the action and keeps it up. This impression is removed by the use of the Continuous. Thus, Past Simple is used when the activity was intended or kept up by the speaker/doer, and Past Continuous is chosen when we wish to avoid such identification and are satisfied with merely naming the elements of the action, i.e. who did what.

i. I came home unexpectedly and guess what I found. He watched her from behind the curtain.
ii. When I came, he was watching her from behind the curtain.
iii. I seldom met her at Peter's.
iv. I was seldom meeting her at Peter's.

Past Simple used in the sentence *i.* sends a strong signal suggesting that the activity was kept up and willed by the doer, whereas Past Continuous removes this suggestion, leaving just a bare statement of fact[21]. In the case of a rule (the sentences *iii.* and *iv.*), Past Simple may be read as a neutral statement of fact or an indication that the continuance of the rule was intended, and that, possibly, the events that made it up were also such. Thus, the sentence *iii.* may be additionally interpreted as stating that the subject seldom made appointments at Peter's. Past Continuous, by removing the element of intentionality, will make an impression that what is being described is a series of accidents.

In the case of a state, since by nature it is involuntary, it can not be represented as willed or kept up. Thus, Past Simple will make a neutral statement of fact (besides, such is the meaning attributed by the Action Aspect, and the latter is primary to the Doer/Speaker Aspect). The use of Past Continuous, on the other hand, will strengthen the impression that what is presented was accidental and unintended.

i. Summing up all the costs at that quite initial level, the enterprise was already costing us a fortune.
ii. Summing up all the costs at that quite initial level, the enterprise already cost us a fortune.

3. Foreground vs. background activity

In a narrative (when permitted by the Action Aspect), the intentional character of the activity suggested by the non-Continuous (Past Simple) makes it a more appropriate form to express the foreground actions, whereas the fact that the Continuous (Past Continuous) is perceived to represent neutrally what was in the middle of happening at a given moment, makes it a more likely choice to present the activities which remained in the background of the main plot.

I entered the room and I saw them occupied. Mary was listening to music and Henry was writing in a notebook. I yelled at them, and they jumped from their seats and ran to me.

4. Direct (blunt) address vs. less direct (more polite) address

Since the non-Continuous is recognised as expressing the intentional character of what is said, it is regarded inappropriate in situations when we wish to show our deference and avoid the impression that we impose on our interlocutor (particularly when asking questions or requesting something - see Continuous Doer/Speaker Aspect). In the situations when we want to show our respect, we will use Past Continuous. If we do not care if we sound blunt or even arrogant, we may use Past Simple.

i. Did you talk to John, Mr Smith?
ii. Were you talking to John, Mr Smith?
iii. Did you prepare the report yesterday?
iv. Were you preparing the report yesterday?

The fact that Past Simple seems particularly blunt in interrogative constructions may be owing to the intentional character of the non-Continuous – its use in the question makes the interlocutor respond in the

---

21 The time clause of the sentence *i.* is different from that of the sentence *ii.* to avoid ambiguity. Although it is not a rule, the more common interpretation of the temporal relation between the activity of the time clause and the main clause when the time clause uses the conjunction *when* and there are non-Continuous forms (which tend to be interpreted as rendering the activity as a whole, not in the middle) in both clauses is that the activity of the main clause succeeds that of the time clause - using Past Simple in the main clause of a sentence of the type of the sentence *ii.*, we must remember that it might also mean that the activity of *watching* was not caught in the middle by the entrance of the subject of the time clause but that the activity followed it.

same construction, which forces him/her to make a statement of a character of a declaration/ a promise. In consequence, the interrogated persons may feel that instead of just describing the situation, they are called to oblige themselves to do something. Consequently, when people feel they are not in a position to demand such declarations (e.g. talking to their superiors), they tend to avoid the non-Continuous forms, here, Past Simple. In the opposite situation, namely when people have authority over others, they are free to choose either the direct but blunt and impolite address of the non-Continuous, or wrap their statements in a more polite, and, therefore, more palatable Continuous form.

Attitudinal Past

In situations when we feel we are required to express extra politeness, we may indicate it by using Past Continuous with reference to Present and Future. The impression that such modification enhances the impression of reverence and politeness crated by our statement and makes it less antagonistic results possibly from the enlargement of the distance between the participants in the conversation and the form in which the situation is rendered by the sentence.

i. I hope you will give me my leave in June.
ii. I am hoping you will be able to give me my leave in June.
iii. I was hoping you could give me my leave in June.

The most possibly antagonistic because direct and blunt is the sentence *i*. It confronts the participants in the conversation with the situation in which both parties are rendered in their true shape: the speaker confronts the interlocutor with his hope expressed in the form that suggests that this hope is willed and presented here and now to appeal to the willingness (named directly) of the addressee of the statement. In the sentence *ii.* the antagonistic character is mitigated by the Continuous form of *hope*, which deprives it of the form that suggests that the speaker wishes to 'throw' it in the face of the interlocutor, changing it into a report of a phenomenon that exists as if independently of the conversation. Likewise, the change from *you will give* into *you will be able to give* alters the situation into a more comfortable one for the recipient - he is no longer asked to say if he is willing to give the permission or refuses to give it; now, what is asked of him is to assess if the situation is likely to permit him to grant the permission. In the case of refusal, the situation will be to blame, not the boss. The most polite because the least antagonistic is the sentence *iii.* because it additionally makes an impression that both parties are disassociated from the described situation - *was hoping* and *could give* may be interpreted as either referring to the past (which means that it is no longer here for them to respond) or being hypothetical, i.e. referring to the situation that does not and will not exist and the response to which will put no obligation upon the parties involved in the talk.

Future non-Perfect Tenses

Future Simple vs. Future Continuous

When at the moment of speaking about an action/occurrence, a rule or a state, it has not yet begun and is only expected to happen, the situation is recognised by the grammar as Future. There are two Future tenses which handle the communication in a non-Perfect manner - these are Future Simple and Future Continuous tenses. The choice between the two is dictated by the Aspect Continuous and, therefore, falls into two systems of meaning attribution, Action Aspect and Doer/Speaker Aspect.

Action Aspect

Action Aspect is the primary of the two and conveys the information about the status of the action. When the grammatical form of the verb is the only or primary information about the nature of the action with regard to the Continuous, the meaning attributed to the verb by the choice to use or not to use the Continuous will be determined by the Action Aspect. In consequence, it will fall into three basic categories distinguished by the Action Aspect: a single action/occurrence, a rule describing the regularity with which the actions or occurrences take place, and a state.

a. A single action/occurrence

the non-Continuous (Future Simple)	the Continuous (Future Continuous)
presents the action or occurrence either in its entirety (or continuing - see Doer/Speaker Aspect)	presents the action or occurrence in the middle of being performed

In the Action Aspect, Future Continuous presents a single action or occurrence in the middle of being performed or happening at a specified or implied moment in the future. Future Simple (or: Future non-Continuous) presents it as a whole, in its entirety. One thing, however, has to be remembered - with an exception of punctual verbs, the use of the non-Continuous, here Future Simple, does not mean that we present a homogeneous, solid point, like an event. Most English verbs are durative and non-conclusive, and in such cases, the use of Future Simple must be understood as representing the occurrence seen in its entirety, even though this entirety is not so much a point as a defined period.

In the situations regulated by the Action Aspect, Future Continuous is used to present a single action/occurrence only when there is a specified moment at which the action is perceived as 'caught' in the middle of happening. In all other cases of both punctual verbs and durative, the nature of Future Simple (which, after all, is nothing more than a name of the activity marked as past) is broad enough to render these situations with precision sufficient for the English grammar.

Performative verbs - Future Simple vs. Future Continuous

There is a class of verbs and expressions in whose case the utterance of the phrase is, at the same time, the performance of the action that they denote. Since the utterance and the action is one, in the situation of simple communication of a single action or occurrence, the verb always names the action in its entirety, therefore, the natural form for such verbs is the non-Continuous, hence Future Simple.

i. I will swear that she was with me for at least half hour.
ii. We will promise to remain there till you come back.
iii. I hope you will give her your word that her son will pass the final exams.

Although the verb *give* is not as such a performative verb, in the sentence *iii.*, it is a part of a phrase equivalent to the performative *promise*, and, therefore, in this case, its form is the effect of the same mechanism.

b. A rule

	the non-Continuous (Future Simple)	the Continuous (Future Continuous)
prolonged, uninterrupted activity	presents it as primary, permanent, endless (at the moment of reference)	presents it as temporary/transitory, secondary
a series of events	presents them as governed by a rule - orderly, predictable, primary	presents them as disorderly series of accidents, transient, subsidiary

When we talk about a rule in the Continuous Action Aspect in English, we make a choice within two binary oppositions:
- permanent, primary vs. transitory, secondary,
- orderly vs. accidental.

The use of Future Continuous presents the rule either as temporary/transitory (in the case of prolonged uninterrupted activities as *work, live*), or as a disorderly series of occurrences (in the case of a series of disconnected actions). When we use Future Simple, the natural assumption will be that we wish to mark the rule as opposite in nature to the above, namely, as primary, permanent and orderly. However, we must remember that the non-Continuous does not mark the rule as specific in any way, stating merely the existence of the activity or a series. Thus, the interpretation that the rule expressed by Future Simple is primary, permanent must be understood not so much as communicated by the grammar as rather a permitted inference from the fact that instead of the Continuous, the non-Continuous is used. In other words, Future Simple may be used both to represent a permanent/primary and a temporary/secondary rule, though the common natural assumption is that the choice of Future Simple is an indication of a wish to mark the rule as primary, permanent and orderly.

A separate question is the criterion that is to be employed in determining whether a future rule should be regarded as permanent or temporary (after all, when juxtaposed with the true timelessness, all rules are temporary). The circumstance that decides this question is the knowledge or attitude of the subject of the rule - if for this person at the moment of which we speak the rule will be permanent, orderly, the form proper for this situation will be Future Simple; if, however, for this person, the rule will be temporary, disorderly series of accidents, the form preferred will be Future Continuous.

The student of English needs to remember that the choice of the Continuous, indicative of the fact that the rule is of a temporary nature, is not obligatory and will only be made if one wishes to inform with the use of grammar about this fact. It would not be ungrammatical to use in such a situation the unmarked non-Continuous - the only difference between the two forms in this case is the fact that the Continuous would be more precise in rendering the nature of the situation. However, if we judged that our interlocutor does not deserve to be informed so precisely (being e.g. merely an inquisitive barber or pumping station attendant, etc.) or that we do not need to state the fact because it is already known to the listener, the non-Continuous (Future Simple) would be an equally acceptable choice.

An additional consideration that must be taken into account in making a choice between the Continuous and the non-Continuous is sometimes the question whether the rule is of a primary, basic type or additional and subsidiary - a good illustration is a permanent job and some temporary, additional one. If the rule is primary, the preferred form will remain the non-Continuous (Future Simple) even if the end of the rule is known at the moment of which we speak, like, e.g. in the situation when a person already knows the date of his retirement - talking about the remaining years or months of his working there we would be likely to prefer Future Simple to Future Continuous.

c. A state

The Continuous is to a large extent antagonistic to what is intuited as constituting the nature of a state, therefore, the combination of the Continuous with the stative verb frequently not so much enriches its meaning as rather alters it, modifying certain elements making up the character of the described phenomenon. Thus, whenever, in the future, we wish to present a state in its 'natural', commonly intuited form, we use Future Simple. The addition of the Continuous will change significantly certain properties of the state described (a detailed discussion will be found in the chapter on Aspect Continuous). An additional consideration that must be borne in mind is that the actual shape of the modification of meaning produced by the Continuous when combined with a stative verb depends often upon the meaning of the verb, different combinations producing different effects (the list of these verb categories will be found in the chapter on the Continuous Aspect), therefore, the presentation below must be regarded as a certain approximation, not a complete list.

- The Continuous may change a state into a kind of action performed by the subject.
    i. *I am sure a child of such parents will be patient.* (permanent neutral state)
    ii. *I have no doubt she will be being patient with me.* (she will act in this manner)

- The Continuous, in the case of words having also dynamic punctual meaning, like *see*, may be used (as an alternative to the construction with auxiliary *can*) to reaffirm the fact that what is presented will be, at the moment described, an ongoing experience/situation seen in the middle.
    i. *I bet she will find it difficult to believe what she will be seeing.* (future version of BNC - H8M 2191)
    ii. *You may be sure that everything that we will be hearing will be classified.*

- When expressed with the non-Continuous form, a stative verb is intuited as describing a state as an uninterrupted phenomenon. The use of the Continuous may change this intuition, transforming the object of description into a series of similar static instances.
    i. *Once there, you will be hearing many stranger stories.*
The use of the Continuous implies that what is denoted will be neither a single uninterrupted phenomenon, nor a rule but a series of incidents of a similar nature.

- The Continuous may be used to emphasise the temporary nature of the experience, stressing the impression that what is being described will not be a boundless ability but a passing experience.
    i. *I wonder whether she will be understanding what she will be asked to read.* (future paraphrase of BNC - B1Y 1365)
    ii. *I wonder whether she will understand what she will be asked to read.*
In the above examples, the Continuous changes the nature of what is represented by the verb *understand* from the apparently permanent property of the person (i.e. in the non-Continuous form, a stative verb is intuited as describing a state as an uninterrupted phenomenon. The use of. Future Simple suggests that her *understanding* is a stable and final phenomenon) into reference to a particular experience in the shape existing only when it takes place (i.e. her *understanding* acquires a transitional and progressing shape, changing at any moment of her reading, trying to follow the alterations of the sense of the text).

- The Continuous may be used to reflect the fact that the state described will not be natural and 'flat' but characterised by an increased or increasing intensity.
    i. *After devaluation, the food will naturally be costing more and more.*
    ii. *After what she has seen, there is no stopping it - she will be understanding slowly what is her real status.*
    iii. *I'm sure, she will be loving every minute of her stay there.*
All the above three sentences can be rewritten in the non-Continuous but we would lose a warning/indication that the intensity of the state was changing (the sentences *i.* and *ii.*) or had increased (the sentence *iii.*).

- The Continuous may be used to emphasise the fact that the state, at the moment described, will exist not in its final shape but will be progressing towards it.
    i. *I'm sure, in time, he will resemble his father in every respect.*
    ii. *I'm sure when he grows up he will resemble his father more and more.*
    iii. *I'm sure when he grows up he will be resembling his father more and more.*
The sentence *i.* presents the resemblance between the two as a finally established fact, hence the non-Continuous, which merely names the state in its fully-developed shape, is sufficiently precise. The sentences *ii.* and *iii.*, describe a process progressing towards reaching its fullness determined by the meaning of the verb. This fact may be expressed with the use of lexical items alone (*more and more*), but

the fact may be rendered with increased clarity if we use an accompanying structure of the Continuous, stressing the instability of the described phenomenon.

As it was stated at the beginning of the presentation of the state, the above list must be perceived as only an introduction to the consequences of the combination between the Continuous and the stative, the complete presentation to be found in the chapter on the Continuous Action Aspect.

Doer/Speaker Aspect

This chapter presents the cases when the choice of the Continuous signals an intention to inform about the speaker or doer rather than about the activity. Using this fragment of the Continuous Aspect we must remember that it is secondary to the Action Aspect, i.e. that it is recognisable either when the situation or the context has independently established the shape of the Action Aspect as non-Continuous or the non-conclusive nature of the verb makes the distinction of the Action Aspect negligible. There are four types of modifications resulting from such use of the Continuous. Since these are all auxiliary structures, employing the same grammatical form, their use requires exercise of sufficient caution lest the meaning should become ambiguous - as the situations that legitimise the use of the Continuous are not mutually exclusive, the significance of the Continuous in one and the same sentence may be interpreted in different ways, which makes it additionally important to clarify with the syntax or extralinguistic components of the situation, which of the following cases the use of the Continuous addresses.

	the non-Continuous	the Continuous
1.	Neutral presentation of the situation.	It indicates emotional attitude of the speaker to the situation described by the sentence.
2.	It may be intuited as identifying the doer or the speaker as the originator or controller of the action, i.e. somebody who keeps it up.	It removes the information as to who is the originator of the action, leaving it unmarked.
3.	In the narrative, the non-Continuous is the form reserved for the presentation of the foreground action.	In the narrative, the Continuous is the form indicating the background status of the action.
4.	In conversational English, this form is perceived as blunt and inconsiderate.	In conversational English, this form is perceived as more 'polite'.

1. Neutral vs. emotional presentation

When either the Action Aspect is determined as non-Continuous by the context (the rest of the sentence, the situation) or the non-conclusive nature of the verb makes the distinctions of the Action Aspect negligible, the Continuous may be employed to indicate that the speaker/subject will be moved by the described event. Thus, in such cases, Future Simple will represent the situation in a neutral shape, without disclosing any feelings of the speaker or doer whereas Future Continuous will give the utterance a perceivably emotional character. This grammatical modification is most often employed when the non-Continuous nature of the described event is most obvious, namely in the case of talking about a rule and a state, though in the case of a single action/occurrence it is also possible.

i. *Mark my word - he is the kind of person who will forever be forgetting his money at home.*
ii. *He will always forget his money at home.*
iii. *You will see it yourself that the children will want it very, very much.*
iv. *You will see it yourself that the children will be wanting it very, very much.*
v. *I know what you are thinking - you will be meeting this girl again!*
vi. *I know what you think - you will meet this girl again.*

The Continuous alternatives in the above sentences may indicate that the doer was moved by what is described. We must remember that the actual nature of this agitation (i.e. whether it is positive or negative: a sign of admiration or criticism) is not determined by grammar but must be inferred from the context.

2. Activity presented as intended vs. activity presented as merely happening

The non-Continuous creates utterances which seem to point towards the doer/speaker as the one who has initiated the action and keeps it up. This impression is removed by the use of the Continuous. Thus, Future Simple is used when we predict or know that the activity will be intended or kept up by the speaker/doer, and Future Continuous is chosen when we wish to avoid such identification and are satisfied with merely naming the elements of the action, i.e. who will do what.

    i. *I am going to stay home tonight. I will watch the event on TV.*
    ii. *When we come home, he will be watching her on TV.*
    iii. *We will seldom meet in this park.*
    iv. *We will seldom be meeting in this park.*

Future Simple used in the sentence *i.* sends a strong signal suggesting that the activity will be kept up and willed by the doer, whereas Future Continuous removes this suggestion, leaving just a bare statement of fact[22]. In the case of a rule (the sentences *iii.* and *iv.*), Future Simple may be read as a neutral statement of fact or an indication that the continuance of the rule will be intended, and that, possibly, the events that will make it up will also be such. Thus, the sentence *iii.* may be additionally interpreted as stating that the subject will seldom make appointments in this park. Future Continuous, by removing the element of intentionality, will make an impression that what is being described will be a series of accidents.

In the case of a state, since by nature it is involuntary, it can not be represented as willed or kept up. Thus, Future Simple will make a neutral statement of fact (besides, such is the meaning attributed by the Action Aspect, and the latter is primary to the Doer/Speaker Aspect). The use of Future Continuous, on the other hand, will strengthen the impression that what is presented will be accidental and unintended.

    i. *Summing up all the costs at that quite initial level, the enterprise will already be costing us a fortune.*
    ii. *Summing up all the costs at that quite initial level, the enterprise will already cost us a fortune.*

3. Foreground vs. background activity

In a narrative (when permitted by the Action Aspect), the intentional character of the activity suggested by the non-Continuous (Future Simple) makes it a more appropriate form to express the foreground actions, whereas the fact that the Continuous (Future Continuous) is perceived to represent neutrally what will be in the middle of happening at a given moment makes it a more likely choice to present the activities which will remain in the background of the main plot.

    She will enter the room and will see them occupied. Mary will be listening to music and Henry will be writing in a notebook. She will yell at them, and they will jump from their seats and run to her.

4. Direct (blunt) address vs. less direct (more polite) address

Since the non-Continuous is recognised as expressing the intentional character of what is said, it is regarded inappropriate in situations when we wish to show our deference and avoid the impression that we impose on our interlocutor (particularly when asking questions or requesting something - see Continuous Doer/Speaker Aspect). In the situations when we want to show our respect, we will use Future Continuous. If we do not care if we sound blunt or even arrogant, we may use Future Simple.

    i. *Will you talk to John, Mr Smith?*
    ii. *Will you be talking to John, Mr Smith?*
    iii. *Will you prepare the report tomorrow?*
    iv. *Will you be preparing the report tomorrow?*

The fact that Future Simple seems particularly blunt in interrogative constructions may be owing to the intentional character of the non-Continuous – its use in the question makes the interlocutor respond in the same construction, which forces him/her to make a statement of a character of a declaration/ a promise. In

---

[22] The syntax of the sentence *i.* is different from that of the sentence *ii.* to avoid ambiguity. Although it is not a rule, the more common interpretation of the temporal relation between the activity of the time clause and the main clause when the time clause uses the conjunction *when* and there are non-Continuous forms (which tend to be interpreted as presenting an activity as a whole, not in the middle) in both clauses is that the activity of the main clause succeeds that of the time clause - combining the main clause of the type of the sentence *i.* with the time clause of the sentence *ii.*, we must remember that it might also mean that the activity of *watching* will not be caught in the middle by the entrance of the subject of the time clause but will follow it.

consequence, the interrogated persons may feel that instead of just describing the situation, they are called to oblige themselves to do something. Consequently, when people feel they are not in a position to demand such declarations (e.g. talking to their superiors), they tend to avoid the non-Continuous forms, here, Future Simple. In the opposite situation, namely when people have authority over others, they are free to choose either the direct but blunt and impolite address of the non-Continuous, or wrap their statements in a more polite, and, therefore, more palatable Continuous form.

Perfect Tenses

Present Perfect non-Continuous and Present Perfect Continuous

Present Perfect Continuous and Present Perfect non-Continuous are the Present versions of the Perfect construction of describing a situation or activity (often alternative and interchangeable with the non-Perfect, though with the use of different means - see the chapter on Aspect Perfect). Since the Continuous and the Perfect combine mechanically without altering each other[23], Present Perfect and Present Perfect Continuous are not separate and distinct entities but one and the same Perfect structure enriched by the Continuous or left 'bare', without the additional information conveyed by the Continuous. There is no reason, therefore, to discuss them separately - students are more likely to grasp the peculiarity of these constructions if they regard them independently of the Continuous.

In accordance with the nature of the Aspect Perfect, Present Perfect non-Continuous and Present Perfect Continuous will be used to address three basic situations:
1. to describe a present situation by means of what brought it about, whose effect the present situation is,
2. on the basis of what we see in the present, either to make a guess as to the likely cause or to present information that explains the existing situation by naming its reason (here, contrary to point 1, the speaker uses what is seen to guess at or inform of what possibly brought it about),
3. to state for how long or since when, a single action/occurrence, a rule, or a state present at the moment of speaking, have continued or have been repeated.

The Continuous Action Aspect vs. the Continuous Doer/Speaker Aspect

The meaning of the choice between the Continuous and the non-Continuous is determined by two systems of aspect, one primary (the Action Aspect) and the other, secondary (the Doer/Speaker Aspect). The latter becomes 'visible', recognisable only when either the former is clarified by the context (i.e. the rest of the syntax or the situation), as the non-Continuous (i.e. when the Action Aspect is satisfactorily identified irrespective of the choice of the form of the verb within the Continuous) or when the non-conclusive nature of the verb makes the distinctions of the Action Aspect negligible. The following tables illustrate the consequence of choosing the Continuous or the non-Continuous for the Perfect form of the verb.

---

23 A certain exception to this rule is American English, in which, though the aspects do not modify each other, the Continuous restricts significantly the range of combinations of the Continuous and the Perfect – for details, see the chapter on the Aspect Perfect.

Action Aspect

	Category of the object of description	the Non-continuous	the Continuous
1.	a single action or occurrence	tends[24] to be presented as a whole, in its entirety	presented in the middle of being done
2.	a rule - continued activity	presented as unspecified rule, presumably primary and unrestricted by time, permanent	presented as secondary and restricted by time, understood as temporary, transitory
	a rule - series of acts or occurrences	presented as unspecified rule, presumably controlled, planned, regular	presented as chaotic and accidental or temporary, transitional
3.	a state	presented as not changing its intensity, steady, 'flat'	presented as a dynamic process, changing its intensity (increasing/decreasing its intensity) advancing towards completion

Doer/Speaker Aspect

	the non-Continuous	the Continuous
1.	Neutral presentation of the situation.	It indicates emotional attitude of the speaker to the situation described by the sentence.
2.	It may be intuited as identifying the doer or the speaker as the originator or controller of the action, i.e. somebody who keeps it up.	It removes the information as to who is the originator of the action, leaving it unmarked.
3.	In the narrative, the non-Continuous is the form reserved for the presentation of the foreground action.	In the narrative, the Continuous is the form indicating the background status of the action.
4.	In conversational English, this form is perceived as blunt and inconsiderate.	In conversational English, this form is perceived as more 'polite'.

---

24 Although by nature, the non-Continuous tends to present the activity in its entirety, this potential may not always be realised due to contextual reasons - see the chapter on the Continuous Aspect.

Variant 1

Paraphrasing the structure from which the Perfect originated, in Variant 1, we have structures of the type of *'I have something NOW as a result of the fact that I did or was doing something in the PAST'*.

Present Perfect Continuous vs. Present Perfect non-Continuous

a. A single action/occurrence

In the Continuous Action Aspect of Variant 1, Present Perfect non-Continuous will be used when we wish to communicate that the present situation is an effect of finishing, completing something in the past. Present Perfect Continuous, on the other hand, will be used in the cases when the present situation is a result of merely performing some action, i.e. that to produce the present situation the action specified in the sentence did not have to reach completion, it was enough for it to be being performed. A good illustration of this kind of distinction is the situation when somebody excuses himself that he can not drive as a result of drinking alcohol. His inability may be suggested in two different ways:

i. *I can not drive you home because I have drunk 4 bottles of beer.*
ii. *I can not drive you home because I have been drinking.*
iii. *I can not drive you home because I am drunk/am not sufficiently sober.*

The intended meaning of the utterance is presented directly in the sentence *iii*. The remaining two sentences present what is to be understood indirectly, suggesting it by means of a reference to an accomplished fact (*I finished drinking 4 bottles and as a result I am not capable of driving*) or to performance of something which produces the result (*I was drinking alcohol and as a result I am not capable of driving*).

Past Simple instead of Present Perfect

There are certain situations when Present Perfect must not be used even though a past event is spoken of with an intention to communicate something about the present moment. One such situation is the case when it is material to state in the sentence the moment in the past when the action took place[25]. Such sentence, although grammatically past, in a conversational situation might be made to refer to the present time, however, with extralinguistic means like behaviour of the speaker or context in which the sentence is produced, e.g. in the above situation of responding to a plea to drive somebody home, it would be perfectly clear that our response refers to the present moment even if its adverbial is past like: *I can not drive you home because 20 min. ago I finished drinking this bottle of wine*. We must remember that the sentence itself (*20 min. ago I finished drinking this bottle of wine*) does not refer to the present - each time we feel bound to exploit this possibility offered by Past Simple, we have to make sure that the context in which the sentence appears will be sufficiently clear about which moment in time it really describes - the past (which is its nature), or the present (which is our intention).

As it was stated above, when the Action Aspect has been clarified independently as the non-Continuous, the meaning of the choice between the Continuous and the non-Continuous may be defined by the Doer/Speaker Aspect. Let us take the following pair of sentences:

i. *He has talked to her.*
ii. *He has been talking to her.*

The sentence *i.* will be preferred in the situation when the talking was an initiative of the doer. When, however, the speaker would like to signal the fact that it is not known or immaterial who was the initiator of the talking, he would be likely to prefer the sentence *ii*.

b. A rule

In the situations determined by the Action Aspect, Present Perfect non-Continuous is used when the present situation is a result of the operation of a primary, permanent or regular and controlled rule. Present Perfect Continuous is likely to be preferred when either the rule producing the present result is temporary/transitory and secondary or a chain of accidents. Let us compare:

---

[25] In Present Perfect, which is a form of speaking about the present moment, the past adverbial of time is ungrammatical, since it produces a situation of grammatical incongruence similar to a statement: *I HAVE yesterday*.

i. He knows this place and, therefore, he may tell us where the file can be found.
　　ii. He has worked here for 20 years, and, therefore, he may tell us where the file can be found.
　　iii. He has been working here as her substitute for the past 2 weeks, and, therefore, he may tell us where the file can be found.

The sentence *i.* states the intended meaning directly, namely the fact that he has a thorough knowledge of the place. In the sentence *ii.*, the above is given to understand by representing it as a result of operation of a permanent rule, in the case of the sentence *iii.*, as a result of operation of a temporary rule.

When talking about a rule, the choice of the Continuous may also be determined by Doer/Speaker Aspect. One such possible case is when we wish to represent a rule either as a result of choice or coincidence - let us compare:
　　i. Ask Peter - he knows this wine and will be able to tell you if it is suitable for the occasion.
　　ii. Ask Peter - he has frequently drunk this wine and will be able to tell you if it is suitable for the occasion.
　　iii. Ask Peter - he has frequently been drinking this wine and will be able to tell you if it is suitable for the occasion.

The sentence *i.* states the intended meaning directly, namely that Peter knows this wine, whereas in the case of the sentences *ii.* and *iii.*, it is given to understand. The sentence *ii.* will be recognised as more appropriate in the case when we know that the drinking of this wine has not been a chain of accidents but a result of choice and persistence. In the case of it being a series of accidents, the sentences *iii.* will be perceived as more natural.

c. A state

When the meaning of the choice of the Continuous is defined by the Action Aspect, Present Perfect non-Continuous is used when we wish to present the present situation as an effect of a state characterised by neutral and stable intensity. Let us take the following dialogue concerning the question if somebody is likely to find his way in London:
　　A: Won't he get lost?
　　B: No, he knows London very well.
　　B: No, he has already been to London.

In the first answer, *B* presents the opinion directly, in the second, it is indirectly given to understand in the form of the implied effect of his having been to London already.

Present Perfect Continuous is a likely choice when we wish to make use of any of the modifications of meaning resulting from combining the Continuous with a stative verb (a complete list of these modifications will be found in the chapter on the Continuous Aspect) - in short, the list comprises the following situations:
　　- changing a state into a kind of action performed by the subject,
　　- reaffirming the fact that what is presented is an ongoing experience/situation perceived in the middle,
　　- giving a state the form of a series of static phenomena,
　　- giving a state the form of a passing experience,
　　- reflecting the fact of changing intensity of a state (increasing, decreasing),
　　- suggesting that a state has not yet reached the final form but has only been progressing towards it.

The above list determines the potential of the combination of the Continuous and a stative verb, its realisation in Variant 1 depends, however, on whether we shall find a context that would justify the use of the Perfect Continuous form with a given verb in the structure of describing a situation by means of what brought it about. Such contexts are quite rare, though they exist. For example, being enquired about our understanding of a certain case, we may answer referring to our knowledge directly, or it may be given to understand by means of the Perfect construction:
　　i. We know/understand it very well.
　　ii. We have seen quite a lot of similar cases.
　　iii. We have been seeing quite a lot of similar cases.

The difference between the sentence *ii.* and *iii.* is that the Continuous enriches the answer with an impression that the *seeing* was accidental and, additionally, that it was extended over a period of time in the form of a series of events rather than a solitary experience (though such interpretation of the sentence *ii.* is also possible - the sentence *iii.* merely strengthens these features).

Another situation possibly justifying the use of both Present Perfect non-Continuous and Present Perfect Continuous might be a conversation about a predictable reaction of a person talked about to a projected pulling down of a certain house - let us compare:
  i. A: Won't he be sorry if we pull down the old house?
  ii. Him? No. He will be overjoyed.
  iii. Him? No. He has ever wished it demolished.
  iv. Him? No. He has ever been wishing it demolished.
The sentence *ii.* presents the intended meaning directly, the sentences *iii.* and *iv.*, indirectly. The sentence *iv.* will be preferred in the situation when we wish to be more emphatic about the strength of the person's wish to see the house pulled down.

Still another case in which we might find it convenient to use Present Perfect Continuous instead of Present Perfect is the situation when we would like to avoid misrepresentation of what we describe as a phenomenon existing in its final and complete form and rather present it as an ongoing experience perceived in the middle. Let us compare:
  i. You won't persuade me - I know as much as others do.
  ii. You won't persuade me - I have heard as much as others have.
  iii. You won't persuade me - I have been hearing as much as others have/could.
In the sentences *ii.* and *iii.* the meaning, which the sentence *i.* names directly, is given to understand. The difference between *ii.* and *iii.* is that the sentence *ii.* gives reason to believe that what is being described by the Perfect non-Continuous is a static experience existing in a final and complete form, whereas the sentence *iii.* gives it a shape of an incomplete and passing phenomenon. Besides, the sentence *ii.* might be interpreted as showing the present situation as a result not of a static *seeing* but of dynamic *noticing*, i.e. of a single, conclusive event. The possibility of such interpretation would be diminished if we used the Continuous, as illustrated by the sentence *iii.*

Variant 2

Paraphrasing the definition of Variant 2, in the present it addresses the situations when we wish to say that the cause and explanation of what we see is some event, rule, state in the past. The utterance has the form of - *I guess that what the person has NOW, is an effect of the following event, rule, state located in the PAST.*

Present Perfect Continuous vs. Present Perfect non-Continuous

a. A single action/occurrence

In this variant, Present Perfect non-Continuous will be used when we wish to put forth a guess that what we see at the moment of speaking is an effect of accomplishing, completing something in the past. Should we believe that what we see is a result of mere doing something which is capable of producing a result in the form of what is seen without reaching the end, we would use Present Perfect Continuous. For example, if we imagine friendship with a dramatist, whom, one day, we pay a visit, we may come across the following situation. We know that the dramatist has been working on a drama, and upon entering his room we notice some printed pages - we may comment upon what we see, using one of the following:
- if we believe that the meaning of what we see is that the person worked upon the text:
  Oh, you have been writing your drama.
- if we believe that the meaning of what we see is that the person has finished the drama, e.g on top of a pile of paper, we see a page with a single word - 'End':
  Oh, you have finally written your drama.

We might come across a similar case while paying a visit about the time when somebody has lunch. Judging on what we see on such occasion, we would feel justified to interpret it in the following ways:
  i. Oh, you have had your lunch already.
  ii. Oh, you have been having your lunch.
The sentence *i.* would be proper if we thought that what we see has been caused by completion of the lunch, whereas the sentence *ii.*, would be preferred if we wanted to express a surmise that what we see is an effect of mere having lunch, not necessarily requiring its completion.

At the same time, we must remember that whenever either the Action Aspect is independently determined as the non-Continuous or the non-conclusive nature of the verb makes the distinctions of the

Action Aspect negligible, the Continuous may be loaded with the meanings of Doer/Speaker Aspect. In such a case, the significance of the choice of the Continuous may change. The above situation, when combined with non-conclusive verbs might justify the use or neglect of the Continuous either to signify the doer's resolution to continue the activity (the non-Continuous - the sentence *i.* below), or to present the activity as just happening, without expressing any opinions about its relation to the doer (the Continuous - the sentence *ii.* below):
  i. Oh, you have worked on that new drama.
  ii. Oh, you have been working on that new drama.

b. A rule

In Variant 2, in the cases determined by the Action Aspect, Present Perfect non-Continuous will be chosen when we wish to put forth a surmise that the present situation is an effect of a primary, permanent, regular rule. When, in our opinion, the present situation is a result of a rule that is temporary, secondary or just a chain of accidents, the more likely choice is Present Perfect Continuous. Let us compare:
  i. It seems she has lived here all her life.
  ii. It seems she has been living here for quite some time.
  iii. It seems that they have regularly met here.
  iv. It seems that they have regularly been meeting here.

The sentence *i.* will be a likely choice when the speaker surmises that what he sees is the effect of the operation of a permanent rule (regulating a continuous activity); the sentence *ii.*, when he guesses that the shape of the present suggests that it is a result of the operation of a temporary, short-lived rule. The sentence *iii.* will be preferred to the sentence *iv.* when the speaker understands that the present is an effect of a controlled, regular rule, whereas the sentence *iv.* will seem more proper when the events producing the present situation are guessed to be but frequently happening accidents. The last two sentences (*iii.* and *iv.*) may also be used to put forth notions defined by Doer/Speaker Aspect. In the above case, the fact that we are dealing with a regularity is quite clear, therefore, the Continuous and the non-Continuous may be employed to distinguish between different notions. The Perfect non-Continuous would be recognised as proper to express the regularity which is an effect of will and determination to continue (like in the case of making regular appointments), whereas the Continuous, by removing the intentionality, would be a likely choice to describe a situation of frequent but unintended accidental meetings at a place. Thus, if we wish to say that what we see is probably an effect of the persons spoken of having made regular appointments, we would choose Present Perfect non-Continuous; if we wanted to say that the situation at the moment of speaking suggests that the person in question has regularly come across rather than dated the other person, we would use Present Perfect Continuous.

c. A state

The present may be surmised to have resulted from a certain state in the past - let us analyse the following:
  I gather you have seen her.
The above sentence addresses the case when we realize that the behaviour of the person talked about seems to suggest that he/she saw a certain person.

In Variant 2, in the cases determined by Action Aspect, we are likely to use Present Perfect non-Continuous when we surmise that the present is an effect of a state perceived as neutral and unmarked by any other considerations. Present Perfect Continuous would be recognize as proper if we wanted to put forth a guess that the present has been shaped by the state marked by any of the traits resulting from combining a stative verb with the Continuous form - in short, the list comprises the following situations:
  - changing a state into a kind of action performed by the subject,
  - reaffirming the fact that what is presented is an ongoing experience/situation perceived in the middle,
  - giving a state the form of a series of static phenomena,
  - giving a state the form of a passing experience,
  - reflecting the fact of changing intensity of a state (increasing, decreasing),
  - suggesting that a state has not yet reached the final form but has only been progressing towards it.

The above list presents the potential of the modification of meaning by combining the Continuous with a stative verb, its realisation in Variant 2 depends, obviously, on whether we shall find a context that would justify the use of the Perfect Continuous form with a given stative verb in the structure of expressing a

conjecture about what is being suggested by the shape of the present state. Such contexts are quite rare, though they exist. For example, if we imagine the situation when we start suspecting that the behaviour of a given person reveals that the person is not as ignorant as we previously thought - this case could be addressed with two sentences:
  i. *Apparently, he has understood everything that he saw.*
  ii. *Apparently, he has been understanding everything that he was seeing.*
If we wish to express a guess that the shape of the present suggests that it is an effect of a phenomenon of understanding seen in its entirety, as a single and undivided experience (or we do not care if such impression is made), the form that will be preferred is Present Perfect non-Continuous (the sentence *i.* above). When, however, we want to imply that the present results from the understanding having been not so much a single and final phenomenon but a continuing series of stages or events to be understood separately, the form of choice would be Present Perfect Continuous (the sentence *ii.* above).

As usual, in addition to Action Aspect, the system determining the meaning of the choice between the Continuous and the non-Continuous may be Doer/Speaker Aspect. Let us analyse the following:
  i. *I see you have wanted it badly.*
  ii. *I see you have been wanting it badly.*
The sentence *ii.* would be a more likely choice of the two in the situation when we wish to put emphasis on the presentation of the state of *wanting* indicating its uncommon intensity.

Variant 3

We employ this variant whenever we wish to say that a single action/occurrence, a rule, or a state existing at the moment of speaking has remained in continuation for some time. We must remember that unlike the non-Perfect construction, this type of sentences is not focused on the entire continuation of the activity but solely on the moment of reference located at its end, here, in Present Perfect tenses, the moment of speaking. The information about how long or since when the present activity has remain in continuation has the status of only additional information.

Present Perfect non-Continuous vs. Present Perfect Continuous

a. A single action/occurrence

The combination of Variant 3 of the Perfect and a single action/occurrence may be baffling because it defies the fundamental intuitions acquired at the early stages of English language acquisition (dominated by the Action Aspect of the Continuous) suggesting that the non-Continuous represents a single action/occurrence in its entirety, as a more or less conclusive, independent entity. The actual reality created by the Perfect form is different - due to its nature, Variant 3 imposes its segmental nature on even punctual verbs, presenting everything at a given point of reference (here, in the case of Present Perfect, at the moment of speaking) in the middle of continuation or repetition, i.e. in the middle of an ongoing segment. The meanings attributed by the non-Continuous and the Continuous forms in Variant 3 are determined by the Doer/Speaker Aspect and derive from the opposition between the action presented as willed and kept up by the doer/speaker (the non-Continuous), or just continuing (the Continuous). As a result we can choose between the following pairs of sentences:
  i. *He has written the report for 2 weeks and will probably finish tomorrow.*
  ii. *He has been writing the report for 2 weeks and will probably finish tomorrow.*
  iii. *He has hammered the lock for a couple of minutes and does not seem to be going to stop soon.*
  iv. *He has been hammering the lock for a couple of minutes and does not seem to be going to stop soon.*
  v. *It has rained since 5.*
  vi. *It has been raining since 5.*
All four sentences present an ongoing segment perceived at the moment of speaking. The first pair of sentences (*i.* and *ii.*) present a single durative action seen at the moment when it is talked about, being then in the midst of continuation for 2 weeks. In the second pair (*iii.* and *iv.*), a single punctual action is multiplied into the form of a series perceived at the moment of speaking in the midst of being repeated. In each of the pairs, we have a choice whether to represent the performance as willed and kept up by the doer (sentences *i.* and *iii.* - the non-Continuous), or (after removing the information about who originates or controls the action) just to present the situation identifying who does what and when but withholding

the information about who is responsible for the origination or continuation of it (sentences *ii.* and *iv.* - the Continuous). The last pair features an impersonal natural phenomenon in whose case the question of volition does not apply. In such context, the choice between the two sentences is likely to be governed (still within the meanings of Doer/Speaker Aspect) by the status of the action with regard to the narrative - if the *raining* belongs to the mainstream of what is being described, the likely choice is the non-Continuous (Present Perfect non-Continuous - the sentence *v.*); if the *raining* constitutes an element of background, the preferred construction will be the Continuous (Present Perfect Continuous - the sentence *vi.*).

b. A rule

The fact that a rule, when described by a non-Perfect tense, presents a certain period over which the activity described continues makes the properties of the activity similar to those characterising the modification of meaning imposed upon the verb and the structure of the sentence by this variant of the Perfect. In consequence, the description of a rule in the Perfect and the non-Perfect form look, to some extent, similar with, however, one significant difference. The non-Perfect form (both the Continuous and the non-Continuous) describes a rule in force at a point specified by the sentence, presenting it as being in the middle of operation then (neither at the beginning nor at the end). When we use the Perfect, a rule is also presented at a certain moment but not in the middle of continuation but as having been in force so far, till the moment of reference (as if 'at the end of it so far'). Let us compare the following sentences:

   i. She always goes on holiday in June.
   ii. She is always going on holiday in June.
   iii. So far, she has always gone on holiday in June.
   iv. So far, she has always been going on holiday in June.

The first two sentences, *i.* and *ii.*, present the rule at the moment of speaking in the middle of operation, i.e. the rule started earlier and is expected to continue beyond now, our attention focused upon now. The sentences *iii.* and *iv.* also focus the reader's attention upon *now* and present the same rule but they handle the presentation in a different way - they present the rule not so much in the middle of an ongoing continuum of unspecified boundaries but *now* as having operated so far, till the moment of reference (which is *now*). The latter form excludes the inevitability of future continuation, which is naturally implied in the case of the non-Perfect form (though leaves the question of its continuation open as at least not impossible). The suggestion indicated by the decision to use or not to use the Continuous may be described by the elements of both the Action and Doer/Speaker Aspect - they are quite close. The use of the non-Continuous will indicate that the speaker perceives the rule as originating from and remaining under control of the will of the doer and, in consequence, being 'regular' and 'predictable', whereas the use of the Continuous will remove this suggestion, representing the rule as a series of occurrences or tendency rather than a realization of some policy of the doer. Similar considerations seem to be standing behind the choice of the Continuous and the non-Continuous in the following sentences.

   i. He sometimes drinks tea instead of coffee.
   ii. He is sometimes drinking tea instead of coffee.
   iii. Since 1999, he has sometimes drunk tea instead of coffee.
   iv. Since 1999, he has sometimes been drinking tea instead of coffee.
   v. He never plays with us.
   vi. He is never playing with us.
   vii. Since he has lived there, he has never played with us.
   viii. Since he has lived there, he has never been playing with us

Another of the more obvious modifications of meaning introduced by the selection of the Continuous or the non-Continuous operates between two opposing notions of permanence/predominance of the rule (the non-Continuous) and impermanence/secondariness of it (the Continuous). Let us compare:

   i. I have worked for IBM for 15 years.
   ii. I work in the Accounts Department. But since Friday, I have been working in the Human Resources as Mrs White is away I am substituting for her.

In the sentence *i.*, the non-Continuous was chosen as better reflecting the fact that the work is probably the primary and permanent occupation of the doer (although, as it was stated in the chapter, it is only a conjecture, not a fact determined by grammar). In the sentence *ii.*, the non-Continuous was chosen to warn that the work in the Human Resources has a temporary status, the primary job of the doer being that in the Accounts Dept.

Generally speaking, if the context permits and justifies it, the whole range of meaning modifications described by the Continuous Aspect may be combined with the Perfect.

c. A state

Like in the case of a rule, the natural temporal properties of a state naturally coincide with the characteristics of Variant 3 - both denote an ongoing 'situation' continuing for some time with, however, the same reservation as in the case of a rule. If the state is presented by a non-Perfect tense, it is presented at some point of reference as being in the middle of continuation, stretching, at the same time, naturally into the past and the future of that point. When a state is described by the Perfect form, it is denoted as existing at a moment of reference so far (only), i.e. the description reaches no further than the moment of reference – there is no suggestion (common for the non-Perfect form) that the state is expected to continue beyond the point on which we focus. Let us compare:
  i. *I think he is at home.*
  ii. *I think he has been at home for 2 hours, now.*
Both sentences focus upon now (the moment of speaking), when the state is located. In the case of the sentence *i.*, there is a natural expectation that the state began before and will continue beyond now. The sentence *ii.* 'sees' the state only till now, giving no grounds to suppose that it will be bound to continue.

Present Perfect non-Continuous vs. Present Perfect Continuous

The use of the Continuous (here, Present Perfect Continuous), as in all other cases of the combinations of the Perfect with the Continuous, is regulated by the Continuous Aspect. In the situation when we wish to describe a state as neutral, characterised by the intuitions commonly associated with the state, we will find Present Perfect non-Continuous as a form generally more accurate to represent it. On the other hand, Present Perfect Continuous will be chosen in the situations when we wish to add to the meaning of the verb any of the traits resulting from combining a stative verb with the Continuous form - in short, the list comprises the following situations:

- changing a state into a kind of action performed by the subject,
  i. *He has been quite patient so far.*
  ii. *He has been being quite patient with me so far.*
The sentence *ii.* changes the static, permanent feature of the person described in the sentence *i.* into an ongoing behaviour characterised by patience, akin to showing or offering it.

- reaffirming the fact that what is presented is an ongoing experience/situation perceived in the middle,
  i. *I hope you have seen what the others have.*
  ii. *I hope you have been seeing what the others have.*
The sentence *ii.* disambiguates the meaning of the sentence *i.* which can be interpreted both as describing a single involuntary occurrence, similar to 'notice' (a situation rather for Variant 1) or as presenting a state of seeing. Thanks to the intuitions connected with the Continuous, the sentence *ii.* fixes the meaning in the form of an ongoing experience seen in the middle

- giving a state the form of a series of static phenomena,
  i. *We have seen many stranger cases (since she returned).*
  ii. *We have been seeing many stranger cases (since she returned).*
The Continuous in the sentence *ii.* makes much more prominent what in the sentence *i.* is only one of two possibilities, namely, that what is being described is not an ongoing single experience but a series of such.

- giving a state the form of a passing experience,
  i. *I have kept an eye on them to make sure that they have understood everything that they have read.*
  ii. *I have kept an eye on them to make sure that they have been understanding everything that they have been reading.*
The meaning of the sentence *i.* inclines towards the description of a final state of understanding reached by the subject, whereas the natural tendency of the Continuous added to the Perfect in the sentence *ii.* is to represent it as something ongoing, not necessarily heading towards any completion.

- reflecting the fact of changing intensity of a state (increasing, decreasing),
    i. *Since mother started taking that new drug, she has seen better every day.*
    ii. *Since mother started taking that new drug, she has been seeing better every day.*
Although the meaning of both sentences (*i.* and *ii.*) is similar, the fact that the state keeps growing in its intensity is presented more clearly by the sentence *ii.*

- suggesting that a state has not yet reached the final form but has only been progressing towards it.
    i. *She claims that his leadership has always resembled authoritarian dictatorship.*
    ii. *She claims that over the years his leadership has increasingly resembled authoritarian dictatorship.*
    iii. *She claims that over the years his leadership has increasingly been resembling authoritarian dictatorship.*
    iv. *She believes that since the beginning of this new experimental treatment, most of her patients have forgotten that traumatic event.*
    v. *She believes that since the beginning of this experimental treatment, most of the patients have steadily been forgetting that traumatic experience.*

In the sentence *i.*, the state of resembling dictatorial rule is presented as existing in its complete, final shape. The sentences *ii.* and *iii.* describe the process advancing towards the final, complete form but at the moment described perceived somewhere in the middle, before the final stage has been reached. The replacement of *always* with *increasingly* sufficiently clarifies the changing, incomplete nature of the phenomenon but the Continuous form, by adding dynamism to the description, makes the meaning more distinct. In the case of the sentences *iv.* and *v.*, the meanings are made emphatically different by the Continuous Aspect, the sentence *iv.* presenting the state/occurrence in its final, complete shape, and the sentence *v.*, in the form of an ongoing process seen in the middle. Like in the other instances of the use of the Continuous discussed above, both sentences present more or less the same meaning. However, the fact that the subject has not yet reached the state of final resemblance but is steadily progressing towards it is more clearly expressed by the Present Perfect Continuous of the sentence *ii.*

Present Perfect tenses in subordinate clauses

Using Present Perfect in subordinate clauses like adverbial clauses of time or conditional clauses, we must remember the specific way in which the Perfect relates the action of the main and subordinate clause. Making a choice between the non-Perfect and the Perfect, we choose between referring the main clause to the location of the entire action of the subordinate clause (the non-Perfect) or (in the case of the Perfect) to the location of the moment when the action of the subordinate clause exists either in the form of an effect (like the use of the type of Variant 1), or (like in Variant 3) in the form of an activity perceived at a moment of reference preceded by what of the activity has been being accomplished by that point (i.e. at a given point, the activity of the subordinate clause has been in continuation for some time). In other words, whenever we wish to define the temporal location of the action of the main clause by reference to the moment in time when the entire action of the time clause is placed, we use the non-Perfect tenses in the time clause. Thus, the main action will be located as remaining e.g. 'before' or 'after' the entire action of the subordinate clause. Whenever we wish to describe the placement in time of the main action by reference to the moment when the action of the subordinate clause exists in the form of effect or at a moment when it has existed so far, we shall use the Perfect form. Let us compare:
    i. *I will phone you before we watch the show.*
    ii. *I will phone you before we have watched the show.*
    iii. *I will phone you before we have been having watching the show for an hour.*
(Perfect Continuous and Perfect non-Continuous in the sentences *ii.* and *iii.* respectively is also possible but with a change of meaning determined by the Aspect Continuous)

As it is suggested by the choice of the non-Perfect in the time clause of the sentence *i.*, the action of the main clause will take place before the entire *watching* of the show. The use of the Perfect in the time clause of the sentence *ii.* and *iii.*, indicates that the moment of reference is either the point when the *watching* came to an end (*ii.*) or before the expiration of one hour of watching it (*iii.*). Thus, the most obvious difference between the three sentences is that, in the first, the action of the main clause will precede the entire action of the time clause, whereas in the second and third, it may happen during the action of the time clause but before its end or the expiration of the time specified. In the case of the sentences of the kind of the sentence *ii.* the choice between the Perfect and the non-Perfect makes little

difference when we use the conclusive verbs, particularly those which denote the beginning or end of activity like *finish, end, start* or *begin*, e.g.
   i. *He will leave before we finish lunch.*
   ii. *He will leave before we have finished lunch.*

As the difference between 'finish something' and 'have something (as) finished'[26] is negligible, in the case of such verbs, the choice between them has no other function as stylistic - the Perfect places emphasis on the fact of completion of the action at the moment described.

Another significant consideration that has to be borne in mind while making our choice of the Perfect or the non-Perfect in the subordinate clauses, particularly time clauses, is the discrimination between the situation when the time clause describes the beginning of succession of events or prepares a static 'stage' for the events. As it was stated above, the nature of the modification of meaning resulting from employing the Perfect form derives from its origin, i.e. from the structure similar to 'having something (as) done'. Due to this fact, the Perfect is all the more likely when the character of the object of description is close to a static situation, which is the substance of this 'having something (as) done'. When the nature of the object of description is more akin to a dynamic succession of events, the non-Perfect forms are considered to reflect this fact better. With regard to this fact English employs two different forms in what seemingly are identical contexts - let us compare:
   i. *When you open the case, the mouse will jump out and escape.*
   ii. *When you have opened the case, you will be able to start sorting the clothes out to make a selection.*

In the sentence *i.* the *jumping* and *escaping* succeed directly the *opening* of the case, the latter being treated as a complete event, followed by the others. In the sentence *ii.*, the situation is presented differently - instead of presenting the *opening* as an entire, conclusive event, which, therefore, is 'ready' to be succeeded by other similarly complete events, the structure describes the moment when the doer 'has the case (as) opened', thus moving the focus onto the static situation suggested by the verb 'have' and, therefore, transforming the time clause into a kind of background to the events rather than a conclusive beginning of a series.

Past Perfect non-Continuous and Past Perfect Continuous

Past Perfect Continuous and Past Perfect non-Continuous are the Past versions of the Perfect construction of describing a situation or activity (often alternative and interchangeable with the non-Perfect, though with the use of different means - see the chapter on Aspect Perfect). Since the Continuous and the Perfect combine mechanically without altering each other[27], Past Perfect and Past Perfect Continuous are not separate and distinct entities but one and the same Perfect structure enriched by the Continuous or left 'bare', without the additional information conveyed by the Continuous. There is no reason, therefore, to discuss them separately - students are more likely to grasp the peculiarity of these constructions if they regard them independently of the Continuous.

A significant consideration that must be borne in mind is the fact that the use of the Perfect in the subordinate clauses is not altogether consistent with the model of the Perfect - such cases will be presented separately in the chapter on Past Perfect in subordinate clauses.

Past Perfect non-Continuous and Past Perfect Continuous in the main clause

In accordance with the nature of the Aspect Perfect, Past Perfect non-Continuous and Past Perfect Continuous will be used to address three basic situations:

---

26 As it was mentioned above, though this structure, which is the origin and predecessor of the Perfect form, is no longer popularly recognised as correct, it still determines the shape of the modification of meaning resulting from putting a verb into the Perfect form. Thus, an easy way to grasp the specific shape of the transformation of lexical content of the communiqué in the Perfect form (so much different from the non-Perfect), it is good to 'translate' it into the original structure, which, for instructive reasons, is going to be repeatedly done in the discussion that follows..

27 A certain exception to this rule is American English, in which, though the aspects do not modify each other, the Continuous restricts significantly the range of combinations of the Continuous and the Perfect – for details, see the chapter on the Aspect Perfect.

1. to describe a past situation by means of what brought it about, whose effect the past situation was,
2. on the basis of what could be seen in the past, we either make a guess as to the likely cause or present information that explains the existing situation by naming its reason (here, contrary to point 1, the speaker uses what was seen to guess at or inform of what had possibly brought it about),
3. to state for how long or since when, a single action/occurrence, a rule, or a state remaining at a moment in the past, had continued or had been repeated.

The Continuous Action Aspect vs. the Continuous Doer/Speaker Aspect

The meaning of the choice between the Continuous and the non-Continuous is determined by two systems of aspect, one primary (the Action Aspect) and the other, secondary (the Doer/Speaker Aspect). The latter becomes 'visible,' recognisable only when either the former is clarified by the context (the rest of the syntax or the situation) as the non-Continuous (i.e. when the Action Aspect is satisfactorily identified irrespective of the choice of the form of the verb within the Continuous), or when the non-conclusive nature of the verb makes the distinctions of the Action Aspect negligible. The following tables illustrate the consequence of choosing the Continuous or the non-Continuous for the Perfect form of the verb.

Action Aspect

	Category of the object of description	the Non-continuous	the Continuous
1.	a single action or occurrence	tends[28] to be presented as a whole, in its entirety	presented in the middle of being done
2.	a rule - continued activity	presented as an unspecified rule, presumably primary, unrestricted by time, permanent	presented as secondary/transitory, restricted by time, understood as temporary, transitional
	a rule - series of acts or occurrences	presented as an unspecified rule, presumably controlled, planned, regular	presented as a chaotic series of coincidences or temporary, transitional
3.	a state	presented as not changing its intensity, steady, 'flat'	presented as a dynamic process, changing its intensity (increasing/decreasing its intensity) advancing towards completion

---

[28] Although by nature, the non-Continuous tends to present the activity in its entirety, this potential may not always be realised due to contextual reasons - see the chapter on the Continuous Aspect.

Doer/Speaker Aspect

	the non-Continuous	the Continuous
1.	Neutral presentation of the situation.	It indicates emotional attitude of the speaker to the situation described by the sentence.
2.	It may be intuited as identifying the doer or the speaker as the originator or controller of the action, i.e. somebody who keeps it up.	It removes the information as to who is the originator of the action, leaving it unmarked.
3.	In the narrative, the non-Continuous is the form reserved for the presentation of the foreground action.	In the narrative, the Continuous is the form indicating the background status of the action.
4.	In conversational English, this form is considered blunt and inconsiderate.	In conversational English, this form is considered more 'polite'.

Variant 1

Paraphrasing the structure from which the Perfect originated, in Variant 1, we have structures of the type of '*I had something ('[as] done')* at a specified moment in the past as a result of the fact that I did or was doing something earlier'.

Past Perfect Continuous vs. Past Perfect non-Continuous

a. A single action/occurrence

In the Continuous Action Aspect of Variant 1, Past Perfect non-Continuous will be used when we wish to communicate that the past situation was an effect of finishing, completing something earlier, i.e. deeper in the past. Past Perfect Continuous, on the other hand, will be used in the cases when the past situation was a result of merely performing some action, i.e. that to produce the past situation the action specified in the sentence did not have to reach completion, it was enough for it to be being performed. A good illustration of this kind of distinction is the situation of somebody excusing himself that he could not drive as a result of drinking alcohol. His inability may be suggested in two different ways:

i. *He could not drive you home because he had drunk 4 bottles of beer.*
ii. *He could not drive you home because he had been drinking.*
iii. *He could not drive you home because he was drunk.*

The intended meaning of the utterance is presented directly in the sentence *iii*. The remaining two sentences present what is to be understood indirectly, suggesting it by means of a reference to an accomplished fact (*he finished drinking 4 bottles and as a result he was not capable of driving*) or to performance of something which produces the result (*he was drinking alcohol earlier and as a result, later, at the moment of reference, he was not capable of driving*).

As it was stated above, when the Action Aspect either has been clarified independently as the non-Continuous or the non-conclusive nature of the verb has made the distinction immaterial, the meaning of the choice between the Continuous and the non-Continuous may be defined by the Doer/Speaker Aspect. Let us take the following pair of sentences:

i. *At 5 yesterday, he had already talked to her.*
ii. *At 5 yesterday, he had already been talking to her.*

The sentence *i.* will be preferred in the situation when the *talking* was an initiative of the doer. If, however, the speaker would like to signal the fact that it is not known or it is immaterial who was the initiator of the *talking*, he would be likely to prefer the sentence *ii*.

b. A rule

In the situations determined by the Action Aspect, Past Perfect non-Continuous is used when the past situation is a result of the operation of a permanent or regular and controlled rule. Past Perfect Continuous is likely to be preferred when either the rule producing the past result is temporary or it is a mere chain of coincidences. Let us compare:

i. He obviously knew the place and, therefore, could be asked where the file was.
ii. He had worked there for 20 years and, therefore, could be asked where the file was.
iii. He had been working there as her substitute for the past 2 weeks and, therefore, could be asked where the file was.

The sentence *i.* states the intended meaning directly, namely the fact that he had a thorough knowledge of the place. In the sentence *ii.*, the above is given to understand as an implied result of operation of a permanent rule; in the case of the sentence *iii.*, the same is suggested but represented as a result of operation of a temporary rule.

When talking about a rule, the choice of the Continuous may also be determined by Doer/Speaker Aspect. One such possible case is when we wish to represent a rule either as a result of choice or coincidence - let us compare:

i. Peter knew that wine, so he was likely to know if it was suitable for the occasion.
ii. Peter had frequently drunk that wine (i.e. he had frequently chosen that wine), so he was likely to know if it was suitable for the occasion.
iii. Peter had frequently been drinking that wine (he happened to have frequently been drinking), so he was likely to know if it was suitable for the occasion.

The sentence *i.* states the intended meaning directly, namely that Peter knew that wine, whereas in the sentences *ii.* and *iii.*, it is given to understand. The sentence *ii.* will be considered more appropriate in the case when we know that the drinking of this wine had not been a chain of coincidences but a result of choice and persistence. In the case of it being a series of coincidences, the sentences *iii.* will be perceived as more natural.

c. A state

When the meaning of the choice of the Continuous is defined by the Action Aspect, Past Perfect non-Continuous is used when we wish to present the past situation as an effect of a state characterised by neutral and stable intensity. Let us take the following dialogue concerning the question if somebody was likely to find his way in London:

A: Was there any danger of his getting lost?
B: No, he knew London very well.
B: No, he had already been to London.

In the first answer, B presents the opinion directly, in the second, it is communicated indirectly in the form of the implied effect of his having been to London already.

Past Perfect Continuous is a likely choice when we wish to make use of any of the modifications of meaning resulting from combining the Continuous with a stative verb (a complete list of these modifications will be found in the chapter on the Continuous Aspect) - in short, the list comprises the following situations:
- changing a state into a kind of action performed by the subject,
- reaffirming the fact that what is presented is an ongoing experience/situation perceived in the middle,
- giving a state the form of a series of static phenomena,
- giving a state the form of a passing experience,
- reflecting the fact of changing intensity of a state (increasing, decreasing),
- suggesting that a state has not yet reached the final form but has only been progressing towards it.

The above list determines the potential of the combination of the Continuous and a stative verb, its realisation in Variant 1 depends, however, on whether we shall find a context that would justify the use of the Perfect Continuous form with a given verb in the structure of describing a situation by means of what brought it about. Such contexts are quite rare, though they exist. For example, talking about somebody's understanding of a certain event in the past, we may refer to this person's knowledge directly, or it may be given to understand by means of the Perfect construction:

i. They knew/understood it very well.

ii. They had seen quite a lot of similar cases.
iii. They had been seeing quite a lot of similar cases.

The difference between the sentence *ii.* and *iii.* is that the Continuous enriches the answer with an impression that the *seeing* was accidental and, additionally, that it was extended over a period of time in the form of a series of events rather than a solitary experience (though such interpretation of the sentence *ii.* is also possible - the sentence *iii.* merely strengthens these features).

Another situation possibly justifying the use of both Past Perfect non-Continuous and Past Perfect Continuous with a stative verb might be a conversation about predictable reaction of a person talked about to a projected pulling down of a certain house - let us compare:

i. A: I believe he must have been sorry that they were intent on pulling down the old house.
ii. Him? No. He was overjoyed.
iii. Him? No. He had wished it so hard...
iv. Him? No. He had been wishing it so hard...

The sentence *ii.* presents the intended meaning directly, the sentences *iii.* and *iv.*, indirectly. The sentence *iv.* will be preferred in the situation when we wish to be more emphatic about the strength of the person's wish to see the house pulled down.

Variant 2

Paraphrasing the definition of Variant 2, in the past it addresses the situations when we wish to say that the cause and explanation of what could be seen at some moment in the past had been some event, rule, state still deeper in the past. The utterance has the form of - *Somebody guessed that what the person had THEN, was an effect of a certain event, rule, state located in the still remoter PAST*.

Past Perfect Continuous vs. Past Perfect non-Continuous

a. A single action/occurrence

In this variant, Past Perfect non-Continuous will be used when we wish to put forth a guess that what could be seen at a particular moment in the past was an effect of accomplishing, completing something in the remoter past (remaining in the anteriority of the moment which is described by the sentence). Should we believe that what could be seen was a result of mere doing something, which was capable of producing a result in the form of what was seen (without reaching the state of completion), we would use Past Perfect Continuous. For example, if we imagine friendship with a dramatist, whom, one day in the past, we paid a visit, we might come across the following situation. We knew that the dramatist had been working on a drama, and upon entering his room we notice some printed pages - we may comment upon what we saw, using one of the following:
- if we believe that the meaning of what could be seen indicated that the person had merely been occupied with working upon the text (without completing it):

He had been writing that drama - it was quite evident.
- if we believed that the meaning of what could be seen meant that the drama had been completed (e.g we found him overjoyed or spotted an empty champagne bottle in the waste basket):

He had written that drama - it was clear.

We might come across a similar case while paying a visit about the time when somebody had lunch. Judging on what we saw on that occasion, we might feel justified to interpret it in the following ways:

i. He had had his lunch already - there was no doubt about it.
ii. He had been having his lunch - there was no doubt about it.

The sentence *i.* would be a proper choice if we wanted to express a guess that what we noticed was an effect of completion of the meal, whereas, the sentence *ii.* would be a better choice if we surmised that what we saw was either a result of just having been having lunch, or that the situation described by the sentence did not require the completion of the meal, mere having been having it would have been enough to produce such effect.

At the same time, we must remember that whenever either the Action Aspect is independently determined as the non-Continuous or the non-conclusive nature of the verb makes the distinctions of the Action Aspect negligible, the Continuous may be loaded with the meanings of Doer/Speaker Aspect. In such a case, the significance of the choice of the Continuous may change. The above situation, when combined with non-conclusive verbs might justify the use or neglect of the Continuous either to signify

the doer's resolution to continue the activity (the non-Continuous - the sentence *i.* below), or to present the activity as just happening, without expressing any opinions about its relation to the doer (the Continuous - the sentence *ii.* below):
   i. He had worked on that new drama - it was clear.
   ii. He had been working on that new drama - it was clear.

b. A rule
In Variant 2, in the cases determined by the Action Aspect, Past Perfect non-Continuous will be chosen when we wish to put forth a surmise that the past situation was an effect of a permanent, regular rule. When, in our opinion, the past situation was a result of a rule that was temporary or just a chain of coincidences, the more likely choice is Past Perfect Continuous. Let us compare:
   i. She had lived there all her life - it was obvious.
   ii. She had been living there for quite some time - it was obvious.
   iii. They had regularly met there - it was clear.
   iv. They had regularly been meeting there - I could tell.

The sentence *i.* will be a likely choice when the speaker surmises that what he saw was an effect of the operation of a primary and permanent rule (regulating a continuous activity); the sentence *ii.*, when he guesses that the shape of the past situation suggested that it was a result of the operation of a secondary and transitory, short-lived rule. The sentence *iii.* will be preferred to the sentence *iv.* when the speaker understands that the past was an effect of a controlled, regular rule, whereas the sentence *iv.* will seem more proper when the events producing the past situation were guessed to be but frequently happening coincidences. The last two sentences (*iii.* and *iv.*) may also be used to put forth notions defined by the Doer/Speaker Aspect. In the above case, the fact that we are dealing with a regularity is quite clear, therefore, the Continuous and the non-Continuous may be employed to distinguish between different notions. The Perfect non-Continuous would be considered proper to express the regularity being an effect of will and determination to continue (like in the case of making regular appointments), whereas the Continuous, by removing the intentionality, would be a likely choice to describe a situation of frequent but unintended chance meetings at a place. Thus, if we wish to say that what we saw was probably an effect of the persons spoken of having made regular appointments, we would choose Past Perfect non-Continuous; if we wanted to say that the situation at the moment of speaking suggested that the persons in question had frequently come across each other rather than dated, we would use Past Perfect Continuous.

c. A state
The past might be surmised to have resulted from a certain state in the still remoter past - let us analyse the following:
   He had seen Mary - it was evident.
The above sentence addresses the situation when the speaker realised that the behaviour of the person talked about seemed to suggest that he had seen Mary.

In Variant 2, in the cases determined by Action Aspect, the speaker is likely to use Past Perfect non-Continuous when he surmised that the past was an effect of a state perceived as neutral and unmarked by any other considerations. Past Perfect Continuous would be considered proper if the speaker wanted to put forth a guess that the past situation had been shaped by a state marked by any of the traits resulting from combining a stative verb with the Continuous form - in short, the list comprises the following situations:
   - changing a state into a kind of action performed by the subject,
   - reaffirming the fact that what is presented is an ongoing experience/situation perceived in the middle,
   - giving a state the form of a series of static phenomena,
   - giving a state the form of a passing experience,
   - reflecting the fact of changing intensity of a state (increasing, decreasing),
   - suggesting that a state has not yet reached the final form but has only been progressing towards it.

The above list presents the potential of the modification of meaning resulting from combining the Continuous with a stative verb, its realisation in Variant 2 depends, obviously, on whether we shall find a context that would justify the use of the Perfect Continuous form with a given stative verb in the structure of expressing a conjecture on what of its origin was being suggested by the shape of the past state. Such contexts are quite rare, though they exist. For example, if we imagine the situation when we started

suspecting that the behaviour of a given person revealed that the person was not as ignorant as we had believed previously - this case could be addressed with two sentences:
  i. *I realised that he had understood everything that happened.*
  ii. *I realised he had been understanding everything that happened.*

If we wish to express a guess that the shape of the past situation suggested that it was an effect of a phenomenon of understanding seen in its entirety, as a single and undivided experience (or we did not care if such impression was made), the form that will be preferred is Past Perfect non-Continuous (the sentence *i.* above). When, however, we want to imply that the past situation resulted from the understanding having been not so much a single and final phenomenon but an ongoing process passing through stages to be understood separately, the form of choice would be Past Perfect Continuous (the sentence *ii.* above).

As usual, in addition to Action Aspect, the system determining the meaning of the choice between the Continuous and the non-Continuous may be Doer/Speaker Aspect. Let us analyse the following:
  i. *I was aware that he had wanted it badly.*
  ii. *I was aware that he had been wanting it badly.*

The sentence *ii.* would be a more likely choice of the two in the situation when we wish to put emphasis on the presentation of the state of *wanting* indicating its uncommon intensity.

Variant 3

We employ this variant whenever we wish to say that a single action/occurrence, a rule, or a state existing at a certain moment in the past had remained in continuation for some time. We must remember that unlike the non-Perfect construction, this type of sentences is not focused on the entire continuation of the activity but solely on the moment of reference located at its end, here, in Past Perfect tenses, a specified or implied moment in the past. The information about how long or since when the past activity had remain in continuation has the status of only additional information.

Past Perfect non-Continuous vs. Past Perfect Continuous

a. A single action/occurrence

The combination of Variant 3 of the Perfect and a single action/occurrence may be baffling because it defies the fundamental intuitions acquired at the early stages of English language acquisition (dominated by the Action Aspect of the Continuous) suggesting that the non-Continuous represents a single action/occurrence in its entirety, as a more or less conclusive, independent entity. The actual reality created by the Perfect form is different - due to its nature, Variant 3 imposes its segmental nature on even punctual verbs, presenting everything at a given point of reference (here, in the case of Past Perfect, at a given moment in the past) in the middle of continuation or repetition, i.e. in the middle of an ongoing segment. The meanings attributed by the non-Continuous and the Continuous forms to a single action/occurrence in Variant 3 are determined by the Doer/Speaker Aspect and derive from the opposition between the action presented as willed and kept up by the doer/speaker (the non-Continuous), or just continuing (the Continuous). As a result we can choose between the following pairs of sentences:
  i. *On Tuesday, he had written the report for 2 weeks and was expected to finish on the following day.*
  ii. *On Tuesday, he had been writing the report for 2 weeks and was expected to finish on the following day.*
  iii. *When she returned, he had already hammered the lock for a couple of minutes and did not seem to be going to stop soon.*
  iv. *When she returned, he had been hammering the lock for a couple of minutes and did not seem he would stop any time soon.*
  v. *It had rained since 5.*
  vi. *It had been raining since 5.*

All four sentences present an ongoing segment perceived at some specified or implied moment in the past. The first pair of sentences (*i.* and *ii.*) presents a single durative action reported at a moment in the past, being then in the midst of continuation for 2 weeks. In the second pair (*iii.* and *iv.*), a single punctual action is multiplied into the form of a series observed at the moment when she returned and being then in the midst of being repeated. In each of the pairs, we have a choice whether to represent the performance as willed and kept up by the doer (sentences *i.* and *iii.* - the non-Continuous), or (after removing the information about who had originated or controlled the action) just to present the situation identifying who did what and when but withholding the information about who was responsible for the origination or continuation of it (sentences *ii.* and *iv.* - the Continuous). The last pair features an impersonal natural phenomenon in whose case the question of volition does not apply. In such context, the choice between the two sentences is likely to be governed (still within the meanings of Doer/Speaker Aspect) by the status of the action with regard to the narrative - if the *raining* belonged to the mainstream of what is being described, the likely choice is the non-Continuous (Past Perfect non-Continuous - the sentence *v.*); if the *raining* constituted an element of background, the preferred construction will be the Continuous (Past Perfect Continuous - the sentence *vi.*).

b. A rule

The fact that a rule, when described by a non-Perfect tense, presents a certain period over which the activity described continues makes the properties of the activity similar to those characterising the modification of meaning imposed upon the verb and the structure of the sentence by this variant of the Perfect. In consequence, the description of a rule in the Perfect and the non-Perfect form look, to some extent, similar with, however, one significant difference. The non-Perfect form (both the Continuous and the non-Continuous) describes a rule in force at a point specified by the sentence, presenting it as being in the middle of operation then (neither at the beginning nor at the end). When we use the Perfect, a rule is also presented at a certain moment but not in the middle of continuation but as having been in force so far, till the moment of reference (as if 'at the end of it so far'). Let us compare the following sentences:

i. When I met her for the first time, she always went on holiday in June.
ii. When I met her for the first time, she was always going on holiday in June.
iii. By the time I met her for the first time, she had always gone on holiday in June.
iv. By the time I met her for the first time, she had always been going on holiday in June.

The first two sentences, *i.* and *ii.*, present the rule at the moment of speaking in the middle of operation, i.e. the rule started earlier and was expected to continue beyond then (the moment when she was met), our attention focused upon then. The sentences *iii.* and *iv.* also focus the reader's attention upon 'the moment when she was met for the first time' and present the same rule but they handle the presentation in a different way - they present the rule not so much in the middle of an ongoing continuum of unspecified boundaries but then, at some moment in the past, as having operated so far, till the moment of reference (which is when she was met). The latter form excludes the inevitability of future continuation, which is naturally implied in the case of the non-Perfect form (though leaves the question of its continuation open as at least not impossible). The suggestion indicated by the decision to use or not to use the Continuous may be described by the elements of both the Action and Doer/Speaker Aspect - they are quite close. The use of the non-Continuous will indicate that the speaker perceives the rule as originating from and remaining under control of the will of the doer and, in consequence, being 'regular' and 'predictable', whereas the use of the Continuous will remove this suggestion, representing the rule as a series of occurrences or tendency rather than a realization of some policy of the doer. Similar considerations seem to be standing behind the choice of the Continuous and the non-Continuous in the following sentences.

i. He sometimes drank tea instead of coffee.
ii. During that trip to Scotland, he was naturally drinking tea rather than coffee.
iii. Till 1999, he had sometimes drunk tea instead of coffee.
iv. Till 1999, he had sometimes been drinking tea instead of coffee.
v. He never played with us.
vi. He was never playing with us.
vii. She told me that since he had lived there, he had never played with us.
viii. She told me that since he had lived there, he had never been playing with us.

Another of the more obvious modifications of meaning introduced by the selection of the Continuous or the non-Continuous operates between two opposing notions namely, that the rule was primary/permanent (the non-Continuous) and that it was impermanent, transitory, secondary (the Continuous). Let us compare:

i. He said that at that moment, he had worked for IBM for 15 years.
ii. I worked (i.e. 'was employed permanently') in the Accounts Department but at the time when we first met, I had been working in the Human Resources for a few days substituting for Mrs White.

In the sentence *i.*, the non-Continuous was chosen as better reflecting the fact that the work was probably the primary and permanent occupation of the doer (although, as it was stated in the chapter, it is only a conjecture, not a fact determined by grammar). In the sentence *ii.*, the non-Continuous was chosen to warn that the work in the Human Resources had a temporary status, the primary job of the doer being that in the Accounts Dept.

Generally speaking, if the context permits and justifies it, the whole range of meaning modifications described by the Continuous Aspect may be combined with the Perfect.

c. A state

Like in the case of a rule, the temporal properties of a state, when described by a non-Perfect tense, coincide with the characteristics of the Variant 3 - both denote an ongoing 'situation' continuing for some time with, however, the same reservation as in the case of a rule. If the state is presented by a non-Perfect tense, it is presented at some point of reference as being in the middle of continuation, stretching, at the same time, naturally into the past and the future of that point. When a state is described by the Perfect form, it is denoted as present at a moment of reference so far, by that moment and continuing for some time since a moment (specified or not) in the anteriority of the point of reference - there is no suggestion (common for the non-Perfect form) that the state is expected to continue beyond the point on which we focus (although it is not impossible). Let us compare:
  i. *When I phoned him, I thought he was at home.*
  ii. *When I phoned him, I thought he had been at home for 2 hours.*
Both sentences focus upon 'then', i.e. the moment of phoning, when the state of being at home was located. In the case of the sentence *i.*, there is a natural expectation that the state began before and would continue beyond 'then'. The sentence *ii.* 'sees' the state only 'till then', giving no grounds to suppose that it was bound to continue.

Past Perfect non-Continuous vs. Past Perfect Continuous

The use of the Continuous (here, Past Perfect Continuous), as in all other cases of the combinations of the Perfect with the Continuous, is regulated by the Continuous Aspect. In the situation when we wish to describe a state as neutral, characterised by the intuitions commonly associated with the state, we will find Past Perfect non-Continuous as a form usually more accurate to represent it. On the other hand, Past Perfect Continuous will be chosen in the situations when we wish to add to the meaning of the verb any of the traits resulting from combining a stative verb with the Continuous form - in short, the list comprises the following situations:

- changing a state into a kind of action performed by the subject,
  i. *The nurse confirmed that he had been quite patient until that moment.*
  ii. *The nurse confirmed that he had been being quite patient with her until that moment.*
The sentence *ii.* changes the static, permanent feature of the person described in the sentence *i.* into an ongoing behaviour characterised by patience, akin to showing or offering it.

- reaffirming the fact that what is presented was an ongoing experience/situation perceived in the middle, not a single event:
  i. *She expressed a hope that he had seen what the others had.*
  ii. *She expressed a hope that he had been seeing what the others had.*
The sentence *ii.* disambiguates the meaning of the sentence *i.* which can be interpreted both as describing a single involuntary occurrence, similar to 'noticed' (a situation rather for Variant 1) or as presenting a state of seeing. Thanks to the intuitions connected with the Continuous, the sentence *ii.* fixes the meaning in the form of an ongoing experience seen in the middle

- giving a state the form of a series of static phenomena,
  i. *They asserted that they had seen many stranger cases since 1980s, when the illness reached there.*
  ii. *They asserted that they had been seeing many stranger cases since 1980s, when the illness reached there.*
The Continuous in the sentence *ii.* makes much more prominent what in the sentence *i.* is only one of two possibilities, namely,the fact that what is being described was not an ongoing single experience but a series of such.

- giving a state the form of a passing experience,
    i. *He assured us that he had kept an eye on them to make sure that they had understood everything that they had read.*
    ii. *He assured us that he had kept an eye on them to make sure that they had been understanding everything that they had been reading.*

The meaning of the sentence *i.* inclines towards the description of a final state of understanding reached by the subject, whereas the natural tendency of the Continuous added to the Perfect in the sentence *ii.* is to represent it as something ongoing, not necessarily heading towards any completion.

- reflecting the fact of changing intensity of a state (increasing, decreasing),
    i. *It was obvious that since mother's last visit at the eye specialist's, she had seen better every day.*
    ii. *It was obvious that since mother's last visit at the eye specialist's, she had been seeing better every day.*

Although the meaning of both sentences (*i.* and *ii.*) is similar, the fact that the state kept growing in its intensity is presented more clearly by the sentence *ii.*

- suggesting that a state had not yet reached the final form but had only been progressing towards it.
    i. *She claimed that his leadership had always resembled authoritarian dictatorship.*
    ii. *She claimed that, over the years, his leadership had increasingly resembled authoritarian dictatorship.*
    iii. *She claimed that, over the years, his leadership had increasingly been resembling authoritarian dictatorship.*
    iv. *She believed that since the beginning of the new experimental treatment, most of her patients had forgotten that traumatic event.*
    v. *She believed that since the beginning of the new experimental treatment, most of the patients had steadily been forgetting that traumatic experience.*

In the sentence *i.*, the state of resembling dictatorial rule is presented as existing in its complete, final shape. The sentences *ii.* and *iii.* describe the process advancing towards the final, complete form but at the moment described perceived somewhere in the middle, before the final stage had been reached. The replacement of *always* with *increasingly* sufficiently clarifies the changing, incomplete nature of the phenomenon but the Continuous form, by adding dynamism to the description, makes the meaning more distinct. In the case of the sentences *iv.* and *v.*, the meanings are made emphatically different by the Continuous Aspect, the sentence *iv.* presenting the state/occurrence in its final, complete shape, and the sentence *v.*, in the form of an ongoing process seen in the middle.

Past Perfect tenses in subordinate clauses

Using Past Perfect in subordinate clauses like adverbial clauses of time or conditional clauses, we must remember the specific way in which the Perfect relates the action of the main clause to that of the subordinate. Making a choice between the non-Perfect and the Perfect, we choose between referring the main clause to the temporal location of the entire action of the subordinate clause (the non-Perfect) or (in the case of the Perfect) to the location of the moment when the action of the subordinate clause exists either in the form of an effect (like the use of the type of Variant 1), or (like in Variant 3) in the form of an activity perceived at a moment of reference preceded by what of the activity has been being accomplished by that point (i.e. at a given point, the activity of the subordinate clause has been in continuation for some time). In other words, whenever we wish to define the temporal location of the action of the main clause by reference to the moment in time when the entire action of the time clause is placed, we use the non-Perfect tenses in the time clause. Thus, the main action will be located as remaining e.g. *before* or *after* the entire action of the subordinate clause. Whenever we wish to describe the placement in time of the main action by reference to the moment when the action of the subordinate clause exists in the form of an effect or at a moment when it has existed so far, we shall use the Perfect form. Let us compare:
    i. *She phoned me before I watched the show.*
    ii. *She phoned me before I had watched the show.*
    iii. *She phoned me before I had been watching/had watched the show for an hour.*

As it is suggested by the choice of the non-Perfect in the time clause of the sentence *i.*, the action of the main clause took place before the entire *watching* of the show. The use of the Perfect in the time clause of the sentence *ii.* and *iii.*, indicates that the moment of reference was either the point when the *watching* came to an end (*ii.*) or before the expiration of one hour of watching it (*iii.* - the difference between the Continuous and the non-Continuous defined by Continuous Doer/Speaker Aspect). Thus, the most obvious difference between the three sentences is that, in the first, the action of the main clause preceded the entire action of the time clause, whereas in the second and third, it may have happened during the action of the time clause but before its end or the expiration of the time specified.

In the case of the sentences of the kind of the sentence *ii.*, the choice between the Perfect and the non-Perfect makes little difference when we use the conclusive verbs, particularly those which denote the beginning or end of activity like *finish, end, start* or *begin*, e.g.

i. *He left before we finished lunch.*
ii. *He left before we had finished lunch.*

As the difference between *finished* and *had it (as) finished* is negligible, in the case of such verbs, the choice between them has no other function but stylistic - the Perfect places emphasis on the fact of completion of the action at the moment described.

Another significant consideration that has to be borne in mind while making our choice of the Perfect or the non-Perfect in the subordinate clauses, particularly, time clauses is the discrimination between the situation when the time clause describes the beginning of succession of events or prepares a static 'stage' for the events. As it was stated above, the nature of the modification of meaning resulting from employing the Perfect form derives from its origin, i.e. from the structure similar to 'having something (as) done'. Due to this fact, the Perfect is all the more likely when the character of the object of description is close to a static situation, the substance of this 'having something (as) done'. When the nature of the object of description is more akin to a dynamic succession of events, the non-Perfect forms are considered to reflect this fact better. With regard to this English employs two different forms in what seemingly are identical contexts - let us compare:

i. *When he opened the case, the mouse jumped out and escaped.*
ii. *When he had opened the case, he was able to start sorting the clothes out to make a selection.*

In the sentence *i.* the *jumping* and *escaping* succeeded directly the *opening* of the case, the latter being treated as a complete event, followed by the others in a cause and effect structure. In the sentence *ii.*, the situation is presented differently - instead of presenting the *opening* as an entire, conclusive event, which, therefore, was 'ready' to be succeeded by other similarly complete events, the structure describes the moment when the doer *had the case (as) opened*, thus moving the focus onto the static situation suggested by the verb *have* and, therefore, transforming the time clause into a kind of background to the events rather than a conclusive beginning of a series.

Past Perfect as 'Past Past' non-Perfect

The above-discussed uses of the Perfect derive from and are consistent with the intuitions embedded in its root form of *having something (as) done*, which, by focusing on the content of *having* rather than on what was *done*, makes it merely an alternative form of presentation to non-Perfect tenses, describing the same moment and the same situation as they do, though with the use of a different structure of communication. Thus, for example Present Perfect, though in its structure contains an activity that is often no longer present, uses it to describe the present moment, which makes it equal and interchangeable with Present non-Perfect tenses (Present Simple, Present Continuous), not with the Past. A good illustration of this phenomenon is the reaction of Present Perfect to Past and Present adverbs of time - although in its structure it uses a reference to a past activity, the use of a past adverb would make the sentence ungrammatical, the only adverbs that can be use are those that refer to the present, which indicates the kinship with the Present non-Perfect tenses, not their Past equivalents.

With regard to the latter considerations concerning reaction of Present Perfect to various adverbs of time, some uses of Past Perfect clearly require additional clarification. Let us analyse:

i. *I have the letter ready, now.*
ii. *I have written the letter now.*
iii. **I have written the letter yesterday.*
iv. *I had the letter ready at 5.*
v. *I had written the letter at 5.*
vi. *She said that she had seen him.*

vii. She said that she had seen him two days before.
viii. I entered the house, told them everything and they abandoned it.
ix. I entered the house and realised that they had abandoned it a long time before.

The sentences *i.* and *ii.*, in the present, and *iv.* and *v.* in the past refer to the same moments and situations, although they describe them with the use of different means – with the use of the non-Perfect, the situation is presented directly, whereas in the case of the Perfect, it is communicated indirectly. The sentence *iii.* is ungrammatical (as indicated by the asterisk) because of the combination of Present Perfect and the past adverb of time, apparently shifting the suggested communicative focus of the structure from the situation hidden under the *having* to the activity of *writing* in the past. However, if this is what makes this sentence ungrammatical, what should be the interpretation of the sentences *vii.* and *ix*? Here, the adverbial structures of time clearly refer to the anteriority of the past moment where the non-Perfect forms reside (e.g. the sentence *ix.*), and, additionally, the Past Perfect structures focus not on the moment indicated by *having* but on the one indicated by *doing*. These sentences are not ungrammatical - they are examples of additional uses to which the Perfect had to be put to keep the capacity of the tense system to distinguish in the past between the situation when an activity is contemporary to the moment of reference or earlier than it (i.e. between 'I saw that he had a car [i.e. he had it at the moment when I saw it]' and 'I saw that he had had a car [i.e. the fact was earlier than when I saw it]'). As we know, when used consistently with their nature, the Perfect forms do not describe an earlier moment in time than a verb in Past non-Perfect forms remaining in the same sentence, e.g. in the sentence *vi.* both the non-Perfect and Perfect predicates refer to the same past moment in time, indicated by the Past non-Perfect *said*, the Perfect being here equivalent to something akin to 'she was aware of (something) about him'. If that were the only possibility, the English would lack structures to address situations past in relation to a past moment (the case similar to the difference between the relation of Past non-Perfect (i.e. Past Simple) and Present Perfect tenses to the moment present - the present moment may be described with the use of Present Perfect and Present non-Perfect tenses, and what is past to the moment of speaking, is described by Past Perfect and Past non-Perfect forms). This problem was solved by enriching Past Perfect construction with a function to address such situations. Therefore, Past Perfect, has two functions, one of them is being a Past version of the Perfect, and the other, which might be called, Past Past Simple/Past Past Continuous, serves to present the events that are merely earlier than the past reference point.

- Performing the role of a Perfect tense, Past Perfect acts as an alternative construction to Past non-Perfect tenses describing, in the manner characteristic for the Perfect aspect, a situation at a past moment. If the sentence contains a non-Perfect Past form, in its Perfect uses, Past Perfect refers to the same moment.
i. When I was still toiling on my report, John had already written his.
ii. When I was still toiling on my report, John was already ready with his.
As the above sentences demonstrate, Past Perfect used as the Perfect is both simultaneous and interchangeable with Past non-Perfect forms.

- Performing the role of a Past Past non-Perfect form (using the traditional terminology: Past-Past Simple and Past-Past Continuous), Past Perfect is used to signify that the activity expressed by it is earlier than other actions or moments represented in the sentence as merely Past. If the sentence contains another predicate in one of the Past forms, in this role, Past Perfect refers not to its contemporaneity but anteriority, i.e. makes the action not contemporary but earlier than this other moment in the past.
i. The archaeologists opened the tomb and found that somebody had broken into it a long time before.
ii. She said she had talked to him a day before.
iii. She said that two hours earlier the child had still been watching TV.
A particularly common situation when the English turns to Past Perfect in this non-Perfect use (as a structure indicating that the activity is earlier than a past moment) is the situation when we enumerate successive stages of some process in a reverse order, i.e. when, after listing a few events which are presented in the order in which they happened, we encounter an activity which happened earlier than the position on which it is placed in relation to other activities preceding it in the sentence. The sentence *i.* above is an illustration of this case (i.e. the *breaking* into the tomb happened earlier than the activities preceding it in the sentence). If the *breaking into* was mentioned at the beginning of the sentence, i.e. the activities were enumerated in the order in which they happened in the past, there would be no need to use Past Perfect:

A long time ago, someone broke into the tomb and when the archaeologists finally found and opened it, it was already empty.

What is additionally interesting, this usage of the Perfect makes it sometimes difficult to recognise whether the Perfect performs the Perfect or non-Perfect role, or both. In the sentence below, the fragment stating that something resulting from her talking to him was at the moment described by the main clause *obvious to everyone* seems to suggest that it is Variant 2 of the Perfect, which we use when we communicate a guess about what brought about something existing at the moment of which we speak. However, the adverbial of time suggests that we are dealing with a structure that focuses on the activity, i.e. the *talking*, rather than on its result hiding under the enigmatic *having*. Or perhaps, the sentence is a blend of the Perfect Variant 2 with the non-Perfect, thus permitting to use an adverbial denoting anteriority in the Perfect usage.

The fact that she had talked to him two days before was obvious to everybody.

The discussion on the mechanisms regulating the usage of Past Perfect non-Continuous/Past Perfect Continuous in clauses that are subordinate to main clauses expressed with the use of Past Perfect will be found in the chapter: **The Reported activity earlier than the act of Reporting**

Hypothetical and non-hypothetical use of Past Perfect

Using and interpreting the sentences using Past Perfect, we must remember that this form is also used to denote the fact that a hypothetical activity was earlier than the moment of speaking about it. Since Past Perfect is the only Perfect form permitted by the hypothetical mood, this hypothetical usage not only blends the Perfect with the non-Perfect while referring to the past of the moment of speaking but also has to be employed whenever we encounter a non-past situation (present or future) which belongs to the cases that are reserved by English for the Perfect form, i.e. the three variant situations of the Perfect. These and other peculiarities of the hypothetical will be found by the reader discussed in detail in the chapter on the hypothetical mood.

Future Perfect non-Continuous and Future Perfect Continuous

Future Perfect Continuous and Future Perfect non-Continuous are the Future versions of the Perfect construction of describing a situation or activity (often alternative and interchangeable with the non-Perfect, though with the use of different means - see the chapter on Aspect Perfect). Since the Continuous and the Perfect combine mechanically without altering each other[29], Future Perfect and Future Perfect Continuous are not separate and distinct entities but one and the same Perfect structure enriched by the Continuous or left 'bare', without the additional information conveyed by the Continuous. There is no reason, therefore, to discuss them separately - students are more likely to grasp the peculiarity of these constructions if they regard them independently of the Continuous.

In accordance with the nature of the Aspect Perfect, Future Perfect non-Continuous and Future Perfect Continuous will be used to address three basic situations:

1. to describe a future situation by means of what will bring it about, whose effect the future situation will be,
2. on the basis of what will be seen in the future, we either make a guess as to the likely cause or present information that explains the situation to arise by naming its reason (here, contrary to point 1, the speaker uses what will be seen to guess at or inform of what will possibly bring it about),
3. to state for how long or since when, a single action/occurrence, a rule, or a state remaining at a moment in the future, will have continued or will have been repeated.

---

[29] A certain exception to this rule is American English, in which, though the aspects do not modify each other, the Continuous restricts significantly the range of combinations of the Continuous and the Perfect – for details, see the chapter on the Aspect Perfect.

The Continuous Action Aspect vs. the Continuous Doer/Speaker Aspect

The meaning of the choice between the Continuous and the non-Continuous is determined by two systems of aspect, one primary (the Action Aspect) and the other, secondary (the Doer/Speaker Aspect). The latter becomes 'visible,' recognisable only when the former is either clarified by the context (the rest of the syntax or the situation) as the non-Continuous, (i.e. when the Action Aspect is satisfactorily identified irrespective of the choice of the form of the verb within the Continuous) or when the non-conclusive nature of the verb makes the distinctions of the Action Aspect. The following tables illustrate the consequence of choosing the Continuous or the non-Continuous for the Perfect form of the verb.

Action Aspect

	Category of the object of description	the Non-continuous	the Continuous
1.	a single action or occurrence	tends[30] to be presented as a whole, in its entirety (or in the middle - see Doer/Speaker Aspect)	presented in the middle of being done
2.	a rule - continued activity	presented as unspecified rule, presumably primary and unrestricted by time, permanent	presented as restricted by time, understood as secondary and temporary, transitory
	a rule - series of acts or occurrences	presented as an unspecified rule, presumably controlled, planned, regular	presented as a chaotic series of coincidences or temporary, transitory
3.	a state	presented as not changing its intensity, steady, 'flat'	presented as a dynamic process, changing its intensity (increasing/decreasing its intensity) advancing towards completion

Doer/Speaker Aspect

		the non-Continuous	the Continuous
1.	Neutral presentation of the situation.		It indicates emotional attitude of the speaker to the situation described by the sentence.
2.	It may be intuited as identifying the doer or the speaker as the originator or controller of the action, i.e. somebody who keeps it up.		It removes the information as to who is the originator of the action, leaving it unmarked.
3.	In the narrative, the non-Continuous is the form reserved for the presentation of the foreground action.		In the narrative, the Continuous is the form indicating the background status of the action.

---

[30] Although by nature, the non-Continuous tends to present the activity in its entirety, this potential may not always be realised due to contextual reasons - see the chapter on the Continuous Aspect.

| 4. | In conversational English, this form is considered blunt and inconsiderate. | In conversational English, this form is considered more 'polite'. |

Variant 1

Paraphrasing the structure from which the Perfect originated, in Variant 1, we have structures of the type of *'I will have something ('[as] done') at a specified moment in the future as a result of the fact that I will do or will be doing something earlier'*.

Future Perfect Continuous vs. Future Perfect non-Continuous

a. A single action/occurrence

In the Continuous Action Aspect of Variant 1, Future Perfect non-Continuous is used when we wish to communicate that the future situation will be an effect of finishing, completing something earlier (it is not material for the use of this construction where on the time line the earlier activity is situated with relation to the moment of speaking i.e. as long as it is earlier that the situation described by Future Perfect it may be future, present or past). Future Perfect Continuous, on the other hand, is used in the cases when the future situation will be a result of merely performing some action, i.e. that to produce the future situation the action specified in the sentence will not have to reach completion, it will be enough for it to be being performed. In the following sentences, the guess that somebody is going to be too tired to join the participants of the conversation at the party is suggested in three different ways – in the sentence *iii.*, it is stated directly (*he will be too tired*); in the sentence *ii.*, it is suggested as a natural result of having been cycling for a very long time; and in the sentence *i.*, it is indirectly communicated as an obvious effect of having covered 130 km by bike.

i. *By the time he reaches the camp, he will have cycled for 130 km and he will be in no mood for a party.*
ii. *By the time he reaches the camp, he will have been cycling far too long to wish to join us at the party.*
iii. *By the time he reaches the camp, he will be too tired to wish to join us at the party.*

The intended meaning of the utterance is communicated directly in the sentence *iii.*, which uses the non-Perfect construction. The remaining two sentences in the Perfect non-Continuous and the Perfect Continuous forms present what is to be understood indirectly, suggesting it by means of a reference to an accomplished fact (the Perfect non-Continuous) or to mere performance of something, which, even if it does not reach any stage of completion, is capable of producing the result (the Perfect Continuous).

As it was stated above, when the Action Aspect either has been clarified independently as the non-Continuous or the non-conclusive nature of the verb has made the distinction immaterial, the meaning of the choice between the Continuous and the non-Continuous may be defined by the Doer/Speaker Aspect. Let us take the following pair of sentences:

i. *I am sure that if you call him at 6 tomorrow, he will already have talked to her.*
ii. *I am sure that if you call him at 6 tomorrow, he will already have been talking to her.*

The sentence *i.* will be preferred in the situation when the talking will be an initiative of the doer. When, however, the speaker would like to signal the fact that it is not known or immaterial who will be the initiator of the talking, he will be likely to prefer the sentence *ii*[31].

b. A rule

In the situations determined by the Action Aspect, Future Perfect non-Continuous is used when the future situation will be a result of the operation of a permanent or regular and controlled rule. Future Perfect Continuous is likely to be preferred when either the rule producing the future result will be temporary or a chain of coincidences. Let us compare:

i. *He will be likely to help his brother because at that moment he will know the people who take these decisions.*

---

[31] One must remember that the choice of the sentence *ii.* (i.e. the Continuous) might be interpreted also in terms of the Action Aspect as suggesting that the speaker believes that there is going to be more than one instance of *talking*.

ii. He will be likely to help his brother because at that moment he will have played in this orchestra for 5 years.
  iii. He will be likely to help his brother because at that moment he will have been playing in this orchestra for 2 weeks.

The sentence *i.* states the intended meaning directly, namely the fact that he will know the people who will be able to help his brother. In the case of the sentence *ii.*, the above is given to understand by representing it as a result of operation of a permanent rule; in the case of the sentence *iii.*, the same is suggested but represented as a result of operation of a temporary rule.

c. A state

When the meaning of the choice of the Continuous is defined by the Action Aspect, Future Perfect non-Continuous is used when we wish to present the future situation as an effect of a state characterised by neutral and stable intensity. Let us take the following dialogue concerning the question if somebody is likely to like a certain product:
  i. A: Is he going to like it?
  ii. B: Naturally, at that time he will have a favourable opinion about the product.
  iii. B: Naturally, by that time, he will have heard numerous good opinions about the product.
  iv. B: Naturally, by that time, he will have been hearing numerous good opinions about the product.

In the first answer (*ii.*), B presents the opinion directly, in the second (*iii.*) and third (*iv.*), it is indirectly communicated in the form of the implied effect of his having heard or having been hearing favourable opinions about the product.

Future Perfect Continuous is a likely choice when we wish to make use of any of the modifications of meaning resulting from combining the Continuous with a stative verb (a complete list of these modifications will be found in the chapter on the Continuous Aspect) - in short, the list comprises the following situations:
  - changing a state into a kind of action performed by the subject,
  - reaffirming the fact that what is presented is an ongoing experience/situation perceived in the middle,
  - giving a state the form of a series of static phenomena,
  - giving a state the form of a passing experience,
  - reflecting the fact of changing intensity of a state (increasing, decreasing),
  - suggesting that a state has not yet reached the final form but has only been progressing towards it.

The above list determines the potential of the combination of the Continuous with a stative verb, its realisation in Variant 1 depends, however, on whether we shall find a context that would justify the use of the Perfect Continuous form with a given verb in the structure of describing a situation by means of what will bring it about. Such contexts are quite rare, though they exist. For example, talking about somebody's understanding of a certain case in the past, we may refer to this person's knowledge directly, or it may be given to understand by means of the Perfect construction:
  i. Theoretically, by the end of their internship, they will know/understand it quite well.
  ii. Theoretically, by the end of their internship, they will have seen quite a lot of similar cases.
  iii. Theoretically, by the end of their internship, they will have been seeing a lot of similar cases.

The difference between the sentence *ii.* and *iii.* is that the Continuous enriches the answer with an impression that the *seeing* was rather a chain of coincidences than pursued program, and, additionally, that it was extended over a period of time in the form of a series of events rather than a solitary experience (though such interpretation of the sentence *ii.* is also possible - the sentence *iii.* merely strengthens these features).

Another situation possibly justifying the use of both Future Perfect non-Continuous and Future Perfect Continuous with a stative verb might be a conversation about predictable form of a boxing champion at the end of the boxing match - let us compare:
  i. Do you think Green will be fresh at the final gong?
  ii. On the contrary. I have a feeling he will be quite tired.
  iii. On the contrary. I think he will have wanted to hear the final bell for a long long time.
  iv. On the contrary. I have a feeling he will have been wanting to hear the final bell for a long long time.

The sentence *ii.* presents the intended meaning directly, the sentences *iii.* and *iv.*, indirectly. The sentence *iv.* will be preferred in the situation when we wish to be more emphatic about the strength of the person's wish to see the end of the boxing match.

Variant 2

Paraphrasing the definition of Variant 2, in the future it addresses the situations when we wish to say that the cause and explanation of what will be perceived or understood at some moment in the future has been some event, rule, state earlier than this situation. The utterance has the form of - *Somebody will express a conjecture (will see, will understand, will notice, etc.) that what a person has at that future moment will be an effect of an earlier event, rule, state*. The structure of this kind, therefore, would contain a main clause, expressed with a Future tense, presenting an act of perception or cognition and a subordinate clause, expressed with a Future Perfect tense, containing the conjecture on the cause or explanation of the situation existing at the future moment identified by the main clause. However, if the main clause, containing the act of perception or cognition (i.e. *You will see..., She will understand...* etc) is to be expressed with the use of a future form, the object of the perception (i.e. the content of the subordinate clause) must not use future forms unless the activities presented by the subordinate clause refer to the future of the main clause. Since the Perfect is a structure which, by nature, links the moment of reference (here, the main clause) with its anteriority, in a complex sentence of the above discussed kind, we will find it difficult, or perhaps impossible to find a situation that would justify using any of Future Perfect tenses - according to the mechanism of tense distribution operating in this situation, they will be replaced with their Present equivalents (see the chapter on the present tenses used to express futurity in the subordinate clauses). As a result, in Variant 2 of the Perfect, Future Perfect non-Continuous and Future Perfect Continuous will be replaced by Present Perfect non-Continuous and Present Perfect Continuous, respectively. The sentences will have the following form:

  i. *If you visit him without a warning, I bet you will easily see that he **has been drinking**.*
  ii. *She will see for herself that he **has not been** his true self for quite some time.*
  iii. *If they see his clothes, they will not fail to understand, I presume, that he **has done** it.*

The rules of distribution of the Continuous will naturally remain the same, respecting the division into Action Aspect and Doer/Speaker Aspect as well as their constituent parts (the interested reader will find them in the chapter on Present Perfect tenses).

Variant 3

We employ this variant whenever we wish to say that a single action/occurrence, a rule, or a state existing at a certain moment in the future will have remained in continuation for some time. We must remember that unlike the non-Perfect construction, this type of sentences is not focused on the entire continuation of the activity but solely on the moment of reference located at its end, here, in Future Perfect tenses, a specified or implied moment in the future. The information about how long or since when the past activity will have remained in continuation has the status of only additional information.

Future Perfect non-Continuous vs. Future Perfect Continuous

a. A single action/occurrence

The combination of Variant 3 of the Perfect and a single action/occurrence may be baffling because it defies the fundamental intuitions acquired at the early stages of English language acquisition (dominated by the Action Aspect of the Continuous) suggesting that the non-Continuous represents a single action/occurrence in its entirety, as a more or less conclusive, independent entity. The actual reality created by the Perfect form is different - due to its nature, Variant 3 imposes its segmental nature on even punctual verbs, presenting everything at a given point of reference (here, in the case of Future Perfect, at a given moment in the future) in the middle of continuation or repetition, i.e. in the middle of an ongoing segment. The meanings attributed by the non-Continuous and the Continuous forms to a single action/occurrence in Variant 3 are determined by the Doer/Speaker Aspect and derive from the opposition between the action presented as willed and kept up by the doer/speaker (the non-Continuous), or just continuing (the Continuous). As a result, we can choose between the following pairs of sentences:

  i. *Tomorrow, he will have prepared for the exam for 2 weeks and I doubt if you manage to persuade him to make a break.*
  ii. *Tomorrow, he will have been preparing for the exam for 2 weeks and I think it should be quite enough.*

iii. *When you return, he will have hammered the concrete on the veranda for a couple of hours and will still have a lot to do before he finishes.*
   iv. *When you return, he will have been hammering the concrete on the veranda for a couple of hours and will still have a lot to do before he finishes.*
   v. *Before the dry summer has come for good, it will have rained here for a couple of months.*
   vi. *Before the dry summer has come for good, it will have been raining here for a couple of months.*

All four sentences present an ongoing segment perceived at some specified or implied moment in the future. The first pair of sentences (*i.* and *ii.*) present a single durative action seen at the specified moment in the future, being then in the midst of continuation for 2 weeks. In the second pair (*iii.* and *iv.*), a single punctual action is multiplied into the form of a series observed at the moment when the person spoken to (i.e. *you*) returns in the midst of being repeated. In each of the pairs, we have a choice whether to represent the performance as willed and kept up by the doer (sentences *i.* and *iii.* - non-Continuous), or (after removing the information about who has originated or controlled the action) just to present the situation identifying who will do what and when but withholding the information about who will be responsible for the origination or continuation of it (sentences *ii.* and *iv.* - the Continuous). The last pair features an impersonal natural phenomenon in whose case the question of volition does not apply. In such a context, the choice between the two sentences is likely to be governed (still within the meanings of Doer/Speaker Aspect) by the status of the action with regard to the narrative - if the *raining* belongs to the mainstream of what is being described, the likely choice is the non-Continuous (Future Perfect non-Continuous - the sentence *v.*); if the *raining* constitutes an element of background, the preferred construction will be the Continuous (Future Perfect Continuous - the sentence *vi.*).

b. A rule

The fact that a rule, when described by a non-Perfect tense, presents a certain period over which the activity described continues makes the properties of the activity similar to those characterising the modification of meaning imposed upon the verb and the structure of the sentence by this variant of the Perfect. In consequence, the description of a rule in the Perfect and the non-Perfect form look, to some extent, similar with, however, one significant difference. The non-Perfect form (both the Continuous and the non-Continuous) describes a rule in force at a point specified by the sentence, presenting it as being in the middle of operation then (neither at the beginning nor at the end). When we use the Perfect, a rule is also presented at a certain moment but not in the middle of continuation but as having been in force so far, till the moment of reference (as if 'at the end of it so far'). Let us compare the following sentences:
   i. *When you return, she will work in the Accounts Dept.*
   ii. *When you return, she will be working in the Accounts Dept.*
   iii. *When you return, she will have worked in the Accounts Dept. for 2 years.*
   iv. *When you return, she will have been working in the Accounts Dept. for 2 weeks.*

The first two sentences, *i.* and *ii.*, present the rule at the moment of speaking in the middle of operation, i.e. the rule started earlier and is expected to continue beyond then (the moment *when you return*), our attention focused upon then. The sentences *iii.* and *iv.* also focus the reader's attention upon the moment *when you return* and present the same rule but they handle the presentation in a different way - they present the rule not so much in the middle of an ongoing continuum of unspecified boundaries but then, at some moment in the future, as having operated so far, till the moment of reference (which is *when you return*). The latter form excludes the inevitability of future continuation, which is naturally implied in the case of the non-Perfect form (though leaves the question of its continuation open as at least not impossible). The suggestion indicated by the decision to use or not to use the Continuous may be described by the elements of both the Action and Doer/Speaker Aspect - they are quite close. The use of the non-Continuous may be intended to indicate that the speaker perceives the rule as originating from and remaining under control of the will of the doer (Doer/Speaker Aspect) and, in consequence, being 'regular' and 'predictable' (Action Aspect), whereas the use of the Continuous will remove this suggestion, representing the rule as a certain coincidence or tendency (Action Aspect) rather than a realization of some policy of the doer (Doer/Speaker Aspect). Similar considerations seem to be standing behind the choice of the Continuous and the non-Continuous in the following sentences.
   i. *Due to doctor's orders, on Fridays, he will drink nothing but water.*
   ii. *Due to doctor's orders, next week, he will be drinking nothing but water.*
   iii. *By next Friday, she will have drunk nothing but water for a year.*
   iv. *By next Friday, she will have been drinking nothing but water for a week.*

Another of the more obvious modifications of meaning introduced by the decision to use the Continuous or the non-Continuous operates between two opposing notions namely, that the rule will be primary/permanent (the non-Continuous) and that it will be impermanent/secondary (the Continuous). Let us compare:
   i. *Tomorrow, he will have worked for IBM for 15 years.*
   ii. *Next Friday, I will have been working here in your department for 2 weeks, substituting for Mrs White.*

In the sentence *i.*, the non-Continuous was chosen as better reflecting the fact that the work will probably have been the primary and permanent occupation of the doer (although, as it was stated in the chapter, it is only a conjecture, not a fact determined by grammar). In the sentence *ii.*, the non-Continuous was chosen to warn that the work in this department has and will have had a temporary status, the primary job of the doer being somewhere else.

Generally speaking, if the context permits and justifies it, the whole range of meaning modifications described by the Continuous Aspect may be combined with the Perfect.

c. A state

Like in the case of a rule, the temporal properties of a state, when described by a non-Perfect tense, coincide with the characteristics of the Variant 3 - both denote an ongoing 'situation' continuing for some time with, however, the same reservation as in the case of a rule. If the state is presented by a non-Perfect tense, it is presented at some point of reference as being in the middle of continuation, stretching, at the same time, naturally into the past and the future of that point. When a state is described by the Perfect form, it is denoted as present at a moment of reference so far, by that moment only and continuing for some time since a moment (specified or not) in the anteriority of the point of reference - there is no suggestion (common for the non-Perfect form) that the state is expected to continue beyond the point on which we focus (although it is not impossible). Let us compare:
   i. *If you phone him at 5, I think he will be at home.*
   ii. *If you phone him at 5, I think he will have been at home for some time already.*

Both sentences focus upon 'then', i.e. the moment of phoning, when the state of being at home will be located. In the case of the sentence *i.*, there is a natural expectation that the state began before and would continue beyond 'then'. The sentence *ii.* 'sees' the state only 'till then,' giving no grounds to suppose that it will be bound to continue.

Future Perfect non-Continuous vs. Future Perfect Continuous

The use of the Continuous (here, Future Perfect Continuous), as in all other cases of the combinations of the Perfect with the Continuous, is regulated by the Continuous Aspect. In the situation when we wish to describe a state as neutral, characterised by the intuitions commonly associated with the state, we will find Future Perfect non-Continuous as a form usually more accurate to represent it. On the other hand, Future Perfect Continuous will be chosen in the situations when we wish to add to the meaning of the verb any of the traits resulting from combining a stative verb with the Continuous form - in short, the list comprises the following situations:

- changing a state into a kind of action performed by the subject,
   i. *If you have persisted in that fashion by the end of the week, you will have been so illogical for a whole month – are you trying to break some world record?*
   ii. *If she has persisted in that fashion by the end of the week, she will have been being nice to us for a whole month – is she trying to break some world record?*

The sentence *i.* presents the *being illogical* as a permanent feature of the person's personality, whereas the sentence *ii.* changes the static, permanent feature of the person (*she is nice*) into just an ongoing type of behaviour merely similar to the behaviour of a person for whom this is a trait of character.

- reaffirming the fact that what is presented will be an ongoing experience/situation perceived in the middle, rather than a single event:
   i. *A natural effect of the combination of a humanitarian crisis like this and the epidemic will be that, by the end of the first year, we will have seen the growth of mortality rate.*

ii. A natural effect of the combination of humanitarian crisis like this and the epidemic will be that, by the end of the year, we will have been seeing the growth of mortality rate.

The sentence *ii.* disambiguates the meaning of the sentence *i.* which can be interpreted both as describing a single involuntary occurrence, similar to 'noticed something once and earlier' (a situation rather for Variant 1) or as presenting a state of seeing. Thanks to the intuitions connected with the Continuous, the sentence *ii.* fixes the meaning in the form of an ongoing experience seen in the middle

- giving a state the form of a series of static phenomena,
   i. By the time we arrive, I bet they will have heard of our coming for quite some time.
   ii. By the time we arrive, I bet they will have been hearing of our coming for quite some time.

The Continuous in the sentence *ii.* makes much more prominent what in the sentence *i.* is only one of two possibilities, namely the fact that what is being described will not be an ongoing single experience but a series of such.

- giving a state the form of a passing experience,
   i. By the end of the semester, you will have understood the implications of this theory much better.
   ii. By the end of the semester, you will have been understanding the implications of this theory much better.

The meaning of the sentence *i.* inclines towards the description of a final state of understanding reached by the subject, whereas the natural tendency of the Continuous added to the Perfect in the sentence *ii.* is to represent it as something ongoing, an unfolding process, not necessarily heading towards any completion.

- reflecting the fact of changing intensity of a state (increasing, decreasing),
   i. Ask her two weeks from now - I bet she will have seen better every day since that visit at the eye specialist's.
   ii. Ask her two weeks from now - I bet she will have been seeing better every day since that visit at the eye specialist's.

Although the meaning of both sentences (*i.* and *ii.*) is similar, the fact that the state will keep growing in its intensity is presented more clearly by the sentence *ii.*

- suggesting that a state has not yet reached the final form but has only been progressing towards it.
   i. I am sure that with a wife like Jane, by the end of the year, you will have forgotten your previous marriage.
   ii. I am sure that with a wife like Jane, by the end of the year, you will have been forgetting your previous marriage.
   iii. She believes that, with this new teacher, by the end of the semester, we will have understood more of this calculus.
   iv. She believes that, with this new teacher, by the end of the semester, we will have been understanding more of this calculus.

The sentence *i.* claims that, at the end of the year, the subject will no longer remember the previous marriage. The Continuous form in the sentence *ii.* removes the suggestion that the *forgetting* is perceived in its final shape, turning it into merely a process advancing in that direction. Similar difference in meaning is indicated by the shift from the non-Continuous to the Continuous in the sentences *iii.* and *iv.* - the meaning of the sentence *iii.* is static, denoting attainment of a new level, whereas the *understanding* of the sentence *iv.* is presented as a dynamic, advancing process seen in the middle and, therefore, free of suggestion of static finality of the sentence *iii.*

Future Perfect used to refer to the present

See the chapter - **Future tenses used to describe a present situation**

Tenses with mixed time reference

Present tenses to describe Past events

Present tenses can be used to describe past events in the narratives when we wish to replace a generally neutral representation of the event by means of Past tenses with a more dramatic form. Let us analyse the following:

A: You won't believe me what happened yesterday. I come home at 5 as usual and see the door open. It is strange so I enter cautiously and find the whole flat changed - furniture, paint on the walls, everything. I stop and stare when suddenly the door to the bathroom opens and a strange woman enters. The moment she sees me she starts screaming, then dashes out and I hear her calling the police. When they finally arrive they find out that I have been so absent minded that by mistake I entered a different staircase (you know I moved in only last week and everything looks alike to me) and consequently, a different flat. I had to apologize and, humiliated I went home. The good thing is I had a good laugh and have made friends with the lady and she is quite pretty.

In the story above, the part of it whose function is merely to present the circumstances of the event is rendered in the Past tense, which locates the situation with reference to the time of describing it. The part which is to be the dramatic core of the story is narrated in Present tense, which moves the speaker and listener as if into the contemporaneity of the event and lets them 'move along' with the story.

Present tenses to express futurity

The use of Present tenses in the main clause to express futurity

Under certain conditions, Present tenses may be used to describe the future directly (unlike the case when they are used in a clause subordinate to a main clause referring to the future, in which case it is the main clause that determines the fact that what is talked about is understood as future). The conditions that have to be satisfied are as follows:
- when we are talking about the future action which has been planned for some time, and now we only talk about what is planned for the future – this construction can not be used to express predictions concerning future or announce decisions taken at the moment of speaking (in both these situations the correct construction will be one of the future tenses),
- the action spoken of must have the nature that makes it possibly dependent on human will, and, therefore, permitting agreeing or deciding about it (it excludes, at least, in non-ironic utterances, the processes independent of human will),
- by nature, present constructions announce an intention to talk about the present, so, if we wish our utterance to be understood as referring to the future, we must make it clear by adding future time reference – the identification of the future time of the action should be either included in our utterance or otherwise inferrable from the context, e.g. our sentence being an answer to a question specifying the future time reference.

The choice of the Present tenses is regulated by the two aspects, Continuous and Perfect, which will now be discussed separately.

Present Non Perfect tenses – Continuous vs. non-Continuous

The above conditions met, we may encounter three basic situations that make specific use of the Aspect Continuous:
1) a single event (determined by the Speaker/Doer Aspect)
2) a single event resulting from a rule (determined by the Action Aspect)
3) a chain of actions (determined by the Action Aspect)

1) – A single decision of the speaker/doer

Usually, when we speak of a single action planned individually for the future, the Continuous Action Aspect seems to be determined by the very situation as that of a single action presented in its entirety. Thus, what is recognised as the difference between the Continuous and the non-Continuous is what is suggested by Speaker/Doer Aspect, namely, the difference between, on the one hand, the presentation of the action as performed as a result of the initiative/intention of the doer/speaker, and, on the other, a mere presentation of the situation together with all its components, with the exclusion, however, of the information concerning the author of the action. It may be illustrated by the following situation: a boss of a company has made a decision that on the following day two of his employees will go on a business trip, one to Berlin, the other, to Paris. Communicating this fact to his employees, he may choose between two forms:

i. John, tomorrow, you go to Berlin, and Helen goes to Paris.
ii. John, tomorrow, you are going to Berlin, and Helen is going to Paris.

The sentence *ii.* is merely a statement of the fact that it has been planned (without specifying, by whom) that, on the following day, one of the employees will go to Berlin, and the other, to Paris. The sentence *i.* contains the same information as *ii.*, plus an indication that the action is to be performed as a result of the decision of either, the doer, (which is in this case impossible), or the speaker. Thus, in the above situation, sentence *ii.* may be used by both the boss (if he does not wish to present the fact as his decision) or by any of the employees (since they do not decide about the fact, only report it). The sentence *i.*, however, may be uttered only by the boss, who is the author of the decision.

2) - A single action resulting from a rule

It may happen that the future event spoken of is a part of a rule, e.g. a schedule. In such a case, as long as we speak of a single event, the choice between the Continuous and the non-Continuous is regulated by the Action Aspect of a single action/occurrence, not that of a rule. Therefore, if the action/occurrence is presented by the sentence in its entirety, the aspect chosen will be the non-Continuous, if, however, the action/occurrence is presented in the middle of being performed at a given moment, the aspect chosen will be the Continuous.

i. What time does the last train to Warsaw leave tonight. ~ It's Saturday today, so the last train leaves at 22:00.
ii. Where can I find him tonight? ~ At the pool. At 7 a.m. he is having a swim.

Although in the sentence *ii.* the verb permits the use of the non-Continuous without a change to Action Aspect, it seems improper since it might be read as suggesting the doer's volition in the case of this single action, whereas the speaker knows it is going to be performed as a result of the operation of a rule, not the unique decision of the doer.

3) - A chain of actions

If what is to be presented is not a single action but a chain of such, the case naturally returns to the regulations of Action Aspect, since it is unlikely that in such situation the Action Aspect will be clarified by the sentence alone. Therefore, what will matter in the case of a single action will be the question whether it is presented in its entirety or in the middle of being done; in the case of a rule, the question whether it is presented as primary, permanent or as temporary; in the case of a state, whether its intensity is neutral or in a way abnormal, i.e. increased/ changing.

i. Brown enters the stage first, then comes Jones, and the next is Green. When Green enters the stage, Jones is still speaking, so...
ii. Tomorrow, we get up at 7 and have breakfast in two groups. The first comes to the dining hall at 8 and has 40 min. to have breakfast. At 7:35, when the first group is about to finish, the second group is already gathering in the hall to be ready to enter the dining room the moment the tables are cleared.

Present Perfect tenses – Perfect vs. non-Perfect

Present Perfect tenses are used to express plans concerning futurity when the situation to be described falls into one of the following categories requiring the use of the Perfect in English:
- when we wish to describe a situation by means of something that has brought it about, of which this situation is an effect,
- when we wish to say that an action, rule or state present at a given moment, has continued for some time which we specify.

In the following sentences, the first illustrates the case when the Perfect describes the situation (the fact that the group is expected to be ready at 8:40) by means of something that may produce such effect. The second sentence is an example of the other situation when we must needs resort to the Perfect because only the Perfect can be used to say that some activity, rule or state present at a given moment in time, has continued for some time or since some moment.

    i. *Tomorrow, we get up at 7 and have breakfast in two groups. The first comes to the dining hall at 8 and have 40 min. to have breakfast. At 8:40 the first group has had its breakfast and the second group is already gathering in the hall, so the moment will be opportune for our guide to give us our tickets.*

    ii. *Tomorrow, I start at 8. First, I put the vegetables into a pot of water and make it boil. Next, I cut the meat into cubes and start frying it. At 9, the vegetables have been boiling for an hour and I can move to the next step...*

Present tenses used to express futurity in subordinate clauses

The grammatical form of the verb in a subordinate finite clause may reflect the following types of relation to a reference point:
- relation to the main clause alone (e.g. in clauses following *wish, would rather, had better*),
- relation to the main clause and the point of speaking (e.g. in Reported clauses in Indirect Reporting),
- relation to the point of speaking alone (e.g. in adverbial clauses of concession, for example after *though* and *although*, in adverbial clauses of cause, for example after *because* etc).

In the case of sentences whose main clause refers to the future (i.e. is expressed by any construction that makes it clear that the sentence refers to the future) and whose subordinate clause belongs to the class in which the verb form reflects the relation not only to the main clause but also to the moment of speaking, the forms of the verb are selected according to the following pattern:
- when the subordinate clause is FUTURE to the main clause, this fact will be indicated by the use of Future tenses,
- when the subordinate clause is PRESENT to the main clause, this fact will be indicated by the use of Present tenses [32],
- when the subordinate clause is PAST to the main clause, this fact will be indicated by the use of Past tenses[33].

Thus, we may encounter sentences similar to the following:

    i. *I will phone you when I come home (not: *... when I will come home).*
    ii. *I will send you a postcard from wherever I'm staying.*
    iii. *Sooner or later, I will buy a cottage in the village where my parents live now.*

In the sentence *ii.* above, the subordinate clause is expressed by a Present tense to show that the state it represents will be contemporary to the action of the main clause. The same Present tense is used also in the sentence *iii.*, although here it indicates that the rule is contemporary to the moment of speaking. Thus, the Present alone can not be taken for an indication of the relation between the moment of speaking and the activity of the subordinate clause of this kind because it may signal the contemporaneity both with the moment of speaking and the moment of the main clause. To reach satisfactory precision we have to clarify the situation with additional syntactic and lexical devices. A different situation will be encountered in the time clauses, which, by reason of their function, as a rule refer to the same moment of time as the main clause - the tense used in the time clause in the sentence *i.* means solely that the action of the subordinate clause refers to the moment when the main clause is located, it makes no indication of what is the relation between the subordinate clause and the moment of speaking apart from what can be deduced from the fact that the main clause to which it is contemporary is located in the future.

At the same time, the student of English must bear in mind that to be able to recognize correctly the character of the subordinate clause and, in consequence, to choose the proper form of the verb, it is not enough to pay attention to conjunctions alone. Sometimes, the temporal conjunctions introduce clauses

---

[32] It must be remembered that with an exception of the adverbial clauses of time, the present form in the subordinate clause may indicate that the action is contemporary to either the action of the main clause or the moment of speaking - it will have to be guessed by the recipient of the communiqué from the context.

[33] Past tenses in the subordinate clause may indicate either that the action of the subordinate clause is past to the main clause alone or also to the moment of speaking.

which are merely similar to time clauses whereas their true syntactic function is entirely different. Let us compare:
   i. *He'll beg for food before he'll ask his parents for money (Quirk et al. 1081)*[34]
   ii. *Pigs will fly before he will become a mathematician (Quirk et al. 1081)*
   iii. *He will return before you finish the letter.*
   iv. *Her mother will tell you when Mary comes home.*
   v. *Her mother will tell you when Mary will come home.*

The sentences *iii.* and *iv.* above are time clauses, whose syntactic function is to locate the main clause in time (therefore, they always refer to the moment in time where the future main clause remains and are more or less contemporary to them), so the tenses chosen for the verbs are Present. The conjunction *before* in the sentence *i.* is equivalent to *sooner than* and does not introduce the time clause but a comparative clause which belongs to a different class of subordinate clauses, namely such whose form reflects the relation to the moment of speaking and whose form is, therefore, independent from the tense of the main clause. The choice of Future tense for this clause indicates that the verb is future to the moment of speaking - the relation to the verb of the main clause will have to be guessed at by the recipient of the communiqué. The subordinate clause in the sentence *v.* is a noun clause, here, an object clause, whose function is not so much to present any of the circumstances in which the action of the main clause takes place but rather to describe the object of Mary's mother's utterance, i.e. the information on when Mary is expected to come home. So, although the clause is apparently introduced by the conjunction *when*, its function is not to present *when* the act of *telling* is going to take place but what the object of this *telling* is going to be.

Present Perfect vs. Present non-Perfect in adverbial clauses of time

Using Present Perfect in subordinate clauses like adverbial clauses of time or conditional clauses, we must remember the specific way in which the Perfect relates the action of the main and subordinate clauses. Making a choice between the non-Perfect and the Perfect, we choose between referring the main clause to the location of the entire action of the subordinate clause (the non-Perfect) or (in the case of the Perfect) to the location of the moment when the action of the subordinate clause exists either in the form of an effect (like the use of the type of Variant 1), or (like in Variant 3) in the form of an activity perceived at a moment of reference preceded by what of the activity has been being accomplished by that point (i.e. at a given point, the activity of the subordinate clause has been in continuation for some time). In other words, whenever we wish to define the temporal location of the action of the main clause by reference to the moment in time when the entire action of the time clause is placed, we use the non-Perfect tenses in the time clause. Thus, the main action will be located as remaining e.g. *before* or *after* the entire action of the subordinate clause. Whenever we wish to describe the placement in time of the main action by reference to the moment when the action of the subordinate clause exists in the form of effect or at a moment when it has existed so far, we shall use the Perfect form. Let us compare:
   i. *I will phone you before we watch the show.*
   ii. *I will phone you before we have watched the show.*
   iii. *I will phone you before we have been having watching the show for an hour.*
   (Perfect Continuous and Perfect non-Continuous in the sentences *ii.* and *iii.* respectively is also possible but with a change of meaning determined by the Aspect Continuous)

As it is suggested by the choice of the non-Perfect in the time clause of the sentence *i.*, the action of the main clause will take place before the entire *watching* of the show. The use of the Perfect in the time clause of the sentence *ii.* and *iii.*, indicates that the moment of reference is either the point when the *watching* came to an end (*ii.*) or before the expiration of one hour of watching it (*iii.*). Thus, the most obvious difference between the three sentences is that, in the first, the action of the main clause will precede the entire action of the time clause, whereas in the second and third, it may happen during the action of the time clause but before its end or the expiration of the time specified. In the case of the sentences of the kind of the sentence *ii.* the choice between the Perfect and the non-Perfect makes little difference when we use the conclusive verbs, particularly those which denote the beginning or end of activity like *finish, end, start* or *begin*, e.g.
   i. *He will leave before we finish lunch.*

---

[34] Quirk, Randolph et al. *A Comprehensive Grammar of the English Language*. London and New York: Longman Group, 1990.

ii. He will leave before we have finished lunch.

As the difference between *finish* and *have it (as) finished* is negligible, in the case of such verbs, the choice between them has no other function as stylistic - the Perfect places emphasis on the fact of completion of the action at the moment described.

Another significant consideration that has to be borne in mind while making our choice of the Perfect or the non-Perfect in the subordinate clauses, particularly, time clauses is the discrimination between the situation when the time clause describes the beginning of succession of events or prepares a static 'stage' for the events. As it was stated above, the nature of the modification of meaning resulting from employing the Perfect form derives from its origin, i.e. from the structure similar to *having something (as) done*. Due to this fact, the Perfect is all the more likely when the character of the object of description is close to a static situation, the substance of this *having something (as) done*. When the nature of the object of description is more akin to a dynamic succession of events, the non-Perfect forms are considered to reflect this fact better. With regard to this fact English employs two different forms in what seemingly are identical contexts - let us compare:

i. When you open the case, the mouse will jump out and escape.
ii. When you have opened the case, you will be able to start sorting the clothes out to make a selection.

In the sentence *i.* the *jumping* and *escaping* succeed directly the *opening* of the case, the latter being treated as a complete event, followed by the others. In the sentence *ii.*, the situation is presented differently - instead of presenting the *opening* as an entire, conclusive event, which, therefore, is 'ready' to be succeeded by other similarly complete events, the structure describes the moment when the doer *has the case [as] opened,* thus moving the focus onto the static situation suggested by the verb *have* and, therefore, transforming the time clause into a kind of background to the events rather than a conclusive beginning of a series.

Futurity and the Past

All the forms which are in use in English to express futurity have their equivalents in the Past, where they function as constructions indicating that the activity spoken of is located in the Future of the Past moment of reference.

i. She said she would go home at once.
ii. He notified us that on Friday at 5 o'clock he would be working in his office.
iii. It was clear that they would have finished the project by September.
iv. The Prime Minister was informed that by the following June the commission would have been working on the project for 2 years already.
v. I visited her yesterday and found her all packed - she was going to Brazil the following week.
vi. When they last met, boss told John that he travelled to Paris on the following day.
vii. She said that she wanted John to get up 2 hours before us the following day so that when we came down to breakfast at 8, he would have had his breakfast already and he could start packing our suitcases.
vi. She said that she wanted to get up at 6 so that when John called she would already have been talking to the doctor.

Future tenses

Future tenses have their equivalents in the tenses called Future in the Past (the difference between them being only the auxiliary which assumes its past form *would*). Their use in non-hypothetical mood indicates that the activity spoken of is represented as future not from the moment of speaking but from a specified moment in the past (see also Futurity from the perspective of the Past).

i. She said: 'I will be watching TV at 5'.
ii. She said that she would be watching TV at 5.

Present tenses

Present tenses used to describe present plans for the future find their equivalents in Past tenses (Present Simple replaced by Past Simple, Present Continuous, by Past Continuous, Present Perfect, by Past Perfect, and Present Perfect Continuous, by Past Perfect Continuous). The use of Past tenses

signifies that we are talking about plans which remain in some specified past moment and refer to the futurity of this past moment.
   i. She said: 'I am going to Warsaw tomorrow'.
   ii. She said that she was going to Warsaw on the following day.

Semi-auxiliaries and auxiliaries

In the finite constructions other than reporting sentences, the set of grammatical devices capable of denoting Futurity to the Past moment of reference comprises only these which have Past forms. Thus, we will find here all semi-auxiliaries, like *be going to do sth, be about to do sth, be on the point of doing sth, have to do sth, be able to do sth, be allowed to do sth*, etc because they all have complete sets of tense forms. Of all the auxiliaries, only *may* and *can* have their past forms, and, therefore, in constructions other than Reporting, only these two will be in our disposal: *may-might, can-could*. However, since auxiliaries are located at the moment of production of the utterance (not necessarily the moment of speaking), in Indirect Reporting sentences (which contain the moment of production of the reported utterance, i.e. the reporting main clause) we will additionally be permitted to use the auxiliaries which do not have Past forms, i.e. *should, ought to, must, needn't, mustn't* (in addition to *might* and *could*, obviously).

Futurity from the perspective of the Past - relation to the moment of speaking

A separate problem that should be remembered when we interpret a past sentence containing a clause referring to the future of the past moment is the relation between the futurity expressed from the perspective of a past moment and the futurity of the moment of speaking. There are two considerations that we have to bear in mind.

a. Unless the future point to which refers the activity expressed by any of the constructions of Futurity in the Past determines the Past character of the activity spoken of, the mere fact that the event is described as Future from the perspective of the Past must not be interpreted as signifying automatically that the activity can be nothing but Past from the moment of speaking - the only thing that is signalled by the use of any of the constructions of Futurity in the Past is that the activity was Future in relation to some moment of reference in the Past, and, therefore, may be actually non-Past from the moment of speaking (i.e. simultaneous with or future to the moment of speaking). For example:
The spokesman confirmed that the vice-President was visiting the site of the explosion tomorrow, although the exact hour has not been determined yet.

b. An activity or an event which are Future not only to the moment of reference in the past but also to the moment of speaking do not have to be expressed with the use of Futurity in the Past constructions but, alternatively, we may use the Future and Present constructions. The Present and Future constructions can not be used when the Future, which was true at the moment in the past, is no longer to happen, e.g. when we know of something that happened after the act of prediction in the past and which cancelled it out:
   i. *Yesterday, we got a letter from Mary saying that she is visiting us tomorrow.*
   ii. *Mary was visiting us tomorrow but two hours ago her mother called and said Mary had had an accident.*

When we wish to use an auxiliary, the question what the combination 'auxiliary+verb' indicates with reference to its position vis a vis the moment of speaking is largely determined by the type of infinitive used. However, due to the complex nature of the role played by the infinitive, caution must be exercised while using it in this context. We must remember that the Perfect infinitive serves both to describe the situations reserved for the Perfect form in English and, additionally, to indicate the fact that an activity belongs to the past of the moment of reference where the auxiliary is located. Whenever there is no identifiable adverb of time locating the activity as future, the Perfect infinitive will serve only as an indicator of the past or unaccomplished nature of the activity. At the same time, we must remember that there are certain constructions like the semi-auxiliary *be to do sth* which, when located in the Past, uses the opposition between non-Perfect - Perfect to indicate possible or impossible, respectively, nature of the activity.

i. I was to have mailed this letter tomorrow but yesterday my aunt called and there is no longer any use in doing it because I could tell her everything on the phone.
ii. He told me yesterday that I was to mail the letter tomorrow, therefore, I must buy some stamps to be ready to send it at once.
iii. He said that the work should have been finished already but one of the employees had had an accident and the whole thing was slowed down.
iv. He said that the work should be finished at 5.
v. He said that the letter should have been written by 5 on the following day.
vi. He said that at 4 his wife should have been at home for some time already.

The combination of *was to+Perfect infinitive* in the sentence *i.* is an indication that the activity named by it will not be accomplished - it denotes a certain plan which, at the moment of describing it, is already known to have been cancelled. The combination of *was to+non-Perfect infinitive* in the sentence *ii.* indicates that the utterance presents an activity still possible, still expected to be accomplished in the specified time. The sentences *iii.-v.* show how the presence or absence of future time reference changes the intuited reference point of *should+infinitive* construction. In the sentence *iii.*, there is no future reference point, therefore, the activity is understood to be located at the moment specified by the reporting clause, to which, as it is indicated by the use of the Perfect infinitive, it is past and unaccomplished. In the sentences *iv., v.,* and *vi.*, there is a future reference point and, thus, the activity refers to this point, defining its relation to it with the use of the Perfect or non-Perfect forms, in accordance with the Aspect Perfect (the sentence *v.*, Variant 1, the sentence *vi.*, Variant 3).

Future tenses to describe a present situation

When a speaker wishes to warn that he is not sure about what he describes as the present situation, he may signal his uncertainty by the use of Future tenses in place of their Present equivalents, i.e. Future Simple for Present Simple, Future Perfect for Present Perfect etc. Let us compare:
i. Don't phone her now. She is now bathing the baby.
ii. Don't phone her now. She will now be bathing the baby.
iii. I think you can safely call him now. I think he has had his lunch already.
iv. I think you can safely call him now. I think he will have had his lunch already.
v. It's nonsense to look for him at school. He is at home already.
vi. It's nonsense to look for him at school. He will be at home already.

In the above sentences, the Present tense versions (*i., iii., v.*) represent just the properties of the situation as it is recognised by the speaker and may be understood as an indication of the speaker's conviction that the situation exists in the shape described by the sentence. Their Future equivalents (*ii., iv., vi.*) additionally signal that the speaker is in doubt about what he expresses.

Passive Voice

English is a language which, because of its non-inflectional nature, is forced to use the position in the sentence order to identify the role performed by a given sentence element in the whole utterance. Therefore, in order not to lose understandability, the observance of the sentence order is quite strict and allows for only few exceptions. As a result, the Passive transformation is practically the only significant modification of the sentence order allowed, hence, its unique status in English. The nature of this transformation consists in moving the object of the sentence, i.e. the recipient of the activity to the position in front of the verb, thus placing it at the location occupied in the Active Voice by the subject, i.e. the doer of the activity. The need for such a shift might arise when we wish to put more emphasis in our presentation on what happened to the recipient of the activity rather than who performed the action. Since the position of recognisable prominence is the front position, by moving the object before the verb we stress its importance - let us compare:

i. *Peter damaged my car.*
ii. *My car was damaged (by Peter).*

The element which seems to be stressed by the sentence *i.* as focused upon by the speaker are *Peter* and *damaged*. The change of position in the sentence *ii.* moves clearly also the suggested focus of the utterance from the doer and/or the activity to the recipient and the effect. In inflectional languages like e.g. Polish, the mother tongue of the author of this book, the position of the doer and the recipient may be freely manipulated without any danger to the understandability of the sentence because in these languages the roles performed by the nouns in the structure of the utterance are indicated by inflectional endings attached to the noun. As a result, in such languages, the utterance retains its original meaning no matter in what order we present it - below are variants of a Polish sentence saying that a policeman caught a thief:

i. *Policjant złapał złodzieja. (a policeman caught a thief)*
ii. *Złodzieja złapał policjant. (a policeman caught a thief)*
iii. *Złodzieja policjant złapał. (a policeman caught a thief)*
iv. *Złapał złodzieja policjant. (a policeman caught a thief)*

All the above sentences have the same meaning - it would change only if we changed the inflectional endings:

i. *Policjant złapał złodzieja. (a policeman caught a thief)*
ii. *Policjanta złapał złodziej. (a thief caught a policeman)*

In the sentence *i.* it is a policeman that caught a thief, in the sentence *ii.*, a thief caught a policeman. In English, the cost of such manipulation would be an irretrievable loss of understandability the moment we would abandon what is dictated by the prescribed order, e.g. there is no grammatical or syntactic indication left in the following sentence that it is the policeman who does the *catching*:

i. *A thief caught a policeman.*
ii. *Caught a thief a policeman.*
iii. *A thief a policeman caught.*

Because this language lacks the inflectional endings, the role of the noun in the utterance is indicated in a different way - <u>in English, the fact that the element preceding the verb is not the doer but the recipient is indicated by the form of the verb.</u> The form of the verb showing that the element preceding it is the recipient of the activity is different from the form of the verb showing that what precedes it is a doer - the former, the passive form is composed of two elements mechanically attached to each other:

- the verb *be* in the form of the active voice of the structure in which it appears[35],
- the main verb in the passive form, i.e. the form indicating that the element it describes is the recipient - it is the form of Passive Adjectival Participle[36], e.g. *done, written, washed* etc. sometimes called Past Participle, or the third form. No matter what construction, finite or infinite we employ, the form of the main verb remains unchanged, i.e. it remains the passive form of the verb.

The fact that the above two syntactic elements do not constitute a solid whole but are simply mechanically juxtaposed is attested by the fact that in complex predicators the adverbs may be placed not only after the auxiliary but also between the whole form of *be* and the main verb in the passive form - for example:

i. *It had already been written when she came.*
ii. *It had been already written when she came.*
iii. *At 5, he had already been writing it for 3 hours.*
*iv. *At 5, he had been already writing it for 3 hours.*

In the Active Voice, whose object of description is a single entity, it is not allowed to insert anything inside the predicator apart from the position following the auxiliary. In the Passive Voice, such structure is permitted, suggesting the fact that this form is actually composed of two separate and independent entities, the verb *be* and the main verb.

As the above shows, since the Passive transformation is an indication of the relation between the activity and the noun, the transformation must not be done without simultaneous moving of the Object to the position in front of the verb, otherwise, we change the meaning of the sentence, i.e.

i. *A policeman caught a thief.*
ii. *A policeman was caught by a thief.*
iii. *A thief was caught by a policeman.*

The sentence equivalent in meaning (though with different placement of emphasis) to the sentence *i.* is the sentence *iii.*, whereas the sentence *ii.* creates a different reality, in which the policeman was caught, not the thief. Sometimes, when, instead of composing a sentence directly in Passive Voice, we make transformations of sentences in the Active Voice into Passive, we may encounter situations when such changes are blocked - it happens when the main verb of the Active Voice sentence is an intransitive verb. Intransitive verbs name activities which are not performed on any Objects but are conducted by the Subject alone. Naturally, in the case of such sentences, it is nonsense to try to change the verb alone into the Passive without altering the syntax, i.e. placing the Object (non-existent here) upon the position before the verb because it changes the meaning of the utterance - let us compare:

i. *John was walking the horse. - The horse was being walked by John.*
ii. *Helen was walking in the park. - Helen was being walked in the park (by whom?).*

In the first pair of sentences above, the sentences have generally the same meaning. In the example *ii.*, the change of the verb without moving the Subject, altered the whole meaning from a description of an independent walk into a situation when a person is forced to walk or supported in doing so by somebody else. Making such transformations we must remember to adjust the number of the verb *be* in Passive Voice sentence to the changed Subject (obviously, only when the number has changed), e.g.

i. *He was making pictures.*
ii. *Pictures were being made by him.*

---

[35] The form of the verb used by Passive Voice construction is not unique and dedicated solely to the use with the Passive Voice. It is the same form as is or would be used in a given construction in other applications, e.g.
- *He is patient - The contract is drawn in Spanish.*
- *He is being patient - The letter is being written.*
- *The letter was in my pocket - The letter was written.*

[36] There are two adjectival participles: active and passive. When they are used to 'describe' a noun, the former presents the noun as the doer of the activity that the participle denotes, whereas the latter, shows the noun as a recipient, for example:
i. *boiling water,*
ii. *boiled egg.*

In the group *i.*, the water performs the boiling, in the group *ii.*, the egg receives the effects of boiling. Therefore, the former may be called Active Adjectival Participle, the latter Passive Adjectival Participle.

Passive Voice and the Aspect Continuous

Reviewing the forms assumed by verbs in the Passive Voice, a number of grammar books recognise the majority of the Continuous forms as awkward, infrequent or, perhaps, even incorrect. The Continuous forms in question comprise all Continuous tenses (with an exception of Present non-Perfect Continuous and Past non-Perfect Continuous tenses, i.e. Present Continuous and Past Continuous) and Continuous infinitives. An interesting question arises what is the reason for this avoidance - is it because the addition of the verb *be* in the Passive Voice makes the Continuous redundant or, perhaps, because in the Passive Voice, the non-Continuous sentences become so general that they cover with equal accuracy the Continuous and non-Continuous meanings? To be able to answer these questions with satisfactory precision, we must first address two specific problems:

1. is the static nature of the verb *be* capable of conveying all the meanings that can be communicated by the Aspect Continuous, both Action Aspect and Doer/Speaker Aspect,
2. what is the object of the Continuous modification in the Passive Voice, i.e. when we choose the Continuous or the non-Continuous form of the component *be* in the Passive construction, do we modify the meaning of the verb *be* or the main verb.

As the chapter on the Aspect Continuous shows, the modifications of meaning resulting from expressing a single action/occurrence, a rule, or a state in the Continuous go far beyond the mere indication that what we present is perceived not in its entirety but in the middle (which might be regarded as the general difference between a state and a dynamic event). The range of shades of meaning, suggestions, innuendoes is so wide that it would be ludicrous to claim that they can be rendered with satisfactory accuracy by any generic use of the verb *be* in its non-Continuous form. Let us analyse the following cases of the use of the Continuous with the Passive and the Active Voice:

i. Gerald **was always being chided** for something or other: his wife had never entirely lost her Portuguese liking for matriarchal discipline, order and cleanliness --; qualities that were not often found among the Husseys. (BNC EWH 613) - [probable Active Voice variant of the same:] Gerald's wife **was always chiding** him for something or other...

ii. Gerald **was always chided** for something or other: his wife had never entirely lost her Portuguese liking for matriarchal discipline, order and cleanliness --; qualities that were not often found among the Husseys. (non-Continuous paraphrase of BNC EWH 613) - [probable Active Voice variant of the same:] Gerald's wife **always chided** him for something or other...

iii. These included speaking more slowly, facing the client, and checking that the advice **is being understood**. (BNC - B0N 183) - [probable Active Voice variant of the same:] ... checking that the client **is understanding** the advice.

iv. These included speaking more slowly, facing the client, and checking that the advice **is understood**. (non-Continuous variant of BNC - B0N 183) - [probable Active Voice variant of the same:] ... checking that the client **understands** the advice.

The probable Active Voice variant of the sentence *i.* (i.e. *Gerald's wife was always chiding him for something or other*) is a case of the Continuous used to modify the meaning of a rule. What seems to be added by the Continuous is, on the one hand, a kind of emotional colouring of the presentation, suggesting critical attitude of the speaker towards the fact presented, and, on the other, perhaps also increased intensity and frequency of the chiding and possibly its disorderly character. All these innuendoes can easily be detected in the Continuous version of the Passive, being at the same time, inaccessible in the sentence *ii.* in the Passive Variant. The latter is clearly nothing but what can be found in its probable non-Continuous Active Voice variant. If we now take the probable Active Voice variant of the sentence *iii.* (i.e. *... checking that the client is understanding the advice*), the Continuous enriches the meaning of *understand* with a suggestion that what is presented in the sentence is not a final and static form of a state of understanding, but an intellectual experience perceived in the form of an ongoing process progressing along some durative activity (here, *giving advice*). This additional meaning is made quite clear by the Continuous variant of the Passive Voice, being, at the same time, unrecognisable in the non-Continuous Passive Voice variant in the sentence *iv*.

Thus, it seems that it is justified to answer the question 1 above in the negative, dismissing the hypothesis that the Continuous form is no longer needed in the Passive Voice because due to the addition of the verb *be*, all the possible shades of meaning conveyed in the Active Voice by the Continuous form are rendered recognisable by the verb *be* alone in the non-Continuous form - it is clearly not the case.

Similarly, the obvious answer to the point 2 above, suggested by the above analysis is the fact that the use of the Continuous clearly seems to be dictated by the considerations to be found in the grammatical or lexical aspect of the main verb rather than any aspectual modifications of the static verb *be* seen as an independent element - whenever the Continuous is used in the Passive Voice, its purpose is to modify the meaning of the main verb rather than the verb *be*, which turns to be rather a grammatical marker of the Passive than the independent lexical element. Thus, the difference between the Continuous and the non-Continuous Passive Voice in the case of a single action/occurrence, rule, or state will be equivalent to the Active Voice modification of the meaning of the single action/occurrence, rule, or state rather than the modification of the stative verb *be*.

Conclusive and non-Conclusive in Passive Voice

Another very important consideration that must be borne in mind while we determine the form of the Passive predicate with regard to Aspect Continuous is the conclusive or non-conclusive nature of the main verb. Let us begin by analysing the following examples:

i. *They will prepare the play next Friday.* - *The play will be prepared next Friday.* (conclusive verb)
ii. *They will be preparing the play next Friday.* - *The play will be being prepared next Friday.*
iii. *Next Friday, they will perform the play.* - *Next Friday, the play will be performed.* (non-conclusive verb)
iv. *Next Friday, they will be performing the play.* - *Next Friday, the play will be being performed.*

As it is illustrated by the sentences *iii.* and *iv.*, the differences between the Continuous and the non-Continuous within the Action Aspect seem, in the case of non-Conclusive verbs like *perform*, negligible, the Continuous admittedly looking quite redundant in the Passive Voice.

The interpretation of the sentences *i.* and *ii.* is more complex. As we remember from the discussion about the Continuous Aspect, the sentence *i.* may have conflicting meanings - it is equally correct to understand it as meaning that the process of preparation will be completed on that day, as that it will proceed throughout without reaching any conclusion, the choice of the non-Continuous in the latter meaning motivated (as dictated by the pattern of Doer/Speaker Aspect) by a wish to present the preparation as kept up by the doer. Both these interpretations may be found in the Passive variant of the sentence *i.*, enriched, however, by an addition of one more possible meaning, namely, that on Friday next, the play will simply be ready (having been actually prepared earlier).[37] Thus, we can see, the interpretation of the non-Continuous form of the Passive is made more difficult as a result of the fact that the structure '*be* plus passive participle' is clearly shared by two constructions: the Passive Voice (denoting some action, activity) and the construction of the copula verb *be* complemented by a passive participle in its adjectival function. If we wished to pinpoint grammatically the meaning that the play will be in the process of preparation during the day, one of the solutions would be to resort to the Continuous version of the Passive (though at a possible cost of both diminishing the prominence of the suggestion that the preparation will be completed on that day and losing the identification of the doer as the person initiating or keeping the activity up). Thus, instead of being redundant, the Continuous may be preferred in the Passive Voice even if it was absent in the probable Active Voice variant. In the situations requiring the Perfect Aspect, the frequency of such situations seems only to increase, because this additional meaning in which the passive participle is only an adjectival complement of the verb *be* is even more prominent - for example:

i. *In 2015, the play will have been performed for 2 years.*
ii. *In 2015, the play will have been being performed for 2 years.*
iii. *In 2015, the book will have been written for 2 years.*
iv. *In 2015, the book will have been being written for 2 years.*

Similarly to the non-Perfect tenses analysed above, there is little that we gain by using the Continuous in the Passive Voice of the non-conclusive verbs like *perform* (the sentences *i.* and *ii.*). In the case of the

---

[37] The structure composed of the verb *be* and the passive participle may be simply a combination of copula verb *be* plus a predicate passive participle like for example in the following sentence:
Look at this jacket - it is soiled. It has been soiled since Friday.
The above is not the case of the Passive Voice, i.e. not the Passive version of the presentation of a situation when something is performed, but a presentation of a certain state, the state of *being soiled*. The soiling was performed on Friday and since that time it is the state of being soiled that has continued till now, not soiling itself.

conclusive verbs (the sentences *iii.* and *iv.*), the situation changes - in the sentence *iii.*, we may identify the following interpretations:
1. the Passive Voice describing an activity of *writing for 2 years* (with an emphasis, resulting from the use of the non-Continuous, on the volition of the doer identified as the originator of the activity) being a version of Variant 3 of the Perfect,
2. and, additionally, the version of the 'be plus passive participle complement' construction, presenting the *writing* as having been completed 2 years before the time specified in the sentence and remaining completed till that time, that time included.

In the Passive Voice interpretation, what will have been continued will be the activity of writing, whereas in the 'be plus passive participle', the object denoted as going to have been extended will be the state of being ready, i.e. written. Like in the examples above, we may grammatically disambiguate the communiqué by choosing the Continuous variant of the Passive (the sentence *iv.*), which, on the one hand, places emphasis on the continuation of 'doing,' and, on the other, excludes the interpretation of 'be plus passive participle', i.e. of 'having been ready'.

Thus, it seems that the answer why the Continuous forms in the Passive (apart from Present Continuous and Past Continuous tenses) are looked upon with suspicion though they clearly exist and remain in use in the current English will not be found in the grammar or syntax - these systems sometimes actually seem to prefer the Continuous to the non-Continuous. The possible explanation of this phenomenon is likely to be the length of the Passive forms of the Continuous Passive - in the more complex tenses like the Future Continuous or Perfect Continuous tenses, the length of the form of the verb may make an impression of academic formality. Perhaps, it is more consistent with the style of the everyday use to replace the Passive in these cases with some other means, lexical or grammatical, that are considered to be more appropriate in the context of the everyday exchanges.

Passive forms of verbal constructions

Tenses

Past Simple
She wrote the letters.
The letters were written by her.
Past Continuous
She was writing the letters.
The letters were being written by her.
Present Simple
She writes the letters.
The letters are written by her.
Present Continuous
She is writing the letters.
The letters are being written by her.
Future Simple
She will write the letters.
The letters will be written by her.
Future Continuous
She will be writing the letters.
The letters will be being written by her.
Past Perfect
She had written the letters.
The letters had been written by her.
Past Perfect Continuous
She had been writing the letters.
The letters had been being written by her.
Present Perfect

She has written the letters.
The letters have been written by her.
Present Perfect Continuous
She has been writing the letters.
The letters have been being written by her.
Future Perfect
She will have written the letters.
The letters will have been written by her.
Future Perfect Continuous
She will have been writing the letters.
The letters will have been being written by her.

Infinitives

Non-Perfect non-Continuous
She should write the letters.
The letters should be written by her.
Non-Perfect Continuous
She should be writing the letters.
The letters should be being written by her.
Perfect non-Continuous
She should have written the letters.
The letters should have been written by her.
Perfect Continuous
She should have been writing the letters.
The letters should have been being written by her.

Participles

Present participle
John looking after the kids, I could devote my attention to mum.
The kids being looked after by John, I could devote my attention to mum.
Perfect participle
John having prepared all the documents, we could lodge our tender.
All the documents having been prepared by John, we could lodge our tender.

Gerund

Present Gerund
I don't mind Jane sending the letter.
I don't mind the letter being sent by Jane.
Perfect Gerund
I suspected mother having seen them.
I suspected them having been seen by mother.
She attested to his not having mentioned these facts before signing the agreement.
She attested to these fact not having been mentioned by him before signing the agreement.

Passive Voice of di-transitive verbs

There is a number of verbs (e.g. *buy, give, grant, lend, offer, pay, promise, refuse, sell, send, show, tell*) that are followed not with one but two objects - Direct Object[38] and Indirect Object[39]. In the case of such sentences, we have a choice of two possible Subjects of the Passive Voice sentence (although many grammar books suggest that it is more common to compose sentences with Indirect Object, it actually depends on the context, which justifies laying emphasis on Direct or Indirect Object). At the same time, it must be remembered that whenever Indirect Object is left alone at the position following the verb, it has to assume the prepositional form (despite the fact that in the Active Voice it is largely up to the speaker) - let us analyse:

i. He gave Mary a book.
ii. He gave a book to Mary.
iii. A book was given to Mary.
iv. Mary was given a book.

No matter which of the first two sentences we may think to have been the original sentence, Indirect Object *Mary*, when left alone following the verb, will have to return to the prepositional form.

Placement of preposition following the prepositional verbs

A number of verbs in English can only be followed by a fixed preposition (e.g. *comment upon, dispose of, insist on, look at, object to, refer to, rely on, yell at* etc.). Among these verbs are also cases in which the choice of the preposition indicates one of the specific meanings of the verb, i.e. they build their meaning on a combination of the verb plus a preposition that follows it. As a result, it is not the same if we *look at somebody* or *look after somebody*. For such reasons, there is a general tendency in English to keep, in the case of these verbs, these two items together, since their separation might make it difficult to grasp the exact meaning of the sentence. In Passive Voice constructions, the preposition tends to remain with the verb rather than moves with the Object to its new position in front of the verb - for example:

i. People often talk of him - He is often talked of.
ii. We sometimes read to mother in the evenings. - Mother was sometimes read to in the evenings.
iii. I will look into this matter. - This matter will be looked into.

Prepositional verbs followed by two objects

Prepositional verbs followed by two objects constitute a special case of di-transitive verbs. Unlike the sentences using the other di-transitive verbs listed above, the structures with prepositional verbs permit a passive transformation only with the object which precedes the preposition in the active form of the sentence, not the one that follows it – for example:

i. Monkeys often throw pieces of debris at creatures that anger them.
ii. Pieces of debris are often thrown by monkeys at creatures that anger them.
iii.(?) Creatures that anger monkeys are often thrown pieces of debris at by them.
iv. She has accused him of murder.
v. He has been accused of murder by her.
*vi. *Murder has been accused him of by her.*
vii. I have informed him of your misfortune.
viii. He has been informed of your misfortune (by me).
*ix. *Your misfortune has been informed him of (by me).*

Indefinite agent omission

English has no subjectless affirmative constructions of finite sentences, since the absence of a noun in front of a verb may suggest that the sentence is an interrogative one. To solve the problem of constructing sentences when we do not know who exactly is the subject of the activity, the language uses a range of indefinite subjects. However, in Passive Voice the necessity to have the indefinite Subject vanishes, for now it is the Object that performs the function of the Subject. Besides, a Passive Voice sentence alone, when left without the specification of the doer of the activity, means the same as is denoted by an

---

38 Direct Object is a kind of complement to the verb simultaneously restricting its meaning and clarifying it, e.g. restricting the meaning of *giving* to *giving a book*.
39 Indirect Object informs to whom or to what the activity of the verb is directed/addressed, e.g. *giving a book* is addressed to *Mary* which performs the role of Indirect Object here.

indefinite Subject, i.e. that the activity is performed by any~ or everybody. Therefore, unless we wish to place some emphasis on the fact that something is to be performed by ANY or EVERYbody, the indefinite subjects are omitted when we compose the sentence in the Passive Voice order - for example:
  i. *People* often visit this place - This place is often visited.
  ii. *Somebody* told her to come at once. - She was told to come at once.
  iii. To justify a lie, *one* must tell a second lie. - To justify a lie, a second lie must be told.
  iv. *We* could not do it immediately. - It could not be done immediately.
  v. *They* knew him very well in the neighbourhood. - He was known very well in the neighbourhood.
  vi. *You* could depend on him. - He could be depended on.
  vii. People gave me a lot of flowers. - I was given a lot of flowers.
  viii. John gave me beautiful flowers. - I was given beautiful flowers by John.

In the sentence *vii.*, the accuracy of understanding of the meaning is not affected by the omission of the agent, because it is indefinite (the same meaning is communicated by Passive Voice alone). However, the agent, i.e. John, can be omitted in the sentence *viii.* only when it is implied independently by the situational context of the sentence, i.e. when it has already been mentioned or it is obvious to the participants in the conversation.

Passive Voice of compound verbs and verb groups

English makes an ample use of verbal forms which consist of more than one element. Some of these structures are complex structures of one lexical verbal item (and these might be called **compound verbs**), others combine more of them into one chain (these might be called **verb groups**). A good illustration of the compound verb structure are for example the predicates in all tenses save Present Simple and Past Simple (in affirmative structures):
  i. He **came** home at 8.
  ii. He **will come** home at 8.
  iii. He **ought to have been doing** it for 3 hours, now.

In the above examples, the sentence *i.* presents a simple form of a verb (consisting of only one element, *came*), whereas the sentences *ii.* and *iii.* show different forms of compound verbs (i.e. made up of more than one element, *will come* and *ought to have been doing*).

A verb group is different form a compound verb because its components, although related, are independent lexical items – for example:
  iv. I ought to be doing it already.
  v. I want to be doing it already.

The sentence *iv.* is the case of a complex form of a single verb (the verb *do*), whereas the sentence *v.* is a verb group made up of two verbs (*want* and *do*). The difference between the two phenomena is particularly significant in the case of Passive Voice, since the passive transformation manipulates the position of an agent and object of an action (the verb), 'revolving' them round the verb to which they relate. Thus, the Passive Voice versions of the above examples, *iv.* and *v.* are:
  iv. **It** ought to be being done already.
  v. I want **it** to be being done already.

In sentence *iv.*, the Object *it* becomes the Subject of the whole verb form, in the sentence *v.*, it is moved to the position in front of the verb *do*, since it is the Object of this verb only, and not of the verb *want*.

Thus, the passive transformation in the case of a **complex verb** requires merely the reconstruction of the active form of the main verb on the verb *be* (it is to acquire identical form as the main verb has in the Active Voice) and addition of the main verb in the form of a passive participle (so called, 3rd form) – for example:
  vi. He *is writing* books. - Books *are being* written by him.
  vii. She *will have written* books. - Books *will have been* written by her.
  viii. At 5, they *ought to have been writing* that report for 2 hours already. - At 5, that report *ought to have been being* written for 2 hours.

Since in the Passive Voice the form of the verb *be* takes over from the main verb the role of an indicator of the tense and aspect, in the above sentences, the forms of *be* simply reconstruct the tense and aspect of the forms of the main verbs in the Active Voice (*is writing=are being*; *will have written=will have been*; *ought to have been writing=ought to have been being*). On the other hand, the correct passive transformation of the **verb group** requires more – first of all, we have to identify the component elements making up the group, and then, compose the passive form of the structure of the verb plus its Object,

seeing to it that we do not overstep the border between the elements of the verbal group (the passive transformation is to affect only one element, leaving the rest intact). For example (the element of the group plus its Object underlined):
   ix. *I would like to dress her myself. - I would like her to be dressed by myself.*
     *She would like to be dressed by myself.

Passive Voice in the sentences containing a non-finite component

An area of equally frequent uncertainty and confusion is the problem of complex sentences with infinite component like infinitive, participle or gerund.

Infinitive constructions

Infinitive Object clause

In the case of verbs which may be generally classified as presenting the mental/sensual relation between the Subject and the reality (e.g. *want, see, make, hear, expect, prefer* etc.), it is possible to use, as an Object, a complete subordinate noun clause containing a predicate in the form of an infinitive. Majority of these verbs are followed by a 'full' infinitive clause (i.e., infinitive preceded by *to*), but there is also a group followed by a 'bare' infinitive clause (i.e., infinitive without *to*). These clauses make an interesting case because the Subject of the subordinate noun clause is at the same time treated as an independent Object of the main clause, i.e. independent of the subordinate clause of which it is a part. As a result, the sentence contains three Objects offering three different options for a passive transformation:

1. Passive transformation within the subordinate clause:
   i. *Mother wanted him to read **this book**.*
   ii. *Mother wanted **this book** to be read (by him).*

2. Passive transformation within the main clause with the subject of the subordinate clause:
   i. *Mother wanted **him** to read this book.*
   ii. ***He was wanted** (by Mother) to read this book.*

3. Passive transformation within the main clause recognising as Object the whole subordinate Object clause (though with modification because the mechanical moving of the subordinate clause to the position of the Subject of the main clause makes an awkward construction):
   i. *Mother wanted him to read this book.*
   ii. *That he should read this book was wanted by Mother.*
   iii. *(?) Him to read this book was wanted by Mother.*

The example 3 is obviously a variant of a sentence *It was wanted by Mother that he should read this book* which is rather similar in meaning than identical grammatically with the sentences analysed in the examples 1 and 2.

If, after passive transformation, the subordinate clause refers to the same Subject as the main clause, the Subject in the subordinate clause is reduced in accordance with the rule of reduction of redundancy:
   i. *She likes her pupils to call her Madam. -*
   ii. *She likes (herself) to be called Madam (by her pupils).*

While, as it is illustrated above, the operation of the rule of passive transformation within the segment of structures containing the 'full' infinitive is quite predictable (with an exception of *get*[40]) as it is fully consistent with the mechanisms of passive transformation operating in already discussed finite and

---

40 In the case of *get*, the speakers tend to avoid the constructions in which the subordinate clause were to contain a reflexive pronoun and, in such situations, are likely to rephrase the sentence with a different verb, e.g.
i. *She gets them to call her Madam.*
ii. *She gets herself to be called Madam.*
iii. *She asks to be called Madam.*
iv. *She demands being called Madam.*
v. *She insists on being called Madam.*
Among the above sentences, the variant offered by the sentence *ii.* seems to be the least popular (although it is in use).

infinite clauses, in the case of the 'bare' infinitive, the change into passive includes a number of irregularities. In the case of the verbs followed in the object clause with a 'bare' infinitive (i.e. *make* and *have* meaning 'force/cause'; *let* meaning 'permit'; sensual verbs and verbs denoting 'observing'), the full form of infinitive returns when we make the passive transformation with the main verb of the main clause (with the exception of *let* which does not occur in the passive form and is replaced by *be allowed to* or *be permitted to*), whereas in the case of the passive transformation in the subordinate clause, the verb *be* is omitted. Let us compare the operation of the rule in the case of the 'full' and 'bare' infinitive:

a. 'Full' infinitive clauses:
   i. She wanted him to write the report.
   ii. <u>He was wanted</u> to write the report.
   iii. She wanted <u>the report to be written</u> by him.

b. 'Bare infinitive' clauses
   iv. She made him write the report.
   v. <u>He was made **to**</u> write the report.
   vi. She <u>made the report (be) written (by him)</u>.

The above sentence *vi.* is rather unusual. Typically, in that context, the verb *make* would be replaced with *have* in the same meaning like in the sentence *ix.* below:

   vii. She had him write the report.
   viii. He was had **to** write the report. (rather awkward, usually replaced by the construction *v.* with the verb *make*)
   ix. She <u>had the report (be) written (by him)</u>.
   x. I saw them put the case on the carriage.
   xi. <u>They were seen to</u> put the case on the carriage.
   xii. I saw <u>the case (be) put</u> on the carriage (by them).

A similar reduction of the verb *be* in the passive version of the subordinate clause may be found as an alternative in the case of such clauses following the verb *want*:

   xiii. She wants <u>you to clear the tables</u> immediately.
   xiv. She wants <u>the tables to be cleared</u> immediately
   xv. She wants <u>the tables cleared</u> immediately.

The construction Nominative with the Infinitive

In the case of complex sentences with impersonal passive construction in the main clause referring by means of expressing verbal or mental attention (e.g *allege, announce, believe, claim, consider, expect, hear, know, presume, prove, report, say, see, state, suppose, think, understand*) to the Subject of the subordinate clause, it is possible to reduce the number of Subjects by moving the Subject of the subordinate clause to the position of the main Subject, introducing necessary changes – the steps leading to the final form are as follows:

   i. People say that he once talked to the Queen.

The above indefinite personal Subject may be replaced with an indefinite impersonal Subject with passive transformation:

   ii. That he once talked to the Queen is said. → It is said that he once talked to the Queen[41].

The impersonal Subject may be removed by replacing it with the Subject of the subordinate clause. However, in such a case, we have to construct a verbal group, which requires transformation of the subordinate predicate from the finite form into infinite, here, infinitival:

   iii. He is said once to have talked to the Queen.

It must be remembered that the form of the infinitive has to reflect the time and aspect relation between the original actions, i.e., if the original subordinate action was reported as Continuous, we should choose one of the Continuous forms, if it was earlier than the action of the main clause, we should choose the Perfect infinitive, if it was not earlier, then the infinitive chosen should be one of the non Perfect infinitives[42].

---

41 The replacement of a long Subject clause with an 'empty,' formal subject 'It' accompanied with simultaneous moving of the Subject clause to the position following the predicate is called 'Anticipatory It' transformation.
42 There are four forms of infinitive in English:
Non-Perfect non-Continuous – *do / be done*
Non-Perfect Continuous – *be doing / be being done*

iv. It <u>was</u> considered that she <u>was working</u> on her new novel. - She was considered <u>to be working</u> on her new novel.
v. It <u>was</u> claimed that he <u>owned</u> that house. - He was claimed <u>to own</u> that house.
vi. It <u>was</u> claimed that he <u>had owned</u> that house. - He was claimed <u>to have owned</u> that house.
vii. It <u>is</u> claimed that he <u>owns</u> the house. - He is claimed <u>to own</u> the house.
viii. It <u>is</u> claimed that he <u>owned</u> the house. - He is claimed <u>to have owned</u> the house.

As it is illustrated by the examples above, the choice of the Perfect or non-Perfect form of the infinitive depends on the relation between the subordinate clause verb to the main clause verb and not on the relation to the moment of speaking.

Participle constructions

In Object clause in the form of infinitive discussed above, the infinitive may be replaced with a participle with consequences described by the Aspect Continuous. These structures can also be transformed into passive – for example:
i. We heard Mary calling Jim.
ii. Mary was heard calling Jim.
iii. We heard Jim being called by Mary.
iv. I saw him making that declaration.
v. He was seen making that declaration.
vi. I saw that declaration being made (by him).[43]

Verbs followed by passive participle

In the case of the verbs followed by a passive participle (e.g. sensual verbs like *see*, *hear* or verbs like *want, expect, have,* etc), it must be remembered that the verb in the subordinate clause (the passive participle verb) is already a part of a passive construction[44]. Therefore, the only passive transformation may be done by making the Subject of the subordinate clause, the passive Subject of the main clause, which, however, enforces changes in the subordinate clause as well – for example:
i. I actually heard this fact mentioned.
ii. This fact was actually heard <u>to be</u> mentioned.
iii. We wanted the confession sent before the Jury by the following Friday.
iv. The confession was wanted <u>to be</u> sent before the Jury by the following Friday.

Gerund constructions

Gerund, though recognised as a noun, is a complex though impersonal structure which may have a predicator and its Object. In certain cases, the Gerund clause may have either Active or Passive form. For example:

Perfect non-Continuous – *have done / have been done*
Perfect Continuous – *have been doing / have been being done*
More information on infinitive forms will be found in the chapter 'Hypothetical mood'.
43 Perhaps it does not have any significance for the practical usage of the above constructions, but the progressive form of verb (i.e. *verb+ing*) in the subordinate clause may be regarded (more consistently with the rest of the mechanisms already discussed) as a reduced form of the progressive infinitive, with its auxiliary *'be'* clipped off:
i. We heard Mary (~~be~~) calling Jim.
ii. Mary was heard (~~to be~~) calling Jim.
iii. We heard Jim (~~be~~) being called by Mary.
iv. I saw him (~~be~~) making that declaration.
v. He was seen (~~to be~~) making that declaration.
vi. I saw that declaration (~~be~~) being made (by him).
44 It must be remembered that the construction of the subordinate Object clause containing the predicate in the form of the Passive Participle is simply a segment of the Infinitival construction - in the Object clauses which in the Active Voice contain a predicate in the form of a 'bare' infinitive, in the passive construction the verb *be* is omitted, thus, the result is a clause containing the Passive Participle functioning as a predicate. The full and real shape of the structure, revealing also the hidden parts, will be found in the case when the main clause is transformed into the passive form, which requires addition of the particle *to* to the verb *be*, thus forcing *be* to the surface of the sentence. Therefore, the examples above may be rewritten into the form revealing the elements which normally remain invisible:
i. I actually heard this fact <u>(be)</u> mentioned.
ii. This fact was actually heard (by me) <u>to be</u> mentioned.
iii. We wanted the confession <u>(be)</u> sent before the Jury by the following Friday.
iv. The confession was wanted (by us) <u>to be</u> sent before the Jury by the following Friday.

i. I don't mind *your talking to her*.
ii. I don't mind *her being talked to (by you)*.

Additionally, it must be remembered that no matter its length, when Gerund occupies the position of the Object of a verb, it may become a Subject of the passive transformation of this sentence. For example:

iii. John mentioned *your having bought his house*.
iv. *Your having bought John's house* was mentioned by him.
v. *John's house having been bought by you* was mentioned by him.(possible, though awkward)

Reported Speech

Tenses in Reporting

Reporting sentences are complex sentences joining in one syntactic structure the act of reporting and the object of it, i.e. some meaningful act (an utterance, thought, feeling). The structure has two major variants: Direct Reporting (sometimes called Direct Speech) and Indirect Reporting (often called Indirect Speech or Reported Speech). Generally speaking, a reporting sentence consists of two clauses:
- the main clause which is the reporting clause, in which we may identify the nature of the speech act to be reported, i.e. whether it is an affirmative sentence, a question, an order or interdiction etc.,
- the subordinate clause which is the reported clause, in which the reported meaningful act is presented.

The major distinction between the Direct and Indirect Reporting consists in the relation between the main and the subordinate clause. In the easier of the two, the Direct Reporting, the reported act is simply quoted without any changes to its grammatical or syntactic structure. In the Indirect Reporting, the reported act is 'described,' having been first incorporated into the structure of the main clause. As a result, both the grammatical and syntactic structure of the reported meaningful act must be adjusted to the structure of the main clause (place, time, participants etc.).

Direct Reporting

The sentences constituting this variant comprise two independent clauses, the reporting main clause and the reported subordinate clause which has the form of a quotation of the reported utterance presented in the shape in which it originated. The structure of the subordinate clause is not influenced by any of the elements of the main clause. Additionally, the main clause may but is not obliged to reflect the nature of the reported utterance (i.e. whether it is an interrogative, affirmative or any other syntactic structure). Since the component sentences are not interrelated in any way, there are no grammatical rules that have to be observed to be able to unite them into one structure - the following, therefore, should not be represented as a presentation of all possible patterns because there are none, what is presented is only a selection of Direct Reporting possible equivalents of what is going to be discussed in connection with the much more complex Indirect Reporting.

i. *He said to her: 'I like it'.*
ii. *He will say to her: 'I like it'.*
iii. *He says to her: 'Do you like it?'*
iv. *He said to her: 'Don't go there now!'*
v. *He said to her: 'Come home as fast as you can'.*
vi. *He will say to her: 'I will come as soon as possible'.*
vii. *He said to her: 'He was here yesterday and I think he will be here again tomorrow'.*

As it is illustrated by the above sentences, no element of the subordinate sentence is modified in consequence of the fact that the utterance has become a subordinate clause - neither the personal pronouns, nor the tenses, adverbs of time and space, nor any syntactic structures present in the original of the subordinate clause.

Indirect Reporting[45]

Similarly to Direct Reporting variant, the structure of an Indirect Speech sentence is made up of two clauses, the reporting main clause and the reported subordinate clause. However, unlike in Direct Reporting sentences, the subordinate clause is not a quotation of the original of the reported utterance but a 'description' of it, incorporated into the grammatical and lexical structure of the main clause through the process of adaptation.

This process of adaptation of the structure of the original form of the utterance to the changed situation resulting from the possible change of speaker, place and time reference of the activities spoken of is the natural consequence of turning what once came into being as an independent speech act, whose properties reflected a certain situation into a subordinate part of another speech act, produced in and reflecting possibly different circumstances. In the following discussion the constituent elements of this process of adjustment will be analysed separately.

Personal and possessive pronouns in Indirect Reporting

The choice of personal and possessive pronouns always reflects the situation existing at the moment when a given speech act is produced. The first person singular is reserved for the speaker, the second, for the addressee/s, and the third, for the objects of the discourse. When a sentence is produced, the elements of its structure naturally reflect the existing circumstances. If, however, a sentence produced in a particular situation becomes a part of a sentence produced in changed circumstances, the pronouns used in the original sentence will have to be adjusted to the change. Let us analyse the following phone conversation:

i. (Mary to Susan) I want you to visit me.
ii. (Susan to her husband standing by her) She says that she wants to visit us.

In the sentence *i.*, the first person singular is used because the speaker (Mary) is speaking of herself. In the sentence *ii.*, however, the speaker has changed (it is now Susan), and the first person singular denotes now a different person. In the new situation, since Mary is no longer a speaker but a person spoken of, she becomes a third person singular. In the Direct and Indirect Reporting sentences, the above situation would be presented in the following way:

Direct Reporting
(Susan to her husband) *Mary says: "I want you to visit me".*

Indirect Reporting
(Susan to her husband) *Mary says that she wants us to visit her.*

A similar mechanism determines the choice of possessive pronouns and adjectives - after incorporating the original of the reported sentence into the structure of the reporting, the pronouns and adjectives have to be adjusted to reflect the new situation.

---

45 The presentation of mechanisms working in Indirect Reporting is often illustrated by pairs of 'equivalent' Direct=Indirect Reporting sentences, which might be interpreted as suggesting that this structure is a kind of mechanical, one-to-one translation of sentences of Direct Reporting - the reader must be cautioned that it is not true. The real Indirect Reporting sentence stems from the communicative act of the original sentence but deals with it quite freely both on the lexical (i.e. choice of words) and syntactic (i.e. choice of sentence type) level. In a normal situation, an Indirect Reporting sentence is not a translation of the original sentence but a communicative 'play' upon the meaning of it as it is perceived by the speaker - it is the meaning which is the point of departure and the object of manipulation. The speaker usually builds the sentence independently, trying to render the meaning (in a form suiting the purpose and character of the discourse) and not the exact structure of the original. Therefore, only very rarely shall we encounter situations which 'determine' the shape of Indirect Reporting sentence - much more often the result is the speaker's choice of elements of meanings and structures to render it which depend on the speaker and his perception of situation - for example:
i. He said to her: 'Get out!'
ii. He urged her to leave the place.
iii. He gave an exclamation of anger telling her at the same time to remove herself from the place.
iv. He yelled at her to get out.

The above Indirect Reporting sentences are just some possible versions of the sentence *i.*, reported by different speakers to suit different purposes.

He said: 'To the left, you will find your room, and to the right, mine'.
He said that to the left we would find our room, and to the right, his.

Adverbs of time and space and demonstrative pronouns

There is a class of adverbs of time, and adverbs of space together with certain demonstrative pronouns whose choice is made <u>to reflect the situation existing at the moment of speaking.</u> If there is a change with regard to circumstances reflected by these elements between the situation when and where the reported and the reporting sentences are produced, this change will have to be reflected in the shape of the Indirectly Reporting sentence. Let us compare:

(John to Mary, standing in front of Susan's seat) *'This is Susan's seat today'*

Direct Reporting

John said to Mary: 'This is Susan's seat, today.'

Indirect Reporting

i. John said to Mary that that was Susan's seat that day (the speaker is not speaking there and the day is no longer the same).

ii. John said to Mary that this is Susan's seat today (the speaker is speaking in front of this seat and the day is still the same, and, additionally, it probably is still Susan's).

iii. John said to Mary that that is Susan's seat today (the speaker is not speaking there but it possibly is still hers and the day has not changed).

iv. John said to Mary that this was Susan's seat that day (the speaker is speaking in front of this seat but it probably is not hers any more and the day has changed).

The question which of the above Indirect Reporting sentences is correct depends on where, in relation to Susan's seat, the Indirect Reporting sentence is produced (i.e. also in front of it or away from it), and on whether the day when the report is made is still the same at the moment when the reporting sentence is made (if it is not, then it should not be referred to as *today*, if it still is, the sentence should not mislead by replacing *today* with *that day*). If the Indirect Reporting sentence is produced in front of Susan's seat, the demonstrative pronoun *this* should not be replaced by *that*, if the sentence is produced elsewhere, we can not use the demonstrative *this* because it would be misleading, suggesting incorrectly that the object spoken of remains in the vicinity of the recipient of the sentence.

The list of demonstratives, as well as adverbs of time and space which are linked to the moment of speaking together with their possible replacements follows:

this	-	that
these	-	those
here	-	there
this month/week/year etc.	-	that month/week/ year
last month/week/year	-	the previous/ the preceding month/week/year, a month/week/year before
next month/week/year	-	the following month/week/year, the next month/week/year
now	-	then
today	-	that day
tomorrow	-	the following day, the next day
the day after tomorrow	-	in two days time
yesterday	-	the preceding day, the previous day, the day before
two days/weeks/months/years ago	-	two days/weeks/months/years before

Tenses

Choosing a tense for a subordinate clause in English, we may encounter three elementary types of system of locating the position of the subordinate clause activity in time:

- the verb form reflects the relation between the subordinate clause activity and the main clause alone (like the verb forms used in the clauses introduced by *wish, would rather, had better*)
- the verb form reflects the relation between the subordinate clause activity and both the main clause and the moment of speaking (e.g. reporting sentences)
- the verb form reflects the relation between the subordinate clause activity and the moment of speaking alone (for example, the clauses introduced by *although, because*).

The verb form of the reported clause belongs to the second type above and is to reflect the relation both to the moment of speaking and the main clause. Consequently, the Indirect Reporting sentence 'is aware' of three moments in time:
- the moment of speaking from which both the action of reporting and that of being reported is viewed,
- the moment occupied by the act of reporting, marked by a tense reflecting its relation to the moment of speaking,
- the moment occupied by the reported activity, marked by a tense reflecting its relation both to the moment of the main clause and the moment of speaking.

Thus, the structure taken into consideration by grammar in determining the tense of the subordinate clause is always a version of the following general pattern:

(*I am saying now that* - moment of speaking) *sb* (*say* - reporting) *that sb* (*say* - reported)

The relation of the subordinate clause to the main clause naturally falls into three basic types of interrelation:
- the subordinate-reported clause precedes (i.e. is earlier than) the main-reporting clause,
- the subordinate-reported clause is contemporary (i.e. runs parallel) to the main-reporting clause,
- the subordinate-reported clause follows (i.e. is later than) the main-reporting clause.[46]

The above three basic relations which the tense of the subordinate clause reflects will have to be additionally modified with relation to whether the subordinate and/or the main clause refer to the past, present, or future of the moment of speaking, i.e. we will need different tenses to mark the subordinate clause as simultaneous with the main clause if the tense of the main clause changes from Future to Present or Past.

To avoid confusion and, at the same time, focus on the situation in the form reflecting the real situation of sentence production, the presentation will follow the changes of the tense of the main clause and will study the consequences that it brings for the tense of the subordinate clause.

The main clause - Present tense

When we choose a Present tense to express the main, reporting clause, by such decision we recognize the fact that grammatically, we, the speaker, occupy the same moment in time as the moment from which the reporting person views the reported activity (of the subordinate clause). Therefore, the tense chosen by the reporting speaker to present the event should not be changed, otherwise, we might change the information about the relation between the reporting speaker and the activity spoken of by him. As a result, in this variant there is very little (if at all) to modify in the form of the verb - let us analyse:

i. *He says: 'I am at home'.*
   He says he is at home.
ii. *She says to her mother: 'Peter visited me last night.'*
   She tells her mother that Peter visited her last night.
iii. *They say: 'We will see her tomorrow.'*
   They say that they will see her tomorrow.

---

[46] If we remember that the reference point of the subordinate clause is the moment of production of the utterance which is to become the subordinate clause, the indication which of the above types of interrelations we are dealing with will be found in the tense of the original utterance:
 - if the original tense was any of the past tenses, we will seek a form reflecting the fact that the subordinate activity is earlier than the main clause,
 - if the original tense was any of the present tenses, we will seek a form reflecting contemporaneity of the subordinate activity with the main clause,
 - if the original tense was any of the future tenses, we will seek a form reflecting the fact that the subordinate activity follows the main clause.

The main clause - Past tense

When we express the main-reporting clause with the use of a Past tense, by so doing, we indicate that the moment of speaking, when the whole sentence is produced is no longer the same as the moment when the reporting clause was produced. This fact changes significantly the situation with regard to the choice of tenses in the reported clause. If we remember, the choice of the tense reflects the time relation between the moment of speaking and the activity spoken of. In the Indirectly Reporting sentence whose main clause is recognized as Past, we confront the problem of dealing with two non-simultaneous moments of speaking in one structure - the moment of speaking of the entire sentence (which is the reference point for the reporting clause) and the moment of the main clause, which is the moment of speaking (and, therefore, the reference point) for the subordinate-reported clause. If we have chosen a Past tense for the main clause, by so doing, we have moved to the Past the reference point of the reported clause. This past point of reference will now determine which tense forms of the reported clause signify that the reported activity in relation to the act of reporting is earlier, simultaneous, or later. Let us analyse these three basic types of relation.

  i. He said: 'I went to the cinema yesterday.'
     He said that he had gone to the cinema the day before.
  ii. She said to him: 'I am writing a letter now'.
      She told[47] him that she was writing a letter (then/at that moment).
  iii. They said: 'We have written our report'.
       They said that they had written their report.
  iv. We said to her: 'You will be transported tomorrow'.
      We told her that she would be transported the following day.

The Reported activity simultaneous with the act of Reporting

The Present tenses in the reported clause, which, originally, meant simultaneity for the reporting person, are now changed into their Past equivalents. It is the consequence of the fact that in the sentence produced by us, the reporting speaker and everything that is simultaneous with him remain in the Past. An interesting problem area is the situation when the reported activity is simultaneous not only with the act of reporting but also with the moment of speaking. The elementary grammar books demand that in such a case the imperative consideration should be the fact that what was contemporary with a past moment should be presented as past - for example, even though the person speaking is still alive and still a Briton, he uses the past form in the reported clause:

I said I was Briton.

The only exception admitted to this rule by the above-mentioned grammar books are proverbial sentences or such that present some commonly accepted wisdom, which naturally is simultaneous both to the moment of reporting and speaking - for example:

  i. The nurse said that an apple a day keeps the doctor away.
  ii. She said that the more you have, the more you would like to have.

At the same time, a random search of the most popular concordancers and particularly the 'wilderness' of the internet publications will bring a multitude (in the case of the internet, millions) of sentences which clearly either ignore the rule or represent cases where the rule does not apply. A question arises then if there is any safe rule to follow in such cases. One such that comes to mind is the time focus of the whole discourse, i.e. if it is a narrative of past events it seems more correct to stick to past tenses even though some of the activities or states are also contemporary to the moment of speaking; if, however, the past reporting act is mentioned in a discourse concerned with the present time, it seems more natural to view the situation predominantly from the point of view of time relation with the moment of speaking. Let us compare:

  i. I told them I was British. They demanded that I should present some papers which I did ...
  ii. You have nothing to worry about. She told them you are British and so you will only have to
      register again at ...

In the sentence *i.*, the reported state (of being British) is a part of a narrative of past events, and, therefore, it seems more natural to use a past form, ignoring the fact that the person is still alive and British at the moment of speaking. The sentence *ii.*, focuses upon the present, i.e. the situation contemporary to the

---

[47] In the Indirect Reporting clause the phrase *say to* is avoided as awkward, not ungrammatical. Quite infrequently but still, such usage can be heard in careless or very formal speech.

moment of speaking, and so, the form better suiting this case is the present form of the state of being British, ignoring now the fact that it is brought into the sentence by reference to the moment in the past with which it was simultaneous.

The Reported activity earlier than the act of Reporting

The Past tenses, which, originally were a signal that the reported activity was earlier than the moment when it was spoken of, will now be expressed with the use of Past Perfect tense used as a form that might be called Past Past Simple, because, unlike the normal Perfect form, it builds it meaning on the main verb rather than auxiliary *have* and is capable to locate the main verb in the anteriority (i.e. in the Past) of a Past moment). At the same time, it must be remembered that Past Perfect still remains the form equivalent to the Perfect form related to the past moment.

A significant factor determining the choice of tenses in Indirect Reporting when the main clause is in the Past is the mechanism which conserves the ability of the tense system to indicate the anteriority, simultaneity and succession of the subordinate clause to the main clause. As the above sentences illustrate, the mechanism works quite efficiently in the situations made up of two reference points. However, if we deal with a situation when the subordinate clause is past to the main clause and, additionally, the subordinate clause is itself a complex structure descending further into the past, we will need an additional modification to the system to keep the above mentioned ability to discriminate between the three relations (past, simultaneous, future). Let us compare:

   i. She said: 'The thief stole the ring which was lying on the table'.
   ii. She said: 'The thief stole the ring which had been bought by my late husband'.

As the past tense of the reported clause indicates, all the events spoken of should be marked, in Indirect Reporting as past to the act of reporting. However, there is a problem because each of the reported clauses contains two actions: in the sentence *i.*, simultaneous; in the sentence *ii.*, the latter is past to the former. If the intervention of the system ended at the recognition of the fact that each of the subordinate clauses is earlier in its entirety than the reporting clause, we would be required to use Past Perfect for both activities of the reported clause (in the sentences *i.* and *ii.*). In such a case, we would lose the ability to discriminate internally between their moments in time, and the simultaneous actions would be represented in the same way as the preceding. The English deals with this situation differently - <u>Past Perfect tense in the subordinate clause is the only indication of the actual order of succession of actions and it is reserved for the situation when the subordinate clause is earlier than the main clause</u> - the main clause to which the subordinate one directly relates. Thus, such a situation is not the case in the sentence *i.*, in which the reported clause within the subordinate clause is not earlier but simultaneous. Therefore, not Past Perfect Continuous but Past Continuous will be used, indicating that the subordinate clause (the state of *lying* on the table) is contemporary to its main clause (here, the act of *stealing*):

   i. She said that the thief had stolen the ring which was lying on the table.

In the situation described by the sentence *ii.*, the subordinate act of *buying* is earlier than the *stealing*, which will thus be indicated by the use of Past Perfect:

   ii. She said that the thief had stolen the ring which had been bought by her late husband.

Naturally, the Continuous Aspect, if it is present in the original sentence does not change.

   i. She said: 'He visited me when I was watching TV'.
   She said that he had visited her when she was watching TV.
   ii. She said: 'He told me what I had been doing at 5 yesterday'.
   She said that he had told her what she had been doing at 5 the day before.

A further complication with the use of Past Perfect in Indirect Reporting that has to be borne in mind is that it may be replaced by the Past non-Perfect whenever the time reference and the nature of the event expressed are independently recognized as earlier than their main clause - in other words, when Past Perfect is not necessary to signal the temporal relationship between the reporting and the reported acts. It is the case predominantly with the events whose location in time is either a common knowledge (e.g. in the case of historical events) or is known to the interlocutors. Let us analyse:

   i. I read recently that the super-continent Pangea broke into two pieces along the line which ran somewhere here.
   ii. The lecturer said that the ice-caps remained in our region for about 3000 years.

The Reported activity future to the act of Reporting

If the reported activity was originally future to the act of reporting, when the reporting moment is moved to the Past, the Future tenses in the reported clause will be changed to their past equivalents, i.e. Future in the Past. The latter are in no way new types of tenses - the past form of their auxiliary (*will* is changed to *would*) signals merely that what is expressed is not future to the moment of speaking of the sentence but to the moment in the past, when the reported sentence was produced. It is due to the fact that the auxiliary *will* invariably marks an activity as future to the moment of speaking, which now is different than originally. If, however, the reported activity is future not only to the moment of reporting but also to the moment of speaking, it may (and many users of English believe it should) be left unchanged lest the recipient of the information should be misled into believing that the actually future moment referred to by the sentence is already past at the moment when the whole sentence is produced - we must remember that the reported subordinate clause belongs to the class whose form reflects the relation not only to the main clause but also to the moment of speaking. Let us compare:

i. She said (a year ago): 'I will see him tomorrow'.
ii. She said that she would see him the following day.
iii. He announced at the meeting (2 hours ago): 'I will pay them a visit tomorrow'.
iv. He announced at the meeting that he will pay them a visit tomorrow.
v. He announced at the meeting that he would pay them a visit (the following day).

The Future tense of the reported clause in the sentence *i.* is transformed into Future-in-the-Past in the sentence *ii.* because the *seeing*, although future to the *saying*, nevertheless, remains in the Past of the moment of speaking. The adverbial of time *tomorrow* which denotes a day following the one in which the utterance is produced has to be replaced with the phrase *the following day* because, in relation to the moment of speaking, it remains in the Past, not in the Future. Indirect reporting of the reported clause of the sentence *iii.* is more complicated. Here, the activity to be reported is future not only with reference to the past act of reporting but also with regard to the moment of speaking. In this case, the speakers have two options. They may report the *paying of the visit* as future merely to the moment of reporting, in which case the correct form will be the sentence *v.* The speakers may also choose to enrich the information communicated to the recipient with an indication that the *visit* is not only future to the moment of reporting but also to the moment of speaking. Then, the correct form would be the sentence *iv.* In the latter case, the transformation of the adverbial of time *tomorrow* into e.g. *the following day* is undesirable because any of the phrases denoting futurity to the past moment would be ambiguous, permitting the interpretation that the day spoken of is in the past rather than in the future of the moment of speaking. At the same time, if we wish to use the version built upon relation to the moment of reporting (i.e. the sentence *v.*), it would be better to omit the adverbial altogether avoiding both the ambiguity of *the following day* and of the combination *would pay a visit* with *tomorrow* (the latter permits the interpretation that we are dealing with hypothetical mood, which is not true).

The main clause - Future tense

The problems that we encounter in Indirect Reporting when the act of reporting is future to the moment of speaking are similar to those which we confront when we deal with multiple subordinate clauses in past reporting sentences - simply speaking, the system runs short of forms that we need to reflect the three relations between the main and the subordinate clause (i.e. anteriority, simultaneity, succession). Let us analyse the following examples:

i. She will say: 'I wrote it a long time ago'.
ii. She will say: 'I like this gentlemen'.
iii. She will say: 'I will call you later'.

If we reported both the situation when the reported clause is simultaneous with the main (*ii.*) and when it follows the act of reporting (*iii.*) with the same Future tense, the system would lose the ability to discriminate between these situations. The solution employed is similar to that used in the case of multiple subordinate past clauses - Future tenses are reserved for the situation when the reported activity is future to the act of reporting, when it is simultaneous, it is indicated by the use of Present tenses. This solution has its price - the system in incapable of discriminating grammatically between, on the one hand, the situation when the reported activity is simultaneous only with the future reporting act and future to the moment of speaking and, on the other, the situation when the reported activity is present both at the moment of speaking and the moment of reporting. Let us compare:

i. She will say: 'I am still considering the problem.'
ii. She will say that she is still considering the problem.

When the speaker uses the Present tense to report that *she is still considering the problem* (which is, after all, the communiqué which reaches the addressee of the sentence), he leaves grammatically unspecified whether what he means is that *she is still considering the problem* only when the utterance will be reported or that *she is still considering the problem* now, as he speaks, or both. Similarly, the use of Past tense in the reported clause is merely an indication that the reported clause is earlier than the act of reporting, being, at the same time, incapable of showing whether with reference to the moment of speaking the reported activity is past, present or future. The above sentence *i.* could be rendered in Indirect Reporting form in one of the following ways:

i. She will say: 'I wrote it a long time ago'.
ii. She will say that she wrote it a long time before.
iii. She will say that she wrote it a long time ago.

The only method of indicating if the reported activity, which is past to the moment of reporting, is or is not past also to the moment of speaking would be the use of other syntactic devices, like the adverb of time. If we use the phrase *a long time before* we leave the activity unmarked for its relation to the moment of speaking (*before* signals only that the activity is past to its moment of reference, here, the act of reporting, leaving unsaid if it is also past to the moment of speaking). If, however, we use *a long time ago*, since the structure containing *ago* always refers to the moment of speaking, the recipient of such sentence will know that the reported activity is past not only with reference to the reporting clause but also to the moment of speaking.

Structures that are not modified by reporting

Indirect Reporting modifies only the structures whose form reflects both the relation to the moment of speaking and the moment of reporting. There is, however, in English, a number of constructions whose structure reflects the relation of an activity only to the moment introducing the construction, be it the moment of producing the original utterance or the syntactic structure which introduces it - these constructions (listed below) will not change in Indirect Reporting.

- Reporting does not change the choice of infinitive, gerund, participle, whose choice (i.e. Perfect or non-Perfect) reflects the relation between the activity expressed by one of these constructions and the moment established by the position of the syntactic element to which these constructions relate:

i. He said: '*Walking* downstairs, I met Mary'.
   He said that, *walking* downstairs, he had met Mary.
ii. He said: '*Having walked* downstairs, I met Mary'.
   He said that, *having walked* downstairs, he had met Mary.
iii. He will tell you: '*Having washed up*, she will start polishing the glass'.
   He will tell you that, *having washed up*, she will start polishing the glass.
iv. They said: 'He is said to *have visited* Rome many times'.
   They noted that he was said to *have visited* Rome many times.
v. They said to us: 'He is said to *be* at home now'.
   They reminded us that he was said to *be* at home at the moment.
vi. She said: 'His *having passed* the exam in time will surprise everybody'.
   She said that his *having passed* the exam in time would surprise everybody.
vii. She said: 'I have no objection to *meeting* him at Mary's'.
   She declared that she had no objection to *meeting* him at Mary's.

- Reporting does not change the structure of the subordinate sentences following *wish, it (be) high time, had better, would rather, as if/as though* (though the latter construction, *as if/as though* only in hypothetical mood):

i. She said: 'It is high time we went.'
   She said that it was high time they went.
ii. She said: 'I wish Peter were working with us'.
   She said that she wished Peter were working with them.
iii. She will say: 'I wish Peter were working with us'.

She will say that she wishes Peter were working with them.
iv. *He said: 'I had better go'.*
He said that he had better go.
v. *He said: 'I would rather Mary was working with us'.*
He said that he would rather Mary was working with them.
vi. *He will say: 'I would rather John had been working with us, not Mary'.*
He will say that he would rather John had been working with them, not Mary.
vii. *She will say to you: 'You look as if/as though you had seen a ghost'.*
She will tell you that you look as if/as though you had seen a ghost.
viii. *They said: 'She looks as if she were ill'.*
They said that she looked as if she were ill.

- Reporting does not change the constructions of attitudinal past (if they are reported - it is more common to cast off these rhetorical structures and present the meaning only):
  i. *She said: 'I was wondering if you could give me a leave tomorrow'.*
  ii. *She said that she was wondering if he could give her a leave the following day.*
  iii. *She asked him (her boss) for a leave on the following day.*
  iv. *She will say: I was wondering if you could give me a leave tomorrow'.*
  v. *She will say that she was wondering if he could give her a leave the following day.*
  vi. *She will ask him for a day off on the following day.*

The more common of the two types (i.e. *ii./v.* and *iii./vi.*) are the sentences *iii./vi.*, though, if the speaker decided to render also the form of the reported utterance, it would have the form of the sentences *ii./v.*

- Modal auxiliaries which do not have their past versions do not change, those that do have the past forms (*can - could, may - might*) change into past forms if the main-reporting clause is past. It is due to the fact that modal auxiliaries are located at the moment when the utterance is produced - in Indirect Reporting sentence, this moment is represented by the reporting clause, therefore, there is no need to introduce any changes if the auxiliary has no past form (like *should, ought to, must*[48], *need (do), needn't (do), mustn't, might, could*).
  i. *He will say: 'I should go home at once'.*
  He will say that he should go home at once.
  ii. *He said: 'It must be Peter'.*
  He said that it must be Peter.

- Reporting does not change sentences in hypothetical mood because it would erase the time distinctions encoded by this construction - let us compare:
  i. *She said: 'If he were at home, he could help us'.*
  She observed that if he were at home, he could help them.
  *She observed that if he had been at home, he could have helped them.
  ii. *She said: 'If he had been at home, he could have helped us'.*
  She observed that if he had been at home, he could have helped them.
  ii. *He told them: 'If you had studied during the semester, you would pass the exam tomorrow'.*
  He told them that if they had studied during the semester, they would pass the exam the following day.

---

48 *Must* always remains unchanged in meanings other than obligation, the latter being the only of the meanings of *must* which has a past equivalent modal semi-auxiliary *have (got) to*. Even in the case of the meaning of obligation opinions vary, and though concordance searches seem to suggest that *have to* is more common in the past reporting sentences, even academic handbooks of usage find it impossible to either disqualify *must* as incorrect or draw a line that would sharply divide contexts into those reserved for *must* and others reserved for *have to*. If there is any preference for any of the modal auxiliaries in any context, it is the following:
- whenever the obligation has the character of a single, everyday phenomenon (i.e. the effect of operation of a law, regulation, contract, treaty, agreement, direct order of an external authority), it is more likely that we shall hear *have to* used by a native speaker,
- whenever *must* is used to express on the one hand, the obligation that either has the character of a universal rule, generally recognized moral obligation, or is an expression of personal intention or sense of obligation, or, on the other, *must* is a form of assessment of probability, it is more likely that *must* will be left unchanged in past reporting sentence.
It must be repeated, however, that the above can not be regarded as a strictly observed rule but rather a common tendency.

Past reporting can not change the sentences because reporting would loose the ability to distinguish grammatically between what is earlier and what is simultaneous - see the sentences *i.* and *ii.*

Syntactic structures – the interrogative, the affirmative, the imperative etc.)

One more significant mechanism responsible for the final shape of the Indirect Reporting sentence is the type of a sentence, namely the question whether what is reported is an affirmative statement, an interrogative, or imperative one, an exclamation or a mixture of any of them. In each of these cases, the language developed specific structures to render the meaning and character of the utterance. The following is not an exhaustive presentation of all possible phenomena that might be encountered in this segment of grammar but rather a reminder of the most general mechanisms at work there.

The choice of the reporting verb

One of the most important elements of the Indirect Reporting structure is the verb chosen to relate the reported activity. Its choice both determines and reveals the character of the utterance (affirmative, interrogative, imperative, exclamatory) as well as its language register (formal-informal, ironic, emotional etc.).

Affirmative sentences

The range of verbs that can be used to report an affirmative statement is quite wide and, apart from the most common - *say* and *tell* - embraces also such as *admit, attest, affirm, agree, boast, claim, insist, object, protest, retort, maintain, note, observe, state, suggest* etc.

As it was already mentioned in the note to Indirect Reporting, this structure aims at reflecting not the form of the original but its meaning, and in the way that suits the individual purpose of the speaker. As a result, a great number of rhetorical forms used in the original utterance will not be 'translated' into their equivalents but shed in the process of constructing a report on a linguistic/meaningful act - what is preserved is the meaning of the original 'described' in a more or less passionless manner - a good illustration of the working of this mechanism is the nature of transformation of the following sentences:

i. He said: *'I would not trust her if I were you'*.
   He suggested that she should not be trusted.
ii. Peter said to me: *'Would you like me to give you a hand with these parcels - they are quite heavy'*.
   Peter offered to help me carry my heavy parcels.

In the above examples, instead of trying to find the form of one-to-one translation of the original sentences, the speakers were satisfied with conveying only the meaning and intention of the originals, ignoring the form in which they were communicated.

Interrogative sentences

The range of reporting verbs signalling the interrogative character of the reported utterance comprises (among others) the following: *ask, question, interrogate, enquire/inquire, want to know*.

The most important modification that is required in Indirect Reporting of questions is the change of the sentence order from the inverted (which is reserved for the main clauses in English) into affirmative. In the case of Specific questions, the presence of the interrogative pronoun is a sufficient indication of the fact that the original form of the reported statement is a question, in the case of General questions, the interrogative character of the reported clause is indicated by an addition of *if* or *whether* (the latter no longer in common use outside of formal language and disjointed questions).

i. She said to him: *'Do you like it?'*
   She asked him if he liked it.
ii. He will ask you: *'Where do you live?'*
   He will ask you where you live.

The inverted order is retained commonly when we ask about the Subject[49], whereas in a similar construction, when we ask about a complement, the inverted order is rather uncommon though still an option:
   i. He says: 'Who wrote the book?' (question about the subject)
      He wants to know who wrote the book.
   ii. She said to him: 'What is your name?' (question about the complement)
      She asked him what his name was.
      She asked him what was his name. (less common of the two)

In the case of reporting past questions with the auxiliary *shall*, we have to reveal in which of the two common meanings (modal auxiliary signalling an obligation or first person future auxiliary) the auxiliary *shall* is used. When the question asks about an obligation, the reported question will render it with the use of the auxiliary *should*; when we ask merely about the future, it is indicated by the auxiliary *would*.
   i. He said: 'Shall we buy flowers?'
   ii. He asked if they should buy flowers. (obligation)
   iii. He asked if they would buy flowers. (future)

Imperative sentences

There is a range of constructions that may be used to report imperative statements, directions, interdictions. The most common construction in the second person singular and plural is the infinitive construction though the constructions used to report the first and third persons are also an option. Unlike the imperative mood, the reporting phrases are quite precise and can only rarely be used interchangeably - in the normal situation usually only one of them is possible, which requires an equal precision and care on the part of the speaker. The following sentences illustrate the most common of these structures:
   i. He said to her: 'Tell me your name.'
      He told her to give him her name.
   ii. She said to him: 'Don't come any closer'.
      She told him not to come any closer.
   iii. She said to them: 'Let us go to the cinema today'. (nothing important, just a proposition)
      She suggested (their) going to the cinema.
   iv. He said: 'Let's not go to the cinema today.'
      He suggested (their) not going to the cinema.
   v. She said: 'Let's find some shelter - a storm is coming.' (she insists, believing it a necessity)
      She suggested (that) they (should) find some shelter because a storm was coming.
   vi. They said: 'Don't let him go home just yet'.
      They suggested (that) he (should) not go home yet.
   vii. He said: 'Let us run, the planes are coming'. (he not only represents it as a necessity but presses to do it instantly)
      He urged them to run for the planes were coming.
   viii. She said to us: 'Don't let us give up on him'.
      She urged us not to give up on him.
   ix. He said: 'You damaged the car - you pay for the repairs'. (it is represented as an obligation of the person)
      He said that she had damaged the car and, therefore, she was to pay for the repairs.

The above sentences represent merely a selection of the more common ways of expressing obligation but the range of possibilities is much wider - for example, equally common alternatives are such phrases as: *encourage sb to do sth, recommend that sb did sth/should do sth, advise sb to do sth* etc.

Exclamatory sentences and exclamations plus incomplete clauses

The most common problem with reporting exclamations, apart from making a correct choice of the reporting phrase, is the fact that exclamations are often incomplete sentences, whose meaning and often

---

49 In fact, the questions about the Subject only look as if they were in inverted order. Since we ask about the Subject, the sentence lacks the element whose position could be inverted. Consequently, the above-quoted sentence (*Who wrote the book*) is not in an inverted but regular order, the interrogative pronoun occupying the position of the absent Subject.

structure have to be reconstructed before they will be turned into subordinate clauses - below will be found a range of examples showing the nature of difficulty.

    i. She will say: 'How glad I am to be here!'
      She will exclaim with pleasure that she is there.
    ii. He said: 'Thank you for your kind offer. I will find a taxi'.
      He thanked her and said that he would find a taxi.
    iii. He said: 'Hello! Where have you been?'
      He greeted her and asked where she had been.
    iv. She said: 'Ouch! I've broken my nail'.
      She cried out with pain that she had broken her nail.
    v. He said: 'What a lovely garden!'
      He exclaimed with admiration that it was a lovely garden.
    vi. He said: 'Oh, what a fool I am!'
      He exclaimed bitterly that he was a fool.
    vii. She said: 'What an awful climate!'
      She complained that it was an awful climate.
      She remarked what an awful climate it was.

When we report short answers, which, in the original, would have been expressed with the use of an auxiliary, we represent them in Indirect Reporting sentences with the use of the auxiliary of the tense used in the reported question - for example:

    i. He said to her: 'Do you like the town?'
      She said to him: 'Yes'.
      He asked her if she _liked_ the town and she answered that she _did_.
    ii. She said to him: 'Have you ever seen a whale?'
      He said to her: 'No'.
      She asked him if he _had ever seen_ a whale and he answered that he _had not_.

Hypothetical mood

The English offers two alternative systems of predication: non-hypothetical and hypothetical.

    - **The non-hypothetical construction**, which is sometimes called predicative mood, is represented by the tenses. When the speaker chooses to communicate with somebody with the use of the non-hypothetical form, namely tenses, it indicates that the speaker presents the situation in the shape in which he believes it existed / exists / will exist. When we encounter sentences like the following, we will not find in their construction an encouragement to doubt that it was / is / will be as it is described.

    i. He was at home yesterday.
    ii. He is watching TV at the moment.
    iii. I will see him tomorrow at 5.

    - When the speaker chooses **the hypothetical construction**, it is a kind of warning that the speaker believes or knows that what he describes did not / does not / will not exist, and that the utterance is merely a kind of supposition on what might have been / might be an alternative shape of reality, different from what the speaker believes to be the actual shape. The grammatical devices developed by the construction to signal its hypothetical character are distinctly different for the main and subordinate clauses and, therefore, have to be presented separately.

The hypothetical in the main clause

In the main clause, the grammatical marker of hypothetical nature of the presented situation is the auxiliary **would** + **infinitive** construction. In consequence of the fact that the location in time of the auxiliaries in their non-past forms is fixed upon the moment of producing the sentence (i.e. they always 'lie' on the moment of uttering the sentence), *would* itself can not be forced to indicate that we are talking about the present, past or future. To signal what is the time reference of the sentence (i.e. if it describes the past, present, or future), the hypothetical construction uses the choice of the infinitive form following *would*. There is, however, a problem - the infinitive construction has developed only two forms, Perfect and non-Perfect (the latter sometimes called Present), whereas the hypothetical mood is forced to employ it to refer to three types of reference: past, present, future. In consequence, two out of three have to share one and the same form - it is the present and future reference. As a result, in the main clause, we have a binary system of indicating the time reference - Past and non-Past, the latter comprising the Present and the Future. The range of forms from which we choose looks as follows:

- *He would have been* at home yesterday at 5...
  He would have been writing a letter at 5 yesterday...
  He would have gone to sleep at 5 yesterday...
- *He would be* at home now...
  He would be writing a letter now...
  He would be asleep now...
- *He would be* at home tomorrow at 5...
  He would be writing a letter at 5 tomorrow...
  He would go to sleep at 5 tomorrow...

Another significant shortcoming of the above solution is that it employs the Perfect form as the only indication of the Past character of the described activity. Therefore, the capacity of the system to signal grammatically the time reference works only as long as we do not encounter any situations that the English describes with the use of the Perfect form. In such a case, the ability of the system to distinguish between the Past, Present and Future vanishes and everything has to be expressed with the same form - for example:

- *He would have been married* for 5 years tomorrow ...
- *He would have been married* for 5 years now ...
- *He would have been married* for 5 years yesterday...

Apart from *would* used as a neutral marker of hypothetical character of the clause, we may employ also modal markers of the hypothetical, namely *might*, *could* and *would* (the latter used to indicate a range of meanings revolving mainly round the notion of volition or likelihood).

The hypothetical in the subordinate clause

Like in the main clause, the English employs in the subordinate clause a binary system of indicating time reference. The system has the following shape:
- Past tenses indicate the non-Past character of the utterance (i.e. that it refers either to the Present or to the Future),
- Past Perfect tenses indicate the fact that we are speaking of events which are earlier than the moment of producing the utterance.

Originally, the non-Past time reference was signalled by Past Subjunctive, which differs from Past tenses merely by one element, it misses the form *was* of the verb *be* - thus, in Past Subjunctive constructions we say *I were, he/she/it were*. As a result, the indication of whether we are speaking about the Past, Present or Future is realised in the following way:

- *If he had been* at home at 5 yesterday, ...
  If he had been watching TV at 5 yesterday,...
  If he had gone to sleep at 5 yesterday,...
- *If he were/was* at home now, ...
  If he were/was watching TV now,...
  If he were/was asleep now,...
- *If he were/was* at home at 5 tomorrow, ...
  If he were/was watching TV at 5 tomorrow,...
  If he were/was asleep at 5 tomorrow,...

Since the system employs the Perfect form in the same manner as in the main clause, namely to indicate the past character of the object of description, the construction will suffer similar consequences as the main clause. Whenever we describe a situation which requires the Perfect form to be expressed, the variety of the system is lost and we have to make do with a single grammatical form to denote the Past, Present, and Future - the following is an illustration of such situation:
- If he **had been married** for 2 years yesterday, ...
- If he **had been married** for 2 years now, ...
- If he **had been married** for 2 years tomorrow, ...

Like in the case of the main clause, the range of forms in our disposal in the subordinate clause includes also modal auxiliaries, but only those that can be used in their Past forms, i.e. *might, could, would, were to*.

The hypothetical used to present hypothetical plans for the future

While interpreting the hypothetical subordinate clauses, caution must be exercised because, apart from signifying merely that a given situation is hypothetical and past, present, or future, this grammatical construction may be employed (like non-hypothetical Past and Present tenses) to signal the fact that what the utterance describes is not a situation happening at a given moment but rather a plan for the future of that moment (the future being possibly both the future with reference to the moment of speaking and the future in the past). For example, the sentences below may describe hypothetical events or plans for hypothetical events:
  i. *If he were driving home at 5 today/tomorrow,...*
  ii. *If he had been driving home at 5 tomorrow, ...*
  iii. *If he had been driving home at 5 yesterday, ...*

The sentence *i.* may mean both *if it happened that he would be driving home at 5 today/tomorrow* and *if there were plans that he would be driving home at 5 today/tomorrow*. The sentence *ii.* is the most unambiguous because the combination of a past construction with the future time reference indicates quite clearly that what is meant are past hypothetical plans for a future event. In the case of the sentence *iii.* like in the sentence *i.*, the meaning may be both *if it had happened that he would have been driving home at 5 yesterday* and *if there had been plans* [earlier, at the moment about which we speak] *that he would have been driving home at 5 yesterday* [later].

A good illustration of how the two parallel systems, hypothetical and non-hypothetical, work are conditional sentences. The conditional construction looks quite cryptic and illogical when we approach it in the form of 0, 1, 2, and 3 conditional. The difficulty disappears, however, when we look upon it as what it really is, namely, two parallel systems of describing reality, hypothetical and non-hypothetical.

Conditional sentences in English
an attempt of systematisation (from 0 to 18, and beyond)

The most common method of description of the phenomenon of conditionality in English recognises four types of conditional constructions and divides them into two general systems: hypothetical (also called, 'counter-factual,' 'unreal') and non-hypothetical (or, 'direct,' 'real'). This basic duality is additionally refined by numerical representation of the types of sentences constituting, allegedly, the whole system - the constructions are referred to as belonging to 0, 1st, 2nd, or 3rd type of conditional sentences. These types are usually listed as basic, the system recognising additionally also the possibility of 'mixing' parts of 2nd and 3rd type, thus encompassing also the 'mixed' types of conditional sentences. The most significant advantage of such description is the facility of identification of the constructions thus represented by their numbers, however, this and any other advantages of it must be regarded as dwarfed by the fact that the overall impression that it makes is fundamentally incorrect and misleading, and, consequently, crippling, sometimes forever, the process of understanding the nature, structure and logic of the phenomenon. Among the most obvious shortcomings of it one could list its incompleteness (the complete number of combinations of the phenomena whose recognition makes it possible to distinguish between 0, 1st, 2nd and 3 rd is not 4 but at least 18) and seeming arbitrariness (which, instead of explaining the conditional sentences with reference to what the student usually already knows when the conditional is introduced, presents it as an independent and mysterious phenomenon). As a result, the conditional constructions, which are no more difficult that any other complex structures in English, traditionally occupy a high position on the list of structures defying understanding of a normal student. This fact is all the more annoying because, in reality, the conditional construction is quite simple, on condition, however, that it is viewed in its completeness.

The conditional construction - the basic recognitions

In its model form, the conditional sentence is a subordinate complex construction consisting of two clauses related to each other, the subordinate conditional clause and the main clause. The relation between them is always a specific realisation of one of two variants of the construction that generally may be described in the following way:

1. IF something happens (in the past/present/future) [being a **cause**], then something else follows [being an **effect**].
2. IF something happens (in the past/present/future) [being an **effect**], then it resulted from something else, which preceded it [being a **cause**].

Thus, the subordinate conditional clause may present either a cause of the activity of the main clause or its effect on the basis of which the speaker formulates a guess what was its cause, the latter presented in the main clause.

I.

Hypothetical vs. non-hypothetical

The first distinction responsible for the proliferation of the conditional structures in English is the recognition of the difference between the hypothetical and non-hypothetical form of a communiqué.

- **The non-hypothetical construction,** which is nothing but what is commonly referred to as the predicative mood, consists of the prosaic tense constructions. When a speaker chooses as the form of communication the non-hypothetical form, i.e. the construction of any of the tenses, it indicates that **the speaker believes that the situation is being presented in the shape in which it existed/exists/will exist**. Consequently, the construction of the following sentences is not expected, in the normal situation, to encourage doubts as to whether what is being described happened/happens/will happen or whether it happened/happens/will happen in the shape described:
 i. *She met him yesterday.*
 ii. *They are watching TV at the moment.*
 iii. *I will phone you tomorrow.*

- **The hypothetical construction**[50], when chosen to describe the nature of the action (rather than the attitude of the speaker - it is one of the structures employed also to make the communiqué more polite), is meant to be a warning that **the speaker believes or knows that the situation did not exist/does not exist/will not exist in the shape in which it is described**, and, therefore, the sentence presents what the speaker believes to have been/to be merely an alternative course of events, which, although possible, actually (in his opinion) never happened/is not happening/will not happen. Therefore, the following

---

50 . Apart from 'hypothetical', the grammatical discourse uses also such terms as 'unreal' and 'counter-factual'. Although neither of the three is actually fully accurate, 'hypothetical' seems to be closest to what the groundwork of the distinction adopted here is, namely between what is real and actual in the opinion of the speaker (the non-hypothetical construction) and what the speaker believes to be only theoretical, speculative construct, alternative to actual reality (the hypothetical construction).A good illustration of this fact are the following sentences, which show that hypothetical communiqués often refer to situations which are not so much impossible as rather not intended:
 i. *If I change my job, I shall earn more.*
 ii. *If I changed my job, I would earn more.*

equivalents of the sentences *i*, *ii*, and *iii*, will be interpreted as presenting what, the speaker believes, actually did not/does not/will not take place.
- iv. You are wrong about her - she <u>would have met</u> him yesterday but in view of what he had done she naturally changed her mind.
- v. They <u>would be watching</u> TV now, but their aunt has come unexpectedly and they have to entertain her.
- vi. I <u>would phone</u> you tomorrow but, since I have met you I may as well tell you everything now.

If the conditional sentences were to be presented in the form of a table, the drawing would have to start from dividing it into two columns:

the Non-hypothetical	the Hypothetical
He is watching TV now.	*He would be watching TV now (but he is not).*

II.

Another distinction which cross-sections the division into the hypothetical and the non-hypothetical, is the time reference. To perform effectively its primary role of locating the activities spoken of with reference to the moment of speaking of them the system naturally has had to develop the capacity of distinguishing between three relations to the moment of speaking: past, present, and future. Thus, the system to serve its purpose has had to work out the capacity to mark the activities as earlier than the moment of speaking (past), parallel to it (present), or following it (future).

At the same time, it must be remembered that the conditional sentences are complex constructions, consisting of a main and a subordinate clause. In the structure of temporal location of the sentence, the primary role is performed by the main clause, which constitutes the reference point of the whole communiqué. Consequently, in the case when both clauses (the main and the subordinate) belong to the same time segment (past, present, future), the main clause serves as the reference point to the subordinate clause, whose form will then reflect not only the relation to the moment of speaking but also to the main clause. Therefore, the construction of the main clause may be different from that of the subordinate clause, even when they belong to the same segment of relation to the moment of speaking (i.e. both refer to past, present, or future).

Time reference in the non-hypothetical constructions

As it was said above, the non-hypothetical construction makes use of the English tense system, and, therefore, will employ:

- Past tenses to speak about the activities completed earlier than they are spoken of:
  - i. If he went to the party yesterday, he probably met Mary.

- Present tenses, to speak about the activities which have already begun but have not been finished yet:
  - ii. If she is at home alone now, I bet she is reading a book.

- Future tenses, to speak about the events that have not started yet, when they are spoken of.
  - iii. If he visits her tomorrow, he will learn everything.

Special cases of tense choice

At the same time, the above-mentioned difference between the form of the main and the subordinate clause results in the fact that in certain situations the verb form of the subordinate clause is subject to a number of further modifications - see the sentence *iii.* above, in which case, although the subordinate

clause refers to the future, it is expressed with a Present tense. In the case of the non-hypothetical conditional sentences, there are two such considerations:
- when both the main and the subordinate conditional clauses refer to the future,
- when the main clause is expressed with the use of Past Perfect.

The main clause and the subordinate clause referring to the Future

When both the main clause and the subordinate clause refer to the Future, in the subordinate clause, the Future tenses are reserved for the situation when the action/event/rule/state of the subordinate clause is Future with reference to the main clause - in all other cases the subordinate clause uses the Present construction to denote the Futurity (of course, one has to remember that in the case of sentences of mixed-time reference of the clauses, the Present form may also indicate that the subordinate clause is simply Present, i.e. simultaneous with the moment of speaking). It may be illustrated by the following sentences:

 i. *If you ask me to, I will buy you a dog.*
 ii. *If it will make you happy, I will buy you a dog.*

The sentence *i.* belongs to the Variant 1 of the conditional constructions, and its subordinate clause, which presents the cause of the event of the main clause, will naturally be located before the main clause activity. As a result, the subordinate clause can not be represented with the use of a Future tense – instead, it is expressed with a Present tense. In the sentence *ii.*, which belongs to the Variant 2 of the conditional constructions, the subordinate clause presents the predicted future consequence of the action of the main clause - as a result, to denote the fact that the subordinate clause does not precede but follows the situation of the main clause, the Future tense is used also in the subordinate clause.

The main clause expressed with a Past Perfect tense

When the main clause is expressed with Past Perfect tenses and the type of the communiqué to which the subordinate clause belongs is non-Perfect (for explanation see blow under the heading Aspect Perfect), Past Perfect in the subordinate clause is reserved for the situation when the subordinate clause is earlier than the main clause expressed with Past Perfect. If the subordinate clause is Past but simultaneous with the main clause expressed with Past Perfect, the subordinate clause will be expressed with Past tenses. This regularity may be illustrated by the following sentences:

 i. *She said that the thief had probably stolen the necklace if it was at home.*
 ii. *She said that the thief had probably stolen the necklace if Jill had neglected to lock it in the safe the previous day.*
 iii. *If, by the time she arrived, he had already visited the museum, they went directly to the concert hall.*

In the sentence *i.*, the subordinate clause is not earlier than the main clause (they are simultaneous), so the clause is expressed with the Past Simple tense, whereas in the sentence *ii.*, in which the subordinate clause is earlier than the main, this fact is indicated by the use of Past Perfect tense. If the type of the communiqué of the subordinate clause is any of the three variants reserved for the Perfect form in English, the past subordinate clause will be expressed with Past Perfect even when it is simultaneous with the main clause expressed with Past Perfect.

At the same time, since the non-hypothetical conditional sentences make use of all the mechanisms at work in the finite syntactic constructions, one may encounter sentences which make a specific use of the Present and Future tenses - there are two situations that might be misinterpreted and, therefore, justify a separate presentation:

Present tenses used to speak about the present plans concerning the future

Whenever the sentence expresses not so much predictions for the future but present plans concerning it, English permits to communicate this fact by the use of Present tenses - primarily Present Continuous and Present Simple[51]. The choice between these two tenses depends on the recognition to which of the following three situation the event spoken of belongs:

a. When the conditional clause presents **a single decision** of the doer/speaker - in such a case the choice between the Continuous and the non-Continuous is regulated by the Doer/Speaker Aspect, Present Simple being used when the activity is intended to be viewed as initiated and kept up by the doer/speaker; Present Continuous, when the clause is meant merely to identify the surface elements of the situation (who does what) without imparting any information as to whose intention or decision determines the action.
   i. *If you go to Berlin tomorrow, you will be able to visit aunt Mary before she has had this operation.*
   ii. *If you are going to Berlin tomorrow, you will be able to visit aunt Mary before she has had this operation.*

The sentence *i.* seems to suggest that the *going to Berlin* is a plan and resolution of the doer (and, therefore, would be correct if we wanted to describe the situation as such), whereas the sentence *ii.*, having removed this information, states only that the activity has been planned and that it will involve the participation of the person specified as the doer. At the same time, it has to be remembered that the fact that the sentence *ii.* does not point grammatically at the doer as the initiator can not be interpreted as a declaration that the person is not the initiator - the sentence *ii.* is not antithetical to the sentence *i.*, it only lacks some of the information presented by the latter.

b. When the conditional clause presents **a single event resulting from the operation of a rule** - in such a case the choice between the Continuous and the non-Continuous is determined by the Action Aspect of a single action/occurrence (not the Action Aspect of a rule). As a result, if the event planned is presented in its entirety, the proper form will be Present non-Continuous, and if it describes it as being in the middle of operation, it shall be expressed with the Present Continuous tenses.
   i. *If he comes home at 5 today, he will not be able to help you before 6.*
   ii. *If, at 13 hours on Monday, Brown is still having lunch, we will have to sort out possible problems on our own.*

c. When the conditional clause presents **a chain of events**, the context alone is usually insufficient to clarify the Action Aspect of the particular actions/rules/states and, therefore, the choice between the Continuous and the non-Continuous returns to be determined by the Action Aspect. Thus, in the case of a single action/occurrence the speaker chooses between the action/occurrence seen in the middle (the Continuous) or in its entirety (the non-Continuous); a rule presented as permanent, regular (the non-Continuous) and temporary/chaotic (the Continuous); a state presented as unchanging, neutral (the non-Continuous) and changing or intensified (the Continuous). For example:
   If you just enter the shop, buy the newspaper and leave, you may still have time to reach the office on time.

If the mechanism controlling the choice of the Continuous is the Action Aspect, even though the speaker might be talking about the present plans of the doer, the choice of the non-Continuous can no longer be regarded as a signal that the actions are intended and kept up by the doer - the non-Continuous form has been chosen to communicate that the actions forming the series happen one after another (each of them presented in its entirety) rather than are seen in the middle of being performed at a specified moment.

The Future tenses used to suggest hesitancy of the speaker as to the present situation

When the speaker is not sure if what he presents is actually the shape of the present situation, he may warn about this fact by choosing a Future tense instead of Present. For example:
   i. *If she is at home, I think she is watching her favourite serial now.*
   ii. *If she is at home, I think she will be watching her favourite serial now.*

As it is determined by the adverbial of time *now*, the sentence *ii.* is not Future but Present, the only difference between it and the sentence *i.* being the fact that it presents the same situation in the form that

---

[51] . Although from grammatical point of view the use of Present Perfect tenses (Continuous and non-Continuous) to express present plans for the future is possible, the combination of the Perfect Aspect with the logic of the subordinate conditional clause make such uses so imprecise that it is difficult to find a situation that would not be more naturally expressed with the use of other grammatical devices - this presentation will, therefore, focus on the use of Present Continuous and Present Simple only.

suggests that the speaker is not sure if it has the shape in which it is described. Although the use of this construction in the subordinate conditional clause can not be altogether disqualified, it, nevertheless, remains practically undetectable in the existing databases, which apparently suggests that the structure is not in use. The possible reasons for this are, on the one hand, the fact that the activity spoken of is to be presented in the conditional clause, which is perhaps a sufficient suggestion of the speaker's uncertainty, and, on the other, the ambiguity of such utterance due to the fact that the use of the future tense and 'will+infinitive' in the conditional clause is already loaded with additional significance.

Time reference in the hypothetical constructions

The grammatical devices developed by English to signal the hypothetical character of an utterance are distinctly different for the main and subordinate clauses and, therefore, have to be presented separately.

Time reference in the hypothetical main clause

In the main clause, the grammatical marker of the hypothetical nature of the presented situation is the auxiliary **would+infinitive** construction. In consequence of the fact that the location in time of the auxiliaries in their non-past forms is fixed upon the moment of producing the sentence (i.e. they always 'lie' on the moment of speaking), *would* alone (as the marker of hypothetical character of the utterance) can not be forced to indicate whether the sentence refers to the present, past or future. To signal what is the time reference of the sentence (i.e. if the activity spoken of remains in the past, present, or future of the moment of speaking), the hypothetical uses the choice of the infinitive form following *would*. There is, however, a problem - the infinitive construction has developed only two forms, Perfect and non-Perfect (the latter sometimes called Present), whereas the hypothetical mood is forced to employ it to refer to three types of reference: past, present, future. In consequence, two out of three have to share one and the same form - in English it is the present and future reference. As a result, in the main clause, there is a binary system of indicating the time reference - Past and non-Past, the latter comprising the Present and the Future. The range of forms from which we choose looks as follows:

 - *He **would have been** at home yesterday at 5...*
 *He **would have been writing** a letter at 5 yesterday...*
 *He **would have gone to sleep** at 5 yesterday...*
 - *He **would be** at home now...*
 *He **would be writing** a letter now...*
 *He **would be asleep** now...*
 - *He **would be** at home tomorrow at 5...*
 *He **would be writing** a letter at 5 tomorrow...*
 *He **would go to sleep** at 5 tomorrow...*

Apart from *would* used as a neutral marker of hypothetical character of the clause, we may employ also modal markers of the hypothetical, namely *might, could* and *would (*the latter used to indicate a range of meanings revolving mainly round the notion of volition or likelihood).

Time reference in the hypothetical subordinate clause

Like in the main clause, English employs in the subordinate clause a binary system of indicating time reference. The system has the following shape:
- Past tenses indicate the non-Past character of the utterance (i.e. that it refers either to the Present or to the Future),
- Past Perfect tenses, indicate the fact that we are speaking of events which are earlier than the moment of producing the utterance.

Originally, the non-Past time reference was signalled by Past Subjunctive, which differs from Past tenses merely by one element, it misses the form *was* of the verb *be* - thus, in Past Subjunctive constructions we say *I were, he/she/it were*. As a result, the indication of whether we are speaking about the Past, Present or Future is realised in the following way:

 - *If he **had been** at home at 5 yesterday, ...*
 *If he **had been watching TV** at 5 yesterday,...*
 *If he **had talked** to Mary at 5 yesterday,...*

- If he **were/was** at home now, ...
If he **were/was watching TV** now,...
If he **had** more than one car now,...
- If he **were/was** at home at 5 tomorrow, ...
If he **were/was watching TV** at 5 tomorrow,...
If he **decided to phone** me at 5 tomorrow,...

Future-in-the-Past in the hypothetical subordinate clause

At the same time, similarly to the non-hypothetical construction, when both **the main clause and the subordinate clause refer to the Future**, in the subordinate clause, the Future-in-the-Past tenses are reserved for the situation when the action/event/rule/state of the subordinate clause is future with reference to the main clause - in all other cases the subordinate clause uses the Past tense/Past Subjunctive construction to denote the Futurity (of course, one has to remember that in the case of sentences of mixed-time reference of the clauses, the Past tense/Past Subjunctive form may also indicate that the subordinate clause is simply Present, i.e. simultaneous with the moment of speaking). It may be illustrated by the following sentences:

i. If you asked me to, I would buy you a dog.
ii. If it would make you happy, I would buy you a dog.

The sentence *i.* belongs to the Variant 1 of the conditional constructions, and its subordinate clause, which presents the cause of the event of the main clause, will naturally be located before the main clause activity. As a result, the subordinate clause can not be represented with the use of a Future-in-the-Past tense - it is expressed with a Past tense/Past Subjunctive. In the sentence *ii*, which belongs to the Variant 2 of the conditional constructions, the subordinate clause presents the predicted future consequence of the action of the main clause - as a result, to denote the fact that the subordinate clause does not precede but follows the situation of the main clause, the Future-in-the-Past tense is used also in the subordinate clause.

Thus, the table presenting the conditional constructions that was begun to be drawn above has to be cross-sectioned to include the three time references.

	the non-hypothetical	the hypothetical	
Future	If he is in Italy tomorrow, he will enjoy nice weather	If he were in Italy tomorrow, he would enjoy nice weather.	Future
Present	If he is in Italy now, he is enjoying nice weather.	If he were in Italy now, he would be enjoying nice weather.	Present
Past	If he was in Italy yesterday, he enjoyed nice weather.	If he had been in Italy yesterday, he would have enjoyed nice weather.	Past

Mixed-time reference

Additionally, it must be remembered that the choice of the grammatical structure in a given clause (whether subordinate or main) is determined (with only the exceptions discussed above) independently by the time reference to the moment of speaking - the grammatical form of a clause is independent and irrespective of what has been chosen for the other clause. Therefore, in the case of the non-hypothetical construction, the grammar of a clause is regulated merely by the non-hypothetical structures, predominantly by tense and aspect, and in the case of the hypothetical system, by the grammar of the hypothetical mood. As a result, the main clause and the subordinate clause may belong to different time references. In consequence, the table drawn above should be enlarged by the addition of cells presenting the results of mixing time reference within one sentence.

	the non-hypothetical	the hypothetical	
Future	If he is in Italy tomorrow, he will enjoy nice weather	If he were in Italy tomorrow, he would enjoy nice weather.	Future
Present	If he is in Italy now, he is enjoying nice weather.	If he were in Italy now, he would be enjoying nice weather.	Present
Past	If he was in Italy yesterday, he enjoyed nice weather.	If he had been in Italy yesterday, he would have enjoyed nice weather.	Past
Mixed-time reference	If he was in Italy yesterday, he will be in France tomorrow. If he is in France today, he was in Spain yesterday. If he will[52] be in France tomorrow, he was in Spain yesterday.	If he had been in Italy yesterday, he would be in France tomorrow. If he were/was in France today, he would have been in Spain yesterday. If he would be in France tomorrow, he would have been in Spain yesterday.	Mixed-time reference

The hypothetical combined with the non-hypothetical in a conditional sentence

In syntactic complex structures the meanings of whose components are not mutually depend, the hypothetical may be freely mixed with the non-hypothetical. The conditional sentences, however, belong to a different type of syntactic constructions - the meaning and logic of their component clauses are mutually dependent. As a result, it is difficult to imagine a situation that would justify using such a hybrid - it would be a variant of two possible structures:
- the speaker suggests that the condition is impossible (and, therefore, did not happen) but the result, possible (and, therefore, it happened),
- the speaker suggests that the condition is possible (so, it happened) but the result, impossible (in consequence, it did not happen).

Small wonder, practically the only use to which such structures may be employed are ironic sentences, e.g.
If the disease is as deadly and contagious as you say, we would have been dead a long time ago.
The construction natural for the above conditional clause is the hypothetical, compatible with the main clause. The use of the non-hypothetical in the subordinate clause may be regarded as an ironic repetition of the non-hypothetical representation of the situation employed by the person on whose beliefs the above sentence is a commentary. The overall intended effect is a negation of what is suggested by the conditional non-hypothetical clause by juxtaposing it with the fact that makes the former obviously wrong.

---

52 It must be remembered that the use of the construction *will+infinitive* in the conditional clause which is subordinate to a main clause referring to the future is possibly loaded with more meaning than just the indication that the conditional clause is future to the main clause. Without going into details, majority of these additional modal meanings generally revolve round two suggestions:
  1. the action of the subordinate clause is 'willed' by the doer, which makes the meaning of *will* roughly equivalent to *wanting* (*will do/will not do = want to do/refuse, not want to do*),
  2. the action of the subordinate clause is not so much presented as predicted to happen but rather as 'likely to happen' in the construction in which the action of the main clause is to precede that of the subordinate clause. The pattern is similar to: if something is likely to happen in the future, somebody will do something else earlier (but in connection with the prediction of the conditional clause).

Aspect Perfect in the conditional constructions

The above table shows the defective nature of the system of time reference based on a modal auxiliary located on the moment of speaking - the hypothetical system fails to distinguish between the present and the future grammatically, having in its disposal only two constructions, Perfect and non-Perfect. In fact the consequences of building the hypothetical on the above-mentioned foundation turn out to be even more serious when we take into consideration the demands of the Aspect Perfect. Without going into details of this grammatical phenomenon, it is enough to remind here that English reserves three types of situations for the Perfect forms (Continuous and non-Continuous):
- when the speaker wishes to describe a certain situation not directly but by means of some activity/rule/state whose effect this situation is - in other words, instead of being described directly, the meaning is given to understand by the speaker,
- when the speaker wishes to express a guess/conjecture on the basis of a situation existing at the point of reference as to what caused this situation,
- when the speaker wishes to say that an activity/rule/state remaining at the moment of reference, have continued for some time beginning earlier.

In each of the above situations, the use of the Perfect form is obligatory no matter whether the character of the sentence is non-hypothetical or hypothetical. Now, while, in the case of the non-hypothetical construction, the inclusion of the Perfect enriches the system of communication, in the hypothetical, the Perfect impoverishes it. Whenever a hypothetical sentence describes any of the above situations, it is forced to use only the Perfect form, which, however, as we remember has been employed to signal the past character of the described event. In consequence, whenever the sentence describes a situation requiring the use of the Perfect form, the hypothetical system of grammatical time reference is reduced to only ONE form employing it to refer to the Past, Present and Future. Thus, in a situation demanding a Perfect form, the above table would look as follows:

	the non-hypothetical	the hypothetical	
Future	If he has been living with them for two months (by/[53]) tomorrow, they will have been quarrelling all this time.	If he had been living with them for two months (by/) **tomorrow**, they would have been quarrelling all this time.	Future
Present	If he has been living with them for two months (by/) now, they have been quarrelling all this time.	If he had been living with them for two months (by/) **now**, they would have been quarrelling for two months now.	Present
Past	If he had been living with them for two months (by/) yesterday, they had been quarrelling all that time.	If he had been living with them for two months (by/) **yesterday**, they would have been quarrelling all that time.	Past

Aspect Continuous in the conditional constructions

The last significant distinction cross-sectioning the time reference grid is the Aspect Continuous. The operation of this phenomenon is responsible for the fact that the above-mentioned 'numerical' representation of the conditional constructions not only distinguishes between the hypothetical (2nd and 3rd type) and the non-hypothetical (0 and 1st type) utterances but also recognizes the difference within the non-hypothetical, namely between 0 and 1. The typical presentation of the two represents 0 type as reserved for a description of rules and truths, using only Simple tenses (usually Present Simple only, sometimes including also Past Simple), and 1st, as used to present all the remaining types of situations. However, the recognition of the fact that the description of a rule determines the choice between the

---

53 The American usage tends to recognise such combination of the time reference consisting of only the point in time (*tomorrow, at 5*, etc) and the Perfect as substandard, recommending that it should be complemented with e.g. a preposition *by*.

Continuous and the non-Continuous form, is in reality a fragment of a larger grammatical phenomenon, namely the Aspect Continuous, which, at the same time, distinguishes not between two but three categories: a single action/occurrence, a rule, and a state. In each of the three, both the Continuous and the non-Continuous is used but with different modification of the meaning of the verb.

Action Aspect

	Category of the object of description	the Non-continuous	the Continuous
1.	a single action or occurrence	tends[54] to be presented as a whole, in its entirety (or in the middle - see Doer/Speaker Aspect)	presented in the middle of being done
2.	a rule - continued activity	presented as unspecified rule, presumably primary and unrestricted by time, permanent	presented as restricted by time, understood as secondary and temporary, transitory
	a rule - series of acts or occurrences	presented as an unspecified rule, presumably controlled, planned, regular	presented as a chaotic series of coincidences or temporary, transitory
3.	a state	presented as not changing its intensity, steady, 'flat'	presented as a dynamic process, changing its intensity (increasing/decreasing its intensity), advancing towards completion, or, paradoxically, used to stress the ongoing character of the described phenomenon[55]

Last but not least, the indications of the Continuous Action Aspect may be modified by the considerations described by the Continuous Doer/Speaker Aspect, which conveys information not on the nature of the activity but the doer or speaker - these also have to be taken in consideration when one tries to determine the meaning of the conditional sentence.

Doer/Speaker Aspect

	the non-Continuous	the Continuous
1.	Neutral presentation of the situation.	It indicates emotional attitude of the speaker to the situation described by the sentence.
2.	It may be intuited as identifying the doer or the speaker as the originator or controller of the action, i.e. somebody who keeps it up.	It removes the information as to who is the originator of the action, leaving it unmarked.
3.	In the narrative, the non-Continuous is the form	In the narrative, the Continuous is the form

---

[54] Although by nature, the non-Continuous tends to present the activity in its entirety, this potential may not always be realised due to contextual reasons.

[55] It must be remembered that it is only an elementary presentation, attempting to show the breath of the phenomenon without burying the reader under all the details - the full range of modifications of meaning is wider, the above serving only as a general introduction.

	reserved for the presentation of the foreground action.	indicating the background status of the action.
4.	In conversational English, this form is considered blunt and inconsiderate.	In conversational English, this form is considered more 'polite'.

Therefore, if the above drawn table presenting all types of conditional sentences is to be complete (at least at the elementary level), both the non-hypothetical and the hypothetical columns have to be divided into three sub-columns, representing the above mentioned categories of the Continuous Action Aspect, i.e. a single action/occurrence, a rule, and a state. The use of the Continuous or the non-Continuous in each of them indicates a different modification of the meaning.

As a result, if we wish to distinguish between 0 and 1st types, the correct and complete (on this level) representation of conditional sentences should further subdivide each of the columns drawn so far into three sub-columns presenting separately the categories recognised by the Action Aspect, i.e. single actions/occurrences, rules, and states - the table should, therefore, look as follows:

	non-hypothetical			hypothetical			
	a single action/occurrence	a rule	a state	a state	a rule	a single action/occurrence	
Future							Future
Present							Present
Past							Past
Mixed-time reference							Mixed-time reference

To conclude, on pages 142-143 below, the above table will be found filled with examples illustrating the extent and flexibility of the system gathered so far. The table should not be, however, represented as illustrating all the possible and all the permitted combinations of verb forms, or verb form variants of conditional sentences. Since, on the one hand, the choice of verb forms is regulated by the tense and the two aspects, and, on the other, the structure permits the use of practically all the remaining finite and non-finite forms (e.g. Gerund, infinitive, imperative mood, modal constructions etc.), the number of combinations is much larger and their meaning is described by the grammar of these phenomena, the table below serving only as a frame, giving some idea of the foundation on which the structure rests. The detailed presentation of all these modifications exceeds the scope of this presentation and has to be sought in publications devoted specifically to these phenomena - it should be remembered, however, that the conditional sentences can use them fairly freely.

Hypothetical versus non-hypothetical conditional sentences - a table

	Non-hypothetical single action or occurrence	Non-hypothetical rule	Non-hypothetical state
Future	If we buy her this dog, she will be very happy. If it will[56] make her happy, we will buy her this dog. If he is watching TV at 5 tomorrow, he will be watching MTV.	If a particle X hits a particle Z, a particle B will be produced. If, in your future job, you work on the other side of the town, you will have to commute for 2,5 h every day.	If he is in Italy tomorrow, he will enjoy nice weather.
Present	If he is swimming across the lake now, you may be sure his dog is swimming with him. If he is watching TV now, he is watching MTV.	If a particle X hits a particle Y, a particle Z is produced. If you heat water, it boils. If he misses his bus, he returns home by taxi. If, this month, he is working in the Oxford St. store, he is commuting with Jane and Tom.	If he is Italy now, he is enjoying nice weather.
Past	If she met him yesterday, I bet she told him everything she knew. If he was watching TV yesterday at 5, he was watching MTV. She said that the thief had probably stolen the necklace if it was at home. She said that the thief had probably stolen the necklace if Jill had neglected to lock it in the safe the previous day. If, by the time she arrived, he had visited the museum, they went to the concert hall.	If a particle X hit a particle Z, a particle A was produced. If he made a promise, he kept it. If he missed his bus, he went home by taxi.	If he was in Italy yesterday, he enjoyed nice weather.
Mixed time reference	If he met her yesterday, my mother will be told about it tomorrow. If he will arrive at 6, he probably left at 1 o'clock.	If he always got up at 5 when he was young, I think he will get up at 4 when he gets old.	If she liked your brother, she will love Mr Jones. If she is so ill now, she probably was at the stadium during the match.

---

56 *'Will'* indicating that the subordinate clause is future to the main clause.

Hypothetical single action or occurrence	Hypothetical rule	Hypothetical state	
If he swam across the lake tomorrow, we could meet in the bar in the marina. If he were/was watching TV at 5 tomorrow, he would be watching MTV. If it would[57] make you happy, I would buy you that dog. If she had completed her project by next Friday, they would have got the next commission by the end of the month. If she would[58] have completed her project by next Friday, they would have got the next commission by the end of the month.	If a particle X hit a particle Z, a particle B would be produced. If, in your future job, you worked on the other side of the town, you would have to commute for 2,5 h every day.	If he were/was in Italy tomorrow, he would enjoyed nice weather. If I had been married to you for 2 years tomorrow, am sure I would have been happy for 2 years then.	Future
If he were/was watching TV now, he would be watching MTV. If he had not been watching TV for 2 hours now, I would have written that letter for you by now.	If a particle X hit a particle Y, a particle Z would be produced. If he were in your place, if he missed his bus, he would return home by taxi. If, this month, he were/was working in the Oxford St. store, he would be commuting with Jane and Tom.	If he were/was in Italy now, he would be enjoying nice weather. If he had been to London so far, he would have understood what I mean. If I had been in this country for 2 years as he is now, I would have known everybody of importance for quite some time already.	Present
If he had been watching TV at 5 yesterday, he would have been watching MTV.	If a particle X had hit a particle Z, a particle A would have been produced. If he had had your job, if he had missed his bus, he would have gone home by taxi.	If he had been in Italy yesterday, he would have enjoyed nice weather.	Past
If she had met him yesterday, my mother would be told about it tomorrow.	If he had drunk a lot in the past, he would drink a lot now and in the future.	If his nose were not so long, he would have been much more confident during all that affair.	Mixed time reference

---

57 *Would* indicating that the subordinate clause is future to the main clause.
58 Modal *would* expressing volition, equivalent to *want*.

About the author

The author is a graduate of English Philology at a Higher Pedagogical School in Opole, Poland in 1986. Since 1985, he has been employed as a teacher of English and other philological subjects in various Teachers' Training Colleges and English language courses. In 1999, Wydawnictwo Naukowe PWN published his first book, a guide to conditional constructions in English with exercises.